Winners and Losers
of the
Information Revolution

Other Books by Bernard Carl Rosen

Adolescence and Religion

Achievement in American Society (co-editor)

The Industrial Connection

Women, Work and Achievement

Winners and Losers of the Information Revolution

Psychosocial Change and Its Discontents

BERNARD CARL ROSEN

PRAEGER

Westport, Connecticut
London

Library of Congress Cataloging-in-Publication Data

Rosen, Bernard Carl.
    Winners and losers of the information revolution : psychosocial
change and its discontents / Bernard Carl Rosen.
        p.   cm.
    Includes bibliographical references and index.
    ISBN 0–275–96277–6 (alk. paper)
    1. Information society.   2. Elite (Social sciences)   3. Social
classes.   I. Title.
HM221.R644   1998
303.48'33—DC21   98–15652

British Library Cataloguing in Publication Data is available.

Library of Congress Catalog Card Number: 98–15652
ISBN: 0–275–96277–6

First published in 1998

Praeger Publishers, 88 Post Road West, Westport, CT 06881
An imprint of Greenwood Publishing Group, Inc.

Printed in the United States of America

The paper used in this book complies with the
Permanent Paper Standard issued by the National
Information Standards Organization (Z39.48–1984).

10 9 8 7 6 5 4 3 2 1

To the memory of my beloved daughter
Michele Beth

Contents

Preface

This book is about the winners and losers of a great social transformation—the triumph of the techno-service economy—and its offspring, the information society. Losing is easy in a great transformation, for massive social change is always disruptive and in some cases devastating. It can adversely affect how people feel about themselves and how happy they are with the groups to which they belong. It creates new cultures and character types that unsettle people, make them anxious, and set them against one another. It creates clusters of angry people who feel dispossessed, out of place, and unwanted, no longer comfortable in their own country—disoriented people who fluctuate between bouts of anger and resignation. This happened in the nineteenth century and it is happening now.

But, of course, many people benefit from a great transformation; these people are winners. Today, they run the new information economy. They are the ones who have the traits, talents, and skills needed to function well in an information-based economy. They are skilled at information collection and processing, adept at manipulating abstractions and symbols, exceptionally proficient in the use of words and images. Society rewards them with generous amounts of prestige, money and power.

In their efforts to cope with demands of a changing society, adaptive people tend to acquire a character structure that is symmetrical with the functions and needs of the new society. In the information society the functional character is the Chameleon—an individual who has the ability and skill to adopt a social coloration that protects him or her from assault by competitors, unfriendly associates, and outright enemies. Unfortunately, Chameleonism has its down side, for it may ultimately sour social relationships. Moreover, it puts the Chameleon under great pressure, and loads him or her down with impossible expectations.

In this book I examine the anxiety and discontent caused by the Great Transformation; by the contradictions inherent in the Chameleon Personality; by the clash between different cultures and character types; by the competition for power between new and old elites; by the struggle within elites as different factions pull the country in opposite directions; and, not least, by the battle between winners and losers.

Over the many years that it has taken me to research, organize and write this book, I was fortunate to have the help of friends, colleagues, students, and institutions to lighten my task, to provide information, and to sharpen my thinking. Frank Young was always ready to encourage me when the work seemed overwhelming. Glen Altschuler read an earlier draft of the manuscript and made helpful suggestions. Cornell University's superb library and its friendly reference librarians were invaluably helpful. My editors, Elisabetta Linton and Gillian von N. Beebe, were supportive and helpful. And not least, my students, by their honest and critical questions, forced me to defend my position and at times to reformulate my argument. To all of these people, I am deeply grateful.

There is still another point that needs to be made. My motivation for writing this book was deeply personal. Like everyone else I have been caught up in the second great transformation. It has affected my life—my social and economic condition and my mood—and the writing of this book has been an exploratory effort to try to comprehend what is happening to me. If what I have discovered helps others, as it has helped me, to better understand the confusing period we are all in, I shall feel well rewarded for my efforts.

PART I

THE AMERICAN DREAM REVISITED

1

The Loser's Lament

Today many Americans feel like losers in a world that respects only winners. A miasma of doubt and cynicism hangs over their lives. They appear uncertain and worried, frightened that the American Dream of ever greater affluence for more people, generation after generation, is disappearing in a fog of fear and social turmoil. The promised land no longer seems a sure thing. No longer do they believe that tomorrow will inevitably be better than today and that with good will and determination all social problems can be solved, the merely difficult at once, the impossibly difficult taking a little longer. Instead they are dubious about the present and worried about the future. Gone is the sense that history is the story of progress.

Skeptics find the loser's picture of America overdrawn and excessively pessimistic. They ask, where is the evidence for it? The losers could point to what people say and do. What people say is clear: for twenty years poll after poll has reported that large numbers of people say they are "dissatisfied with the way things are going in the United States at this time," that the country is "on the wrong track," that it has "lost its bearings," and that they are worried about the present and pessimistic about the future.[1] Of course, as the polls show, attitudes fluctuate up and down like a roller coaster. And there are winners as well as losers. The winners say they are happy with the way

things are going and optimistic about the nation's future. But the
losers are numerous enough to be a matter of concern.

How people feel shows up in their behavior—jumpy and quick to
anger at the least provocation or even without provocation, given to
wide swings of mood, overreacting to good news or bad, grouchy and
cynical. "We're a grumpy country," said Lamar Alexander, former
Secretary of Education in the Bush administration, while campaign-
ing for the Republican nomination for president in 1996. "We're
losing our sense of promise of American life."[2] A November 1994
New York Times/CBS News Poll found that 57 percent of those
surveyed believed that life for the next generation of Americans will
be worse than it is today. Bill Clinton made it official when he told
a group of reporters aboard Air Force One that Americans were insecure and anxious, and that he was "trying to get people out of their
funk." The president went on to explain the mood of the country.
"What makes people insecure is when they feel like they're lost in
the fun house," he said. "They're in a room where something can hit
them from any direction at any time; they always feel that living life
is like walking across a running river on slippery rocks and you can
lose your footing at any time."[3]

The losers say they have good reason to be worried. They point
to the horrendous problems besetting the country—cities torn by
crime and racial conflict, painful unemployment in the midst of conspicuous wealth, huge private and public debt, drug addiction and
family disintegration, and much more. Yet the government seems
helpless or unwilling to solve them. And while the government dith-
ers and politicians play their usual games, conditions continue to deteriorate. Small wonder that of those questioned in a 1995 national
poll 74 percent said they were dissatisfied with the way the country
was going.[4] "There is a ground swell of opinion in the land," opined
John Chancellor, the veteran television commentator, "that in recent
years something has gone terribly wrong here."[5]

What has gone wrong seems painfully clear to lots of people. Divisions by race, sex, age, class, and creed have surfaced almost everywhere, and social pathology seems out of control. The effect of
mounting dissension on the popular temper is striking: people have
taken to calling each other names. It is no longer a novelty to hear
Americans describe other Americans as fascists, racists, sexists, per-
verts, murderers of unborn children, unfeeling bigots, and louts oblivious to the needs and pain of others. Shrill voices fill the air with

complaints, accusations, threats, and demands for reparations and compensation for past and present injustice. The claim of victimhood has acquired social cachet, and for some people a sense of grievance has become an essential element of personal identity. Amidst the clamor of angry voices threatening violence to get their way and being threatened in return, some people think they hear the sound of the nation's fabric ripping apart.

To the winners this conclusion seems incongruous and perplexing. America is fabulously rich and strong. Only the ideologically blinkered or the emotionally depressed could fail to be impressed by the material comforts most Americans enjoy today. You would think the statistics would have made that clear. America's more than eight trillion dollar annual gross domestic product is twice that of its nearest rival, Japan, even granted that not everyone enjoys full access to this abundance. Particularly impressive is the improvement in living standards that has taken place in the twentieth century. Life expectancy marched upward for most of this century, rising from 45 years in 1900 to 75 years in 1995. Materially, life has gotten a lot easier. In 1920 only a third of Americans had telephones, only one-half had indoor flush toilets, and only one in ten families owned an automobile. In 1940 more than half of all households had no electric refrigerator and 58 percent lacked central heating. Average annual income has quadrupled since 1900, and buying power has doubled since 1950. A large segment of the population, once mired in poverty and seemingly doomed to stay there, has moved into the middle class.[6]

But enough of statistics. Cynicism and anxiety will not relax their grip on the spirit merely because statistics do not support the dreary descriptions of contemporary life so often found in the popular media and in the works of the politicized intellectual elite. For what matters it to the losers that child mortality is down and years in school are up, that people are eating better and living longer, that ancient scourges such as smallpox and tuberculosis have been eliminated or controlled, that the economy is strong and productive, that the rate of crime is declining, particularly homicide, when they feel that society is sick and has made them ill.

THE ANATOMY OF ALIENATION

Troubled in spirit, the patient complains of vertigo and disintegration, a feeling of falling down and of coming apart, a sense of impending doom. A physician confronted with this sort of patient would probably conclude that the problem is not organic but functional; the patient suffers from a disorder of the mind, not of the body. In brief, the physician will conclude that the ailment is imaginary, not real.

But the doctor would be wrong. The patient's symptoms of vague misery, of pervasive anxiety and alienation, cannot be dismissed as figments of a morbid imagination. Anxiety is not a trivial distemper, a mysterious mood change that emerges out of nowhere for no particular reason, a momentary disturbance to be treated with soothing words and minor social palliatives. Anxiety is a fever, and like any fever it should be seen as a symptom of an underlying malady. The patient needs help, but there is no need to call in the undertaker; he is not on death's bed. Nevertheless, many Americans are truly troubled, torn by internal conflicts they do not understand, gripped by anxieties whose sources are obscure, and alienated from a society they feel no longer wants them.

Identifying the true causes of anxiety and alienation may not be easy, however, because anxious, alienated people often do not know what is bothering them. They feel troubled and angry, and in their anger they strike out at the presumed cause of their distress; but since they often misjudge the situation, mistaking some particularly disagreeable person or group for the real source of their misery, they may attack the wrong target. And sometimes, in an ironic twist of fate, the target of their hostility is themselves. Unconsciously, they blame themselves for their misery and turn their anger against themselves.

How can we locate the true cause of this alienation and anxiety? Who will help us? Fortunately, or otherwise, there is no shortage of explanations.[7] Some of them are useful. For example, Harry Stack Sullivan thought anxiety occurs when experience is discrepant with self-picture, a painful condition which most often occurs when others refuse to accept or act in accordance with one's inflated self-image. And Alfred Adler and Karen Horney, to round out this brief glance at theorists, believed anxiety to be the product of living in a threatening and abusive world that makes one feel small, insignificant, and helpless. These theories have a common theme—the troubled self and its relationship to an unfriendly environment. But why do so many Americans feel small and insignificant; what image do they have of themselves and society that violates reality; what circumstances make them feel friendless and insecure, victims of hostile forces determined to grind them down?

This book argues that the answer can be found in a massive and as yet insufficiently understood great social transformation—the emergence of the techno-service economy and its offspring, the information society. This transformation has left considerable social rubble in its wake, losers who have been put out of work by new technologies and whose social identities have been shattered. As the old order withers, a new one is taking its place; comfortable and familiar relationships are evaporating or are disparaged. The losers feel their world is changing in ways they can't accept or understand. They have become discombobulated and disoriented, furious at the people who have shunted them aside.

Caught in a revolution not of their own making but from which they cannot escape, unnerved by changes they do not understand, torn from familiar moorings and cast adrift in choppy waters without a familiar harbor in sight, the losers feel bewildered and demoralized. Even if they finally make it ashore they find themselves in a strange world, a cold place, hostile to anyone without the aptitudes and skills the new economy needs. They feel left out—out of step, out of place, and out of the running. They believe their interests are being ignored, their values trashed, their identity disparaged, their country taken away from them, their rightful place viciously usurped by others. They have become alienated and angry.

TRANSFORMATION AND CHARACTER

A transformation this stupendous is rare but not unique. In a single century the United States has experienced two periods of wrenching socio-economic change, one in the latter part of the nineteenth century when manufacturing decisively established its dominion over agriculture, the other in the last decades of the twentieth century when the techno-service economy conclusively demoted manufacturing to second place. The first transformation gave us more efficient ways to produce goods; the second, based on new developments in telecommunications and computer technology, made the creation and delivery of services easier and infinitely faster.

Though separated by a century and different in many ways, the two transformations are eerily similar in important respects: they both influenced how people earned their living, how they saw themselves and the world, what they aspired to become—and in so doing each produced new character types and novel cultures. The first transformation produced the industrial worker, gave birth to Darwinian Man, and fashioned a refurbished version of the old Bourgeois Culture. The second transformation has given us the information processor, the New Elitist, and the Culture of Perfection and Self-Realization embodied in the Chameleon Complex.

Every transformation needs new kinds of workers, people with the talents and skills and values and motivations to make the system work. Whereas the manufacturing system put a premium on industrial workers and entrepreneurs skilled in the production of tangible goods, the techno-service economy focuses on workers who are skilled at dispensing services and processing information, and who find emotional satisfaction in this kind of work. The Second Great Transformation has created a new class of winners, the New Elite, the creators, conservators, and transmitters of the information upon which the techno-service economy depends.

The New Elite can be rightly called winners. They are affluent and powerful. They have established a meritocracy whose status and wealth is based on proven accomplishments, and they admit to their group only people who meet strict standards of training and achievement. They believe they know what is best not only for themselves but for others as well. Consequently, they argue that power should be put in their hands, for only they can be trusted to use it in the interest of all. Certain of their superiority and convinced of their rectitude, the New Elitists are completely impervious to counter-arguments.

Highly educated, skilled in the manipulation of money and finance, adept at the art of creating ideas and images, well-paid and influential, treated with awe by a society that needs their services, the New Elite is in the catbird's seat. Its members are bright, hardworking, and good at what they do. All of which they are quite ready to acknowledge. What they are not so willing to admit, indeed may be unaware of, is that no small part of this success is due to their possessing, in most cases, a unique character structure—the Chameleon Complex.

Human chameleons, like their reptilian counterparts, fend off danger by assuming a protective coloration when danger arises; they seek to blend safely into a hostile environment by behaving congenially and doing as little as possible to arouse suspicion and aggression. Chameleons are skilled at sensing changes in the interpersonal environment and adjusting their behavior to suit the needs of others. Impression management is the name of their game. When it works properly, the Chameleon Complex helps the individual to fend off competitors, defends the ego against the attacks of enemies, and wins over needed clients and friends. This complex is not limited to any one group—chameleons can be found in diverse sexual, racial, ethnic, and social classes and in all age groups. But chameleonism is often found in people whose jobs require them to provide services in highly competitive face-to-face situations.

Since New Elitists work in highly competitive environments, often in close contact with other people, it is not surprising that many of them become chameleons. Processing information in an exacting world, where mistakes can be enormously costly and often unforgivable, is emotionally taxing. Abrupt demotion and dismissal is an ever present danger. Hence it is understandable that many Elitists take refuge in chameleonism. Chameleonism provides them with shelter, and at the same time helps them get the work done. For this reason, even though chameleonism can also be found in other occupational groups where contact with the public is central to the work, I believe it is especially prevalent among New Elitists.

Unfortunately, the Chameleon Complex has a down side. Pretending to be what one is not is demanding work, rife with anxiety. The chameleon must always be on guard. Betrayal may occur at any time, there is little room for error, fear is an ever-present state of mind. Also, the Chameleon Complex is chock full of contradictions which put New Elitists in the worrisome condition of believing one thing and doing the opposite. To handle these contradictions they must shut out unwelcome facts, ignore people whose opinions don't matter, bend others to their will whenever necessary and feasible. But since this often rubs people the wrong way, they tend eventually to make enemies—the very thing chameleons seek most to avoid. All in all, the Elitists, though winners, have their insecurities and worries.

That a great transformation would create its own type of character is not surprising. Most transformations begin as economic revolutions, as major changes in how society produces goods and services. But for the revolution to succeed people must have or be able to acquire the skills and motivations their jobs require. Force or money alone is not enough to ensure that the work gets done. In order for the new system to function smoothly, people must want to do what the system needs them to do, a condition most likely to occur when, as Talcott Parsons observed, the needs of the system and those of the individual become complementary, when in satisfying the needs of society individuals satisfy their own. This is not as unlikely as it may seem, for, to quote G.D.H. Cole, "every age and every people has a character stamped upon it by the way it earns its bread."[8]

In short, in most cases (not all, of course; there are always deviants from the norm), character necessarily bears a complementary relationship to the needs of the society in which the individual works. When things go well the needs of society and those of the individual mesh neatly in a smoothly functioning system.

The people who do not fit well into the new society, the traditionalists who cling to the past, the misfits who cannot find work in the new system, the workers whose skills are outdated or no longer greatly valued—losers all—get little sympathy from the New Elite. Eager to get on with the job of building a new society, the New Elite is impatient with anyone who resists change. But change never sits well with everyone. Revolutionary change, a psychosocial upheaval that alters people's conception of the present and their vision of the future, is especially hard to take. "Revolution," as Mao Tse-tung once remarked in another context, "is not a dinner party."[9] What makes this revolution especially painful is that many people do not fully understand what is going on, do not yet recognize that a new system is in control, and have not grasped the implications of this takeover.

But they cannot help realizing that the price of change is excruciatingly high. The techno-service economy, which began as a rational, innovative, high-tech system of production designed to deliver goods and services with unparalleled speed and efficiency, has become an all-embracing psychosocial convulsion that is dividing the nation into fiercely hostile groups. Most people welcome change that promises a more productive economy; very few want to pay for it with personal emotional turmoil and social conflict.

CACOPHONY OF COMPLAINT

Losers feel they have lost a central part of their lives—the sense of sharing in a common culture rooted in values worthy of preservation. They are angry because they have lost status in a high-tech society that no longer values their contributions, a society that ignores brawn and admires only brain power and college degrees. Losers in the blue-collar class mutter about the arrogance of the knowledge elite and the assertiveness of women who compete with men in the labor force. On the other hand, the winners in the upper-middle class question whether the hard hat is truly committed to liberal democratic values, to the Bill of Rights and the Constitution. Is there not more than a whiff of fascism in the hard hat's denunciations of welfare mothers and homeless vagrants? Is not the working-class male's display of macho masculinity really a cover for doubts about self-worth?

Who do the losers blame for their plight? Not themselves, usually. Most often people blame other people. Who these other people are depends to some extent on the individual's social class, race, or gender. To losers in the working class, the troublemakers are the ones who spread dissension wherever they go: the belligerent marchers with placards who noisily demonstrate in the streets; the smug, smooth college-educated talkers on television who lecture the great unwashed public about the need for tolerance; the angry women and blacks and homosexuals who demand submission to their demands for equality or special preference; the myriad punks, thugs, drug addicts, and vagrants who make the streets and parks and other public places dirty and unsafe.

Some winners, paradoxically, also complain of losing. Though they have good work and receive generous rewards, can avoid subways and buses and other dangerous forms of public transportation; though they live in the suburbs, stay clear of city streets at night, and send their children to private or highly selective public schools—these privileged folk find plenty to complain about. They are not satisfied with the way things are working out. They feel cheated of their birthright. They are furious at being denied a world free of injustice and inequality. They point to the people who despoil the environment or grab an unfair portion of the Gross Domestic Product for themselves. Angry at society for not keeping its promise of guaranteed self-fulfillment, furious at themselves for not achieving a fair and just society, they first attack society for its callous indifference to their needs, and then they turn their anger against themselves for failing to live up to their own expectations.

In this climate of blame-finding and finger-pointing, winners and losers glare at each other across a chasm of suspicion and resentment. Large numbers of Americans no longer feel comfortable with people not exactly like themselves. Hence, it is not surprising that when asked, "What is the problem?" they point to people with different accents or mannerisms or skin color, with peculiar hair cuts and strange dress and exotic styles of life, with pretensions to moral superiority and superior wisdom. But in fact the problem is not that the blameworthy people look, talk and act strange; the problem is that they want things that are utterly unacceptable to some other Americans; the problem is that differences of opinion and interests are felt to be utterly intolerable and incomprehensible.

To the cynical observer the struggle between winners and losers may seem to be only about money and power, and when have Americans not argued about money and power? Still, something new has been added. In the past, these disputes were usually matters for negotiation and rational bargaining, a question of how best to divide the national pie. In the past, Americans have usually been good at settling differences among themselves through negotiation. Isn't this what politics is all about?

Not any longer; times have changed. As Karl von Clausewitz might have predicted, cultural and psychological war has replaced old-fashioned, log-rolling, give-and-take politics. Disputes that once were regarded as negotiable now seem irreconcilable, and claims that once were treated as bargaining ploys are now seriously presented as non-negotiable demands. Emotions have taken over and rational exchange has fallen by the wayside. In these circumstances, compromise feels like losing and concession feels like betrayal. In a war this is what giving in to the enemy usually means. However, this hostility goes far deeper than differences over jobs, promotion, school placement, and the like; it reflects a feeling that one's identity and personal worth are under attack.

The nub of the matter is that people trained in different systems rub each other the wrong way. Selected and educated to function in different systems, moving in separate worlds, professing different values and needs, the people of the old system and those of the new view each other with deep-seated distrust. This is not a disagreement over lifestyles. It is not simply that winners and losers have different tastes in art and music or that they eat different foods and enjoy different movies (James Fallow's remark on the blue-collar worker's wonderment at the upper-middle class's gusto for cheeses with unpronounceable names and foreign films with subtitles is a case in point). It is also that they are emotionally incapable of understanding the point of view of someone outside their group.

Whenever unreason reigns, whenever opponents are seen as mortal enemies, not as fellow citizens to be reasoned with, we can be sure that deep-seated personality needs are at work, muddying the issues and clouding judgment. Winners and losers have come to feel that any compromise with their values, needs, and claims is a threat to personal safety. They believe that true safety is only possible when they are free to pursue their true goals. This rigidity of character, this inability to entertain opposing points of view, this tendency to see any opposition as iniquitous betrayal, blocks understanding, accommodation, and compromise.

Divided by different cultures and characters, winners and losers are moving apart, physically, socially, and psychologically, a separation which only increases the differences between them. This is startling in a people once notable for their similarity across class and ethnic lines. The German economic historian Werner Sombart, writing in 1906, was struck by how much the social classes were alike. The American worker, he wrote, "carries his head high, walks with a lissome stride, and is as open and cheerful in his expression as any member of the middle class."[10] Fifty years later, Frederick Lewis Allen, a popular American writer and editor, was likewise impressed by how similar Americans were across various social strata—in things consumed, in books and magazines read, in movies and sports attended, in social models emulated. But then Allen lived at a time when the rate of social change seemed to have slowed, when, as he put it, "the social distance between extremes is shrinking."[11]

Things are different today. Groups differences jar the sensibilities of people outside the group. A 1995 Newsweek Poll found that 86 percent of those surveyed feel that Americans have less in common and share fewer values than in the past. Asked to explain this state of affairs, most people point to the rampant social ills afflicting the country, principally the rising rates of crime and violence, and the mounting economic dislocations that are robbing workers of jobs and security. Repeatedly over the past two decades, public opinion polls have reported Americans selecting the state of the economy, especially when the rate of unemployment rises to uncomfortable levels, as it has done intermittently since the first oil shock in the mid-1970s, as the number one problem facing the country. And running a close second in the polls (sometimes first) is crime and violence. These explanations satisfy most people; they see no reason to look further.

They are mistaken, but not entirely. A certain amount of doubt and anxiety has always been an intrinsic human condition, and violence and economic dislocation no doubt make matters worse. These evils should not be ignored, but they are not the main reasons so many people are worried and cynical. There is far more to it than that. Still, the fixation on violence and the economy has to be taken seriously. What is troubling people cannot be understood, let alone remedied, until this fixation is put in perspective—which is the task of the next chapter.

2

Round Up the Usual Suspects

That the mood of many Americans has been exasperated by disruptive social change must seem obvious. But a lot of experts disagree among themselves about the causes of human disgruntlement and anxiety. This is not entirely surprising since the experts are mostly intellectuals, and these folk seldom agree on anything. Perhaps for this we should be grateful, for when intellectuals agree on any topic the consequences are often awful. Still, it must be admitted that they have sensitive antennas, and they have sensed that something has gone dangerously wrong.

Expert explanations of anxiety and disgruntlement are varied and sometimes interesting. Nearly always they place the cause of the problem outside the individual, as something for which the average person can not be held responsible and over which he has no control. Thus the learned doctors of the mind and soul—philosophers, theologians, psychoanalysts—talk of existential misery. They dismiss anxiety as inevitable. Man was born to suffer and nothing much can be done about it. Are people worried? Of course they are. How could they not be, when fate has cursed humanity with inescapable afflictions—physical decay and death, the loss of loved ones, natural catastrophe and war, human relationships gone sour, the same old afflictions about which Soren Kierkegaard, Paul Tillich, and Sigmund

Freud wrote so eloquently years ago. Needless to say, these afflictions are still with us.

However, they cannot explain the rise of anxiety in recent years. By definition existential miseries have always been with us, and in order to explain the rise in anxiety it would be necessary to show that existential matters have gotten worse. But they haven't. In fact, in some cases they have improved. For example, modern medicine has slowed the process of physical decay and cured some diseases once thought invariably fatal, particularly among children. And the improved distribution of food has eliminated famine in the United States and even in some foreign lands where starvation was once commonplace.

More politically minded diagnosticians, eschewing philosophical palaver, point to social injustice, to poverty and inequality, to crime and violence, to stagnant economic growth, as the real sources of American anxiety. They put the blame on an economic system that promotes greed and discrimination, distributes income unfairly, and threatens workers who dare to complain with the loss of their jobs. The fault lies not in our existential stars or in the character of the people, say these diagnosticians, but in society. It is society that makes people feel like underlings; it is society that makes everyday life gritty and dangerous; it is society that unnecessarily burdens people with cares and worries and fears.

Adding their share to this discussion are the ecological doomsayers who loathe industrialization and detest city life. They predict ecological disaster and an imminent breakdown of the environment, which they see as nature's visitation of just punishment on mankind for its sins—global warming, the destruction of the ozone layer, the wasting of rain forests and wetlands, overpopulation, and eventual widespread starvation due to the ruinous depletion of our natural resources. Calamity, they warn, awaits impatiently in the wings. But it is questionable that most Americans are losing much sleep over impending ecological disaster. After all, calamity (or the threat of calamity) is nothing new to Americans.

These explanations are serious and I do not wish to dismiss their importance. But it seems reasonable to argue, judging from the available evidence, that they do not figure largely in the popular mind as explanations of their problems. In fact, as I have noted, public opinion polls have repeatedly reported that most Americans believe crime, violence, and economic dislocation are the country's main problems.

For this reason, this chapter will be devoted to examining how valid is their belief that in violence and the perturbations of the economy can be found the causes of the discontent observed in some circles today.

VIOLENCE IN THE LAND

Contributing to the cacophony of complaint about the way things are going in the country is the harsh sound of violence, a piercing dissonant note heard throughout the land, in big cities, in small towns, and even in rural communities. Few Americans can honestly claim to be unaware of the noise of mayhem around them. Watchers of television, listeners to radio, and readers of newspapers cannot help noticing the ubiquity of violence on the American scene—on the streets and in the playgrounds, in offices and hospitals, in restaurants and airports, and even in heavily guarded government buildings and courtrooms. With frightening regularity the media report events of unspeakable savagery and horror. Demented killers rape and murder helpless women and children; rioters set fire to big cities, looting stores, beating and killing anyone who gets in their way; brutal thugs maim and kill innocent bystanders, including children, in bloody gang wars to control a disputed turf; and predators in search of money for a quick fix prowl the streets, mugging and knifing and shooting hapless victims almost at random. Life in America imitates art, and television-style violence has become the fare of everyday affairs.

Many schools, once privileged sanctuaries, are no longer safe. Disorder and violence have reached them as well, even the elementary and middle schools. For example, in Baldwin, California, two boys, one eight and the other ten, robbed a teacher at gunpoint. At another school, this one in Columbus, Ohio, seven students, aged 12 and 13, plotted the murder of their teacher by dumping chemicals in her ice tea. Guns, not fists, are the weapons of choice. A survey in 1994 of 197,735 students, grades 6–12, found that 7.4 percent of high school students carried a gun to school in the past year. So common have guns and knives become in the nation's schools that large sums must be spent on security arrangements. A quarter of all large city schools use hand-held or walk-through metal detectors, a hugely expensive operation. Nor is school violence only a big city problem. In Parkland, a middle-class suburb of Tacoma, Washington, a vice-principal

was issued a bulletproof vest to protect him from vengeful students.[1]
The school may have been acting on the sentiments of former teacher
Thomas J. Gleaton, president of the National Parent's Resource Institute for Drug Education. "If I was [teaching] in a school today,"
said Mr. Gleaton, "I'd ask for a bulletproof jacket."[2]

Ordinarily, young people learn the importance of controlling their
penchant for aggression from their parents and other adult molders
of character. But the family, that keystone of society and a major
source of moral instruction, is by common estimation in serious trouble. Almost half of all marriages, experts predict, will end in divorce;
and single-parent homes, while not yet the norm, have become common. A quarter of the nation's unwed women have become mothers
(the number rises to 85 percent in some inner-city areas), an increase
of almost 60 percent in the last decade.[3] In its weakened condition
the family can no longer be depended upon to do its job, and nothing
has taken its place—not the schools, not the churches, not the social
work agencies. For that matter, the family is no longer necessarily a
safe refuge from violence. This most intimate and protective of all
social environments is itself plagued by conflict, as the numerous in-
cidents of beatings and spousal murder reported in the daily press
graphically show.

Given this horrifying picture of a nation convulsed by mayhem and
murder, it may seem bootless and perhaps even heartless to question
whether in fact violence is the overwhelming problem alarmists claim
it to be—bootless because the conviction that violence, particularly
by juveniles, is out of control is firmly fixed in the popular mind;
heartless because the question seems to mock the fears of decent citizens appalled by the stories of bloodshed rained down on their hapless heads by the media. No mockery is intended. These fears are
genuine enough and based to some degree on harsh reality. To deny
that would be silly.

VIOLENCE REVISITED

Nevertheless, the level of crime in the United States must be put
in perspective. Crime is nothing new, of course; it has always been
high. But the furious gyre of violence was higher in the past than in
the present. Perhaps Ovid Demaris overstates the case when he writes
in *America the Violent* that violence is as American as turkey dinner

on Thanksgiving, but there is no escaping the fact that the record of lawlessness in the United States is as long as it is grim.[4] Beginning with the Pilgrims, who were not the peaceful folk portrayed in sentimentalized history, as their Indian neighbors soon learned when fighting broke out over desecrated Indian burial grounds and stolen grain, each generation of Americans has felt itself threatened by the specter of rising crime and violence. In the eighteenth century crime flourished like a green bay tree. Benjamin Franklin complained in 1767 that felons transported to the colonies by England, which sought to reduce its own substantial criminal element by shipping it overseas, were terrorizing the populace with burglaries, robberies and murders.[5]

A few generations later, in the 1838 speech that first brought him to national notice, Abraham Lincoln argued that violence was the country's primary problem. Speaking to the Young Men's Lyceum of Springfield, Illinois, he expressed alarm at the "increasing disregard for law which pervades the country; the growing disposition to substitute the wild and furious passion, in lieu of the sober judgment of the courts."[6] He warned that the nation's "proud fabric of freedom" was endangered by mob violence, which "pervaded the country, from New England to Louisiana." He called attention to a vigilante outbreak in Mississippi in which "dead men were seen literally dangling from the boughs of trees upon every road side; and in numbers almost sufficient to rival the native Spanish moss."[7]

Lincoln was speaking not only of the provocateurs who were capitalizing on local tensions to make mischief and the criminal elements that flourished then as they do now; he had in mind as well his ordinary fellow countrymen. Although usually genial and kindly, the average American could be prickly and quick to anger when his honor or autonomy or claim to equality was challenged. "Americans of his time," Herbert Croly writes, describing Lincoln's countrymen, "were generally of the opinion that it was dishonorable to overlook a personal injury . . . [The American] was aggressive, unreasonable, quick-tempered, and utterly devoid of personal discipline. A slight or an insult to his personality became in his eyes a moral wrong which must be cherished and avenged."[8] Consequently, injured feelings, disputes over boundaries, and other clashes of interest often led to bloodshed. The beatings, stabbings, and murders that frequently marred the tenor of everyday life in nineteenth-century America give gory testimony to that sad fact.

Further exacerbating many a quarrel was the general use of knives and guns to settle disputes, these weapons being as plentiful then as they are now. A good part of the citizenry went about armed to the teeth. Even members of Congress at times carried firearms into the House and Senate. Nor was the prodigious amount of alcohol consumed by the average American in the nineteenth century conducive to public tranquility. In the first half of the century, absolute alcohol consumption was twice as great as it is today, just under six gallons per head; modern Americans drink on the average about 2.9 gallons.[9] Whiskey and gunpowder in a charged-up, angry person make an explosive mixture, as many victims of violence have found to their sorrow. Indeed, recounts of such explosions made up a good part of the daily content of the local press—as they do now.

Nowhere does violence attract more media attention than in the cities. And yet city violence is an old story, as urban historians know and as city editors and television anchor people should know. Cities have always been dangerous places, American cities more so than most. "Thronged as our city is, men are robbed in the street," a New York City investigating panel lamented in 1842. "Thousands that are arrested go unpunished, and the defenseless and the beautiful are ravished and murdered in the day time and no trace of the criminals is found."[10] So dangerous did life become in the 1860s that law-abiding citizens armed themselves. "People wouldn't think of going out after dark without a weapon," said Robert D. McCrie, a professor of security management at John Jay College.[11]

Nor are gang warfare and urban riots unique to our time. In *The Gangs of New York* Herbert Asbury wrote that in the past rival gangs often battled to control turf, and that then as now innocent bystanders were killed. In 1910, a gangster named Johnny Spanish opened fire on a rival, Kid Jagger, on New York's Forsyth Street, missing him but killing an eight year old girl.[12] Gangs with names like Plug Uglies, Dead Rabbits, and the Bowery B'hoys roamed the streets, robbing and mugging with apparent impunity.[13] Poverty, crowding, ethnic and racial antagonisms, and general misery provoked bloody explosions.

The record shows that in the past criminal behavior contributed to rates of arrest far exceeding those of today. In 1862, the New York City police arrested 82,072 persons, one-tenth of the population; in 1989, the rate was about one-twentieth of the city, 308,164 people—a staggering number but still much smaller proportionately than in the past.[14] Rivaling New York as the nation's crime capital was Chicago, never a slouch in matters criminal. In the twenty years after the Civil War, the murder rate in Chicago quadrupled, and in the late nineteenth century crimes of violence and other kinds of malfeasance resulted in an enormous number of arrests. One Chicago resident in eleven was arrested in 1893 for one crime or another. In the Windy City and in other metropolises the crime rate was on an upward curve throughout the nineteenth century and well into the twentieth century.[15]

In sum, numerous acts of terror and murder have bloodied the history of the country. As historian Sean Wilentz points out, "hardly a decade has passed without deadly rioting, bombing or vigilante brutality" since the first settlement. Consider the year of 1919. In that year, "bombs were directed at dozens of public figures, including the Attorney General of the United States. Race riots broke out in Chicago, Omaha and Washington; strikes by steelworkers and others turned heartland towns and cities into armed camps, and more than 70 blacks, several of them veterans, were lynched."[16] The Currier and Ives portrait of peaceful, bucolic America to the contrary notwithstanding, the United States in the past was a dangerous place in which to live. The notion that America is more violent today than in the past simply will not stand up to scrutiny.

To which the average citizen, worried about burglary and terrified of being mugged when walking alone at night, might respond: yes, you may be right, the past was dangerous. But isn't crime and violence in the present also plentiful and dangerous? Do not crack cocaine and heroin, the ready availability of guns, and gang warfare in inner-city areas make life today dangerous? Of course they do, but how much more dangerous than the activities people engage in every day without giving them a thought?

Actuarially, according to Charles E. Silberman, an expert on crime, the possibility of being hurt in everyday activity is far greater than in collisions with muggers, rapists, murderers, and similar types. "From an actuarial standpoint," writes Silberman, "street crime is a lot less dangerous than riding in an automobile, working around the house, going swimming, or any number of other activities in which Americans engage without apparent concern. The chances of being killed in an automobile accident are ten times greater than being murdered by a stranger, and the risk of death from a fall—slipping in the shower, say, or tumbling from a ladder—are three times as

great. Accidents also cause far more non-fatal injuries than violent
crimes."[17]

All of this underscores the point that when it comes to the public's
reaction to crime, reality and perception can be worlds apart. To
illustrate, the nation's crime rate dropped slightly in 1992, but in a
1992 poll conducted by the Harvard School of Public Health 94 percent of Americans said that crime had gotten worse. The homicide
rate in many of the nation's biggest, most violent cites dropped significantly in 1995, with the fewest killings since crack cocaine
spawned an epidemic of gangs, guns, and violence in the mid-1980s.
Nevertheless, a 1995 *Time*/CNN poll found 89 percent of those surveyed believed that crime was getting worse, and 55 percent worried
about becoming victims themselves.[18] Statistics issued by the Federal
Bureau of Investigation in December 1993 contradicted the public's
perception that violent crime is rising rapidly across the country.[19] In
fact, the homicide rate has not changed much in half a century. It
reached 10 per 100,000 in 1933, slightly above today's rate, 9.3, according to the National Center for Health Statistics. The numbers
also show that the crime rate, for violent and nonviolent offenses
alike, had actually dropped for the previous two years. According to
figures collected by the FBI, the rate of all crimes dropped 4 percent
from 1991 to 1992 and an additional 3.1 percent from 1992 to 1993,
and statistics indicate that the downward trend continued during
1994, 1995, 1996, and 1997.

Michael Rand, a statistician at the Bureau of Justice Statistics, said
that in the 21 years he has been compiling data on criminal behavior,
the rates of crime and violence have not changed much. Nonetheless,
he went on to say, the public always seems to believe that crime is
growing worse. "We've been living at what is a very high plateau of
criminality for a long time," said John Stein, deputy director of the
National Organization for Victim Assistance, "and the public is worn
out by it."[20] As every politician knows, it is perception that counts.
In 1993, Melvin Melman, a Democratic pollster, said that crime was
the number one issue for the mayoral candidates he was advising, in
Seattle and New Orleans, but not because crime was on the rise; it
wasn't. "The real crime rate and people's perceptions are two different things," he said.[21] This is not to say that Americans have no
reason to be apprehensive about violence. They have. But there is
reason to wonder whether their anxiety is proportional to the threat.

IT'S NOT THE ECONOMY

To complicate matters, the economy is undergoing revolutionary change. Manufacturing, long the foundation of the nation's prosperity, is in relative decline and the techno-service sector has become preeminent. And, as noted, in every revolution there are winners and losers. The winners adjusted to the change, acquired highly valuable information-oriented skills, and are doing just fine. The losers are out of luck and out of work. Economic distress, it is said, is making many Americans feel like losers.

The argument goes something like this. Corporate downsizing and global competition are putting people out of work. Jobs are not as secure as they used to be, and good paying work in manufacturing is giving way to lower-paying employment in services—fewer highly paid welders in automobile factories, more minimum-wage hamburger-flippers in fast food drive-ins. The economy may be growing, but most people feel no better off. The fruits of increased productivity go mostly to the rich. Indeed, most people have to work harder just to maintain their standard of living. If this is truly the case, who can blame people if they worry about the future? No one— if economic conditions are as bad as they say.

But just how bad is the economy? Bad as compared with when, with what, and with whom? Answers to these questions require historical perspective, but this is a problem. If, as L. P. Hartley wrote in his novel *The Go-Between*, "the past is a foreign country: they do things differently there," then the past may appear so alien to the modern mind as to be unintelligible.[22] Even so, since the past left a partial record of itself, it pays to look at the record; perhaps something useful can be learned from the past. But alas, possessing a useful knowledge of history has never been an American strong point. Each generation imagines the scroll of time began with its own birth and cannot believe the past has anything to teach it, which may explain why Americans learn so little from past mistakes and why every contemporary social pathology appears so uniquely calamitous.

Ignorant of their history and uninterested in learning more, many Americans do not realize how unusual the course of the American economy in the twentieth century has been. Economists generally agree (this in itself is remarkable, since agreement among economists

is not at all common) that the period between the end of World War
II and the oil shocks of the 1970s was an economic anomaly, perhaps
unique in the history of any country. At the war's end the economies
of America's competitors, the Europeans and the Japanese, were in
shambles, while America had not only escaped unscathed but emerged
from the conflict stronger and richer than when the Japanese had
bombed Pearl Harbor.

Much of the industrialized world, shattered and exhausted from six
years of carnage, desperately needed American food and manufactured goods; and America, eager to trade, grew richer satisfying the
world's needs. In 1950 America generated about half the world's output, and although this portion began to decline in the 1960s, the
country continued to be prosperous, despite periodic recessions.[23] For
not only did postwar America make and sell more goods and services
than ever before, it produced them more efficiently.

But this magical period of fabulous economic growth did not last.
Sometime in 1973 the engine of economic growth hesitated and the
upward movement of family income slowed to a crawl; for some families, income stagnated and for some it declined. This slowdown is
often given as the major cause of anxiety in America. But this idea is
mistaken. To begin with, it begs several critical questions: has income
in fact stagnated? if so, for whom? and what is the relationship between income and anxiety? It is often said that income has stagnated
for almost everyone (except for the rich) and that anxiety increases as
income declines. But is this correct?

The data say no. It is true that annual increases in real income
slowed or stopped for some workers, and that the median wage for
all workers, adjusted for inflation, is nearly 3 percent less than it was
in 1979. On the other hand, women earn 7.6 percent more than in
1979, and women make up 46 percent of the workforce.[24] Indeed, for
most segments of society income increases did not halt. Contrary to
orthodox opinion, real income continued to rise, albeit modestly, for
a majority of Americans. The exception is a segment of the lower
class, young unskilled men with less than a high school education,
many of them inner-city blacks. This group has unquestionably suffered a decline in real income. And it is also true that recent increases
in total compensation, about 2.9 percent in 1995, seem puny compared to the 9 percent won in 1981. But we tend to forget that the
1981 rise was entirely wiped out by an inflation rate of 10 percent.

According to Labor Department data, most Americans have not

done as badly as they seem to think. From 1981 to 1995 wages rose annually, averaging 3.5 percent over the 14-year period. Average wage increases exceeded inflation in 8 out of those 14 years. Compensation (wages plus benefits) rose even more: about 3.5 percent, year over year. Compensation exceeded inflation in 11 of those 14 years.[25] Stagnation, it turns out, means that the economy had stopped delivering the whopping yearly wage increases the average American has come to consider a birthright.

If we look at family income rather than at individual earnings, an interesting picture appears. According to Labor Department statistics, the median family has 12 percent more income than in 1970.[26] Frank Levy, an M.I.T. economist and expert on family incomes, says the true figure is closer to 20 percent. This figure would be higher were it not for the increase since 1970 in single-parent families and immigrants. Both of these groups typically have lower incomes, and their increasing numbers depress the median income. Levy attributes the improvement in median family income to a second breadwinner in the house, usually a husband or wife whose income may equal or exceed that of their spouse. Also, families are smaller: the birth rate dropped from 18.4 per 1,000 people in 1970 to 16 in 1992. As a result there are fewer mouths to feed, fewer teeth requiring expensive dentistry, fewer demands on appliances and hence less repairs, fewer jeans, sneakers, and games to buy.[27]

Furthermore, some economists now argue that the figures on average median family income are misleading. These figures include an adjustment for inflation based on the consumer price index. But as Alan Greenspan, the chairman of the Federal Reserve, recently told Congress the consumer price index may overstate inflation by 1 percent (the president's Advisory Commission to Study the Consumer Price Index concluded that the index overstates the cost of living by 1.1 percentage points), meaning that wage increases have been underestimated by 20 percent over the past twenty years. Leonard Nakamura of the Philadelphia Federal Reserve Bank thinks the statistical inflation deflater overestimates the rate of inflation by as much as 2.5 to 3 percent.[28] If this estimate is correct, most people are living better than they did a decade ago.

DOWNSIZING AS A WAY OF LIFE

But what about the people who have lost their jobs? Losing one's job is painful, no doubt, especially after many years of service with a company. Nevertheless, for the vast majority of the working population the employment picture remains bright. Employment is high and the unemployment rate low—it dropped to below 5 percent in 1997—and the economy is creating a steady flow of new jobs: 26 million since 1980, 18 million between 1985 and 1995, and 8 million in the period 1992 to 1996 alone. In all, as many as 40 million new jobs have sprung up to offset the 32 million downsized into oblivion.[29]

The Austrian economist Joseph Schumpeter thought job loss and company collapse entirely normal aspects of capitalism, purgatives by which the system cleanses and renews itself. Of the twelve companies originally included in the Dow Jones Industrial Index (1896), only one, General Electric, still exists. The rest have merged or gone under, victims, as Schumpeter put it, of capitalism's creative destruction. Joseph Stiglitz, the chairman of President Clinton's Council of Economic Advisers, also believes that downsizing is healthy for the country. "Our economy is changing," he said, "and is doing a very good job."[30] Furthermore, the jobs currently being created tend not to be low-paying positions, as commonly believed. Quite the contrary. A 1996 study by the Council of Economic Advisers found that the new jobs tended to be of good quality: 68 percent of all new jobs created between 1994 and 1996 paid above average wages; 60 percent were managerial or professional positions. Indeed, far fewer workers have been fired than is commonly believed. In 1995 job losers constituted only 2 percent of the workforce, half that of the recession year 1981–82.[31]

Also, the much heralded decline of social mobility has yet to take place. Americans are moving both up and down the income ladder about as fast as they ever have. The Census Bureau measured year-to-year mobility between 1984 and 1992 and found that only once, in the recession year of 1990–91, did more families experience a drop than a rise in income.[32] Growing job churning, another frequently proffered explanation for malaise, is also a myth. A number of researchers, including Henry Farber, a labor economist at Princeton University, recently looked at the data on job security and found no evidence that job tenure is becoming shorter or that long-term jobs are becoming scarcer. On the contrary, economist Paul Yakoboski of the Employee Benefit Research Institute in Washington found that American workers are staying in the same job longer than they did 20 or 30 years ago. Job tenure for women has been lengthening for most of the past 40 years. As for men, length of tenure dipped in the mid-1980s but soon leveled off. The median tenure for men was higher in the 1980s than at any time in the 1950s, 1960s, or 1970s. The Institute concludes that "[a]vailable data do not support the widely held perception that the American work force is becoming increasingly mobile."[33] The truth is that American workers have always been highly mobile. In the late 1970s more than 40 percent of workers stayed at their jobs less than five years, whereas in 1991 the median figure for male workers aged 35 to 44 was 7.1 years. The longing for a return to the stable jobs of old is largely romantic nostalgia for a time that never was.

Why, then, are some people complaining about the economy? When this question was put to Douglas Holtz-Eakin, an economist and researcher, he responded: "I don't know. The statistical measures look good but the mood of the people is not."[34] In 1994, the Gross Domestic Product increased by 4.5 percent; personal income rose by 6 percent; factory orders soared by 10.2 percent, a 15-year record; the "misery index" (inflation, 2.5 percent, plus unemployment, 5.8 percent) was at its lowest level in almost three decades—and yet in that year 53 percent of Americans felt that "there is something seriously wrong with the United States."[35] A May 1996 poll reported that 60 percent of the respondents were unhappy with the way things were going in the country, despite the fact that the economy was growing at a robust 3 to 4 percent rate and the unemployment level had dropped to the 5.3 percent level, the lowest in years.

Far from being in economic trouble, the country is on a roll. If the economy continues to grow at its present rate, between 2.5 and 3.5 percent a year, and assuming a population expansion of about 1 percent a year, the per-capita gross domestic product would increase from its current level of about $28,500 to about $153,500 in a hundred years time, making our descendants far richer than most of us dream of becoming.[36]

If money were the key to understanding anxiety, why is anxiety prevalent among the prospering middle and upper-middle classes, judging by their comments to reporters? (What the upper class is thinking, no one knows. The very rich do not answer the door when poll-takers knock; servants invariably shoo them away.) Interviews reveal that many middle-class people feel deeply unhappy about the condition of the country. But Richard L. Berke, a reporter for the *New York Times* who interviewed people around the country, was struck by how little worry was fueled by personal anxieties over money. "[Many] people interviewed were not particularly pressed financially. And they did not talk about specific issues. . . . Instead, they expressed a general unease about their futures. . . . They also spoke of a broader sense that the country was losing its moral roots and that the ever-corrupt politicians could do nothing about it."[37] Nothing in their comments suggested that they thought the economic sky was falling down.

Even skeptics leery of economic statistics and ordinary folk bored out of their minds by numbers cannot help being impressed by the growth and productivity of the American economy. To grasp the scale of American economic prowess consider these statistics. With less than 5 percent of the world's population, the United States accounts for at least 20 percent of the world's gross product; its closest competitors, Japan and Germany, produce 7.6 percent and 4.3 percent, respectively.[38] America exports and imports more than any other nation. Its stock and bond markets are the world's largest and most fluid; its companies attract more foreign investment and penetrate more international markets than any of its competitors. The United States ranks first among major industrial nations (Japan, Britain, Germany, France, Italy) in labor market flexibility and high-tech exports.[39]

Americans have become richer, on the average, because the country has grown wealthier. Between 1913 and 1950 the Gross Domestic Product (GDP) grew by an average of 1.6 percent a year; between 1950 and 1973 it grew by an annual average rate of 2.2 percent; from 1910 to 1998, the GDP increased from 200 billion to more than 8 trillion. Granted, newly industrializing nations in the Pacific Rim— for example, China, Thailand, Taiwan, South Korea, Singapore— have at times grown more rapidly, achieving growth rates of 7 to 12 percent in the early 1990s. But 2.5 percent is the normal long-term rate for mature industrialized nations.

The expectation that living standards will continue to rise in giant steps year in and year out is so deeply ingrained in the American mind that a growth rate of 2.5 percent gives rise to hysterical talk of stagnation and even of economic crisis. It is true that compared with the 4- to 7-percent growth that characterized some years during the 1970s and '80s, 2.5 percent seems puny. But viewed historically, 2.5 percent annual growth is astonishingly fast, awesome in its consequences; a steady growth rate of 2.5 percent a year is enough to double the Gross Domestic Product every 28 years. In reality, a growth rate of 2.5 percent ought to be a matter of congratulation, not something to moan about.[40]

In fact any growth at all, rapid or otherwise, has been the exception and not the rule for most of history. Stagnation, not steady economic growth, has been the typical human experience. Until modern times the average rate of economic growth, so far as economic historians can tell, was negligible or close to zero. Nor did people expect any different. To be sure, a few individuals—the powerful, the unscrupulous, the lucky—might become richer; and others—the weak, the improvident, the unfortunate—might become poorer; but over the long haul society as a whole grew neither richer nor poorer. This is what people believed and this was in fact, with rare exceptions, the case.

Unless it preys upon its neighbors and exploits hapless conquered peoples, exacting tribute, selling them into slavery, plundering their cities and stealing their wealth—the path to riches taken by the ancient Athenians, Romans, sixteenth-century Spaniards, and most empires at any time—a nation's enduring enrichment can only come about through greater efficiency and increased productivity. (Economic productivity and gross domestic product, though causally related, are different phenomena and are measured differently. The first concerns the amount of goods and services the average worker produces per hour; the second, the amount of wealth that work aggregately creates.) Increased productivity has been the path Americans most admire and the one they have followed, with occasional lapses, with striking success.

The United States economy is now and has usually been throughout the twentieth century the most productive in the world. America's productivity growth in the 50 years before the Great Depression of the 1930s averaged about 2 percent a year. In the grim 1930s it fell to 1 percent or less, and millions of Americans, a quarter of the workforce, lost their jobs. Financial misjudgment in the White House and the Federal Reserve, tomfoolery and misfeasance in the stock market, an obsession with staying on the gold-standard and balancing the budget almost brought the nation to its knees. How long the economy would have lingered in the doldrums no one knows. John Maynard Keynes, pessimistic about the economy recovering on its own, argued for governmental stimulus, later called pump-priming, but as it turned out no government program was needed—the war gave the country the jump-start it required, and the economic machine roared ahead.

Productivity in the United States has risen in every decade since 1940, notwithstanding occasional ups and downs. It is true that some industries carelessly let themselves become slovenly and inefficient during the fat years after the war's end. However, prodded by adversity many have risen, phoenix-like, from their ashes and pulled themselves together, increasing productivity and strengthening their ability to compete in the global market. The American steel industry is one example of an industry that made a near-miraculous recovery when almost everyone had given it up for dead. A dinosaur among goods producers and seemingly slated for extinction, it refused to go silently into oblivion, as worried experts predicted it would. Though almost sinking beneath the weight of cheap imports from low-cost producers, it finally took long-delayed steps to save itself. It closed inefficient mills, bought modern equipment, drastically slashed its workforce, and is once again highly efficient.

Between 1970 and 1994 the Gross Domestic Product grew by 86 percent; meanwhile the population increased by 28 percent.[41] Part of the credit for this remarkable achievement belongs to management, part to the workers. American workers are the world's most productive, turning out more work per hour in more areas than any of their competitors, including the vaunted Japanese and Germans. On average, a Japanese worker is 22 percent less productive per hour, partly because the service sector in Japan is notoriously inefficient, and the German (West) Worker is 14 percent less productive than the average American. Harvard economist Dale Jorgenson estimates that America's overall productivity is 10 to 15 percent higher than that of Japan.[42]

The United States has become the low-cost producer of a medley of products, everything from steel coil to cardboard boxes. No one knows this better than America's competitors. Foreign companies, recognizing the advantages of manufacturing in a low-cost country with a highly motivated, skilled labor force, have been moving factories to the United States in record numbers, among them Sony,

Toyota, BMW, and Daimler-Benz (now Daimler-Chrysler), the maker of the much-admired Mercedes, which built a factory in Vance, Alabama.

In the long run, higher productivity means higher wages, as any student in elementary economics will tell you. It is not surprising, therefore, that per-capita income is higher in the United States than in any other major industrialized nation. Using the economically sensible Purchasing Power Parity Index as a measure of income, a recent per-capita figure for the United States was 22,200 dollars, as compared with 19,500 dollars for Germany and 19,107 dollars for Japan. These figures certainly do not support the notion that America's economy is crumbling, that it is stumbling and slipping into decrepitude, overtaken by its competitors and headed for second-class status. Quite the reverse: the economy of the United States is thriving.[43]

THE BOOMER'S COMPLAINT

Yet strange to say, in a country blessed with enormous natural resources and an economy without peer, many discontented citizens complain about the economy, even though, as noted, aside from those unfortunate workers who have lost their jobs to structural change, and the ecologically-correct gentry who worry about the effects of economic growth on the environment, few have just cause to complain. Yet, even though bad-mouthing the economy is unwarranted, complaining has its uses. Complaints often come from people whose private agendas coincide with economic decline. The notion of economic slowdown delights their hearts.

Among the complainers are disaffected intellectuals who revel in any sign of American decline, seeing it a long overdue punishment for American imperialism and hubris; or corporate lobbyists who find it useful to be able to point to economic slowdown as justification for higher tariffs and subsidies to protect their clients, often inefficient companies unable or unwilling to compete in the global market; or labor leaders in uncompetitive industries who worry about unemployment, declining union membership, and dwindling union influence; or myriad functionaries and officers in private foundations, universities, and governments who willingly enlist in the war against poverty when it is popular and who, when the war goes badly, blame their failures on economic decline—the only war in which a defeated army and its generals blame their failures on society and get away with it. All of them find the idea of American decline decidedly useful and encouraging.

No group has been noisier in its complaints about the American economy than the Baby Boomers. This humongous cohort, about 78 million people born between the end of the war and 1965, only slightly less than a third of the population, whines that the country— most particularly its political leadership, its incompetent managerial class, its crass, bumbling, recession-prone market system—has let them down, broken its promise to hand them the good life so many of their doting parents had said was their inalienable right. Said J. Walker Smith, a partner at Yankelovich Partners, a polling outfit that has studied this rambunctious group, "Boomers [feel it is] more or less their birthright to spend a lot of time in creative leisure pursuits, to focus on self-fulfillment and self-experience."[44] Sad to say, the world doesn't always see it their way, and they feel cheated and betrayed.

The Baby Boomers' sense of disappointment is real enough, no doubt. But their complaints about how the economy treats them are groundless. Most Boomers are doing better than they think, at least in a material sense. Of course many individuals have suffered reverses, but in what generation has this not been the case? The facts are, notwithstanding their cries of disbelief, the Boomers' standard of living, on the average, has been going up over the past two decades. This conclusion is based on a study by a team of economic demographers led by Richard Esterlin of the University of Southern California. The team concluded that the Boomers, on the average, have much higher family incomes, higher individual earnings, and higher net worth than did their parents at the same age. A study by the Urban Institute confirmed this conclusion. It found that the boomers had incomes, adjusted for inflation, that are half again as high as were their parent's incomes in 1960; consumption is 27 percent higher.[45] High-flying Boomers are doing very well indeed. A recent Merrill-Lynch survey found that 2 percent of the Boomers were worth $1 million or more (beyond home equity), and an additional 17 percent have $100,000 to $1 million.[46]

In rebuttal, the Boomers argue that it takes two people to earn these higher incomes, whereas in their parent's generation one earner was sufficient. To which the researchers responded that smaller families, hence fewer child-related expenses, coupled with higher average income and company medical and pension plans, still put the Boomers in a better financial position than the one-income, three-child family of their parents' generation. The leading edge of the Boomer generation, now in its early fifties, has a median income 50 percent higher than did its parents at that age, adjusted for inflation and family size. Sad and puzzling it is that many relatively prosperous people feel out of sorts, dissatisfied with themselves and society.

Money is not every thing, of course—though people who have been poor at some time in their lives and rich at another, generally say that rich is better—and granted that man (or woman) cannot live by bread alone, the arts and other refinements being necessary for a civilized life, money still is important. I'm not suggesting that it isn't. But money alone will not explain worry in the midst of plenty. We need to look elsewhere for the explanation.

The true cause of the anxiety and discontent felt by many Americans, I submit, can be found in the stupendous economic transformation that is changing the structure of the nation and the character of the people. It is to an analysis of these changes that this book is devoted.

PART II

THE FIRST GREAT TRANSFORMATION

3

We've Been There Before

Every great transformation leaves social debris in its wake. Not everyone benefits from change, not everyone can be a winner, many are losers. The losers lack the skill and motivation to adjust to change. They lose the power to influence events; their jobs disappear into maws of machines or into the hands of eager natives in less developed countries, who are happy to work for less pay, fewer benefits, and no fussing about pollution and workers' rights. Losing is painful everywhere in the world. But in America losing is more than painful—it is a sin.

Two social transformations of immense magnitude and consequence have roiled life in the United States in the last one hundred years. The first occurred during the last third of the nineteenth century when manufacturing dethroned agriculture as the reigning economic force. The second, the techno-service revolution, which achieved definitive ascendancy in the last decades of the twentieth century and is still going on, demoted manufacturing to a position secondary to the service industries. Each transformation created clusters of angry people who felt dispossessed and cheated of their rightful place in the sun; and who felt threatened by upstarts whose uncouth, strange habits and manners were seen as showing a deep contempt for traditional American institutions and values. This threat to their security and traditions disoriented many people, who fluc-

tuated between bouts of anger and resignation. In some cases, overwhelmed by feelings of powerlessness, they fell victim to anomie.

Few social critics in the nineteenth century attributed this anxiety
specifically to economic change. Most analysts blamed fear of war,
frenetic commercial activity, and the growing gap between the rich
and the poor—a list of explanations still around today. When it comes
to explaining the American mood, nothing much has changed in the
last hundred years. What they did not fully understand, or at any rate
did not make special mention of, was that America was undergoing
wrenching change, a transformation such as it had never experienced
before and would not again for another hundred years.

Attention was given, however, and sympathy proffered to the losers
in the social upheavals of the time, and a look at them may help us
understand what is happening today. But since these unhappy folk
were numerous and fell along a broad social spectrum, I will focus
on just two groups, the farmers and the factory workers. Even this
somewhat more limited task must be approached gingerly, because
comparisons across historical epochs are always risky. No two periods
are identical. Even when things seem similar, they may have been
provoked by different circumstances. Nevertheless, comparisons between the two great transformations seem to be in order, since the
similarities between the last decades of the nineteenth century and
the last third of the twentieth century are truly remarkable.

Both periods were marked by extraordinary technological change.
Stunning improvements took place in production, transportation, and
communication, due in large part to improvements in steam and gas-
oline combustion driven machinery in the first case, and to chemically
and electrically energized equipment in the second. Both periods witnessed heightened tensions between races and social classes, between
immigrants and native born, and between agrarians and city folk.
Both epochs experienced extraordinarily rapid increases in national
wealth. For despite occasional economic turndowns, the furious gy-
rations of stock markets, wantonly foolish speculation in land, Ponzi-
type schemes to build financial towers on the quicksand of false
promises, and other mischief to which market economies are subject,
the real gross national product doubled in the nineteenth century and
doubled again in the twentieth.

Vast fortunes were made and lost in both periods, and often the
newly rich displayed their wealth openly, in brazen, arrogant indifference to public opinion or in naive ignorance of the perils of envy-

induced hatred. The inequality produced in both periods boggles the mind and enrages the sensibilities of egalitarians shocked by the immense disparities between the incomes of the rich and the poor. Today, as everyone knows, the megawealthy have grown prodigiously rich in land and stock speculation, in the entertainment and computer industries, in office and housing development.

But we tend to forget how rich the very rich were in the last decade of the nineteenth century. Between 1892 and 1899, at a time when the average garment worker was making 650 dollars a year, John D. Rockefeller's personal dividends from Standard Oil amounted to between $30,000,000 and $40,000,000. Andrew Carnegie received, in 1900, $23,000,000 from his numerous steel companies. And, as there was no income tax at that time, Rockefeller and Carnegie got to keep these tidy sums intact.[1] It was more than favorable tax laws that made these men fabulously rich. Both had the good fortune to live at a time when the United States was undergoing rapid urbanization and industrialization.

AMERICAN URBANIZATION

Thomas Jefferson had a dream. He envisioned an America that would be forever agrarian, a democracy of small farmers tilling their own land. Granted, there would be in his ideal America artisans and shopkeepers in the towns and a handful of big merchants and industrialists in a few cities along the Atlantic coast. But these people would not be the heart of the country, nor should they be. "While we have land to labor," he wrote, "let us never wish to see our citizens occupied at a work bench, or twirling a distaff, for those who labor in the earth are the chosen people of God."[2] He hoped that most people would live out their lives uncontaminated by contact with the city and free of its distractions and vices.

When Jefferson died at age 83, in 1826, his dream seemed reasonable, for in that year the United States was overwhelmingly a rural land. In 1830 only 8 percent of the population lived in communities of 2500 persons or more, and only 83 communities were classified as towns and cities. At mid-nineteenth century, America was still an agricultural country; five times as many people lived on farms as in cities.[3] But even when Jefferson's dream seemed most secure, the seeds of its destruction—urbanization and industrialization—were being planted. For even as agrarian dreamers were celebrating their good fortune, factories and cities were busy at work undermining the structure on which bucolic America rested. Though at the time they may not have noticed, the basis for an explosive growth in cities had already been put firmly in place, and that nemesis, industrialization, with its accompanying revolution in transportation and communication, was growing strong in scattered areas of the country remote from beloved plantations and farms. Changes were underway that would transform America.

These changes would provide fabulous opportunities for ambitious men, including some talented youths. One such youth, Abraham Lincoln, seized his opportunity for advancement, and left the farm to enter the city. Ambition, a muddied relationship with his father, and restlessness had made life at home unsatisfying. Nature had blessed him with exceptional strength, a gregarious personality, a talent for making friends, and a first-rate mind. Not even the harsh environment of the frontier, nor his lack of much formal education, could suppress his natural genius. Marshaling his mental and physical assets, with no money to speak of and only his youth and energy to offer the world, he left his rural home to make his fortune in the city, first in New Salem and then in nearby Springfield, Illinois.

The urban world Lincoln entered would strike the modern American as quaint and quiet, lacking many amenities, without the fast-paced rhythm and ethnic diversity now associated with cities. When Lincoln moved to Springfield it had but 1,500 residents, seventeen dry goods stores, seven groceries, six churches, four drug stores, four hotels, two newspapers, and one book store.[4] Even the largest American towns and cities in the late eighteenth and early nineteenth centuries were small. Philadelphia, the nation's largest city, had a population of only 42,444 in 1790, while New York, which ranked second, had 33,131; only five cities had populations of 8,000 or more. By 1840, the number of such cities had grown to forty-four, although only about 11 percent of the nation lived in communities with 2,500 or more inhabitants.[5] At mid-century rural America's future seemed bright.

But, as we know, it was soon dimmed; the city's future was even brighter. When the Civil War broke out, only one in five Americans lived in an urban area, and only three cities had a quarter of a million or more residents.[6] And yet by 1870 more people lived in cities (one in four) than had inhabited the entire country in 1820. During the

1880s, while the total population grew by 22 percent, the urban population increased by over a third; by 1900 almost 40 percent of Americans lived in urban communities and there were fifteen cities with 250,000 or more inhabitants. Between the end of the Civil War and the start of World War I, the urban population increased sevenfold, while the rural population merely doubled.

The rural-urban balance tipped in favor of the city at some time during the second decade of the twentieth century; the 1920 the census showed 51 percent of the population living in urban areas. By 1970, 73 percent lived in urban communities, and 56 cities had 250,000 or more inhabitants. From that point on the figures changed only slightly. The 1990 census showed 76 percent of Americans living in urban areas. Not surprisingly, the number of farmers dropped dramatically. Today, there are only 600,000 full-time farmers in the United States, and many of these could not survive without the income from a spouse working in town. Indeed, the number of full-time farmers living on farms has fallen so drastically that the Census Bureau will no longer bother counting them as a separate category in future censuses. So much for Thomas Jefferson's hope that the United States would remain forever a nation of independent tillers of the soil.

The transition from an essentially rural nation to an urban one was painful. Many people loathed the city and all its works, especially farmers bred in the Calvinistic tradition, who considered the cities dens of iniquity. Wicked things went on there. City people drank too much and spent their evenings in ubiquitous saloons, when it would have been better had they stayed at home. According to one account, an observer of a single New York City block found 20 grog shops. On one Sabbath he "counted for five hours the number of persons who went in but two of them. There were 450 men, 445 women, 82 boys and 68 girls."[7] City people played cards and gambled, reprehensible practices in the best of circumstances and utterly depraved when the money lost at cards came out of meager family budgets. They danced wantonly, gave wild parties, and enjoyed sex when they could get it, which was often, it was said, since city women were reported to be as loose as their men.

Cities condoned prostitution. Almost every large city, and some small ones as well, had a section set aside for vice, the red light district in which men debauched wayward girls for small sums, receiving sexual release and often venereal infection in return. Syphilis was a pan-

demic terror. In Baltimore a vice commission found only 3.4 percent
of the prostitutes uninfected, and in New Bedford, Massachusetts, 90
percent were ill. In the late nineteenth century New York City was
reporting 243,000 cases of syphilis a year. Innocent lives were destroyed. "Every doctor again and again saw children born with congenital syphilis, innocent wives who had picked up the disease in the
course of a few youthful visits to a brothel."[8] Syphilis was the AIDS
of its day, though even more widespread, and like AIDS no sure cure
had been found.

Venereal infection, loose morals, drunkenness, frivolity, and un-
restrained hedonism were not the city's worst sins. More frightening
was the spread of industrialization across the country. Nothing could
stand in its way, and for this calamity country folk blamed the city.
For in the minds of rural folk industry was the child of the city, and
industry was a threat to the farmer's traditional way of life. Industry
undermined the family, the keystone of the community, forcing people to work with strangers, and erasing the bonds of work that once
kept the family intact. Farmers were repelled by the city's impersonality, its unfeeling marketplace, its noise and confusion, its frantic
pursuit of money and love of change—in short, its citified approach
to life.

Rural Americans could not separate the city from the new industrial
system; both seemed inexplicably strange, unacceptably vulgar, threats
to everything they held dear. The embodiment of this threat was the
city dweller. Individualized and deracinated, competitive and impersonal, without ties to the larger community, bound to no goal other
than self-advancement, the urbanite affronted the deepest values of
the villager, to whom neighborliness, cooperativeness, and collective
responsibility were qualities far more valued than money, success, and
fame, the quintessential urbanite pursuits.

Country folk charged city people with meddling in other people's
business. Farmers detested the city reformer who wanted to eliminate
the one-room school house and consolidate school districts. They
despised the city agricultural expert who sought to "replace traditional patterns of farming with strange and impractical ideas hatched
in some head or laboratory far removed from the realities of farming."[9] Furious at city meddling, suspicious of city motives, frightened
of city power, rural voters fought urban reform, voted against labor
laws, opposed humanitarian measures such as the abolition of capital
punishment, and held tightly to their over-representation in the state

legislatures. Reformers should have known that farmers would fear city politicians who sought control of rural affairs. They should have foreseen that the farmer was not about to give in to outsiders and would fight back, often successfully. Not for the last time reformers discovered that expertise and good intentions are not enough to change an erring world. It is a lesson many of them still have not learned.

Intellectuals put the countryman's fears and hostilities into words, fashioning in books, plays, and speeches a forceful indictment of urbanization that is still popular in some intellectual circles today. To many nineteenth-century intellectuals the city was a place of dark satanic factories whose smokestacks belched grime and dirt into the air, making it almost impossible to breathe, and whose effluents turned rivers into putrid sludge and poisoned the soil. Urbanization filled their minds with frightful images of people forced from the land, crowded into ghastly slums, proletarianized and exploited. The city, they said, is a cold, hard, impersonal place, rife with violence, where rootless people drift through fragmented and anonymous lives, where even pleasure is tawdry and sterile, for without traditional culture to sustain them life has no meaning. In sum, as the intellectual saw it, urbanization was a disaster, a catastrophe that left many city dwellers stunned, helpless, and broken.

This grim description of the city has a long history. It could have been found in the conversations and letters of eighteenth-century gentlemen in England and America who distrusted cities and detested industrialization. Thomas Jefferson, for example, wrote that a yellow fever epidemic plaguing Philadelphia should not be considered a tragedy "since it would discourage the growth of cities, and I view great cities as pestilential to the morals, the health, and the liberties of man."[10] Poets, novelists and literary critics echoed these sentiments. Their aversion to the city was keen, shrill, deep, and articulate. Many ordinary people shared this point of view. To the jobless and homeless, to the worker sweating in miserable shops and factories for meager wages, crowded in dank, dirty tenements, cut off from the life-giving culture of the village, the city was indeed a hellhole. Some could not adjust and died of disease, loneliness, and overwork.

To these city dwellers the farmer's hostility seemed unwarranted and unfair. The condition of many factory workers, after all, was not enviable; fate had not been kind to them. Like the farmer they were caught in a firestorm of social change. The question was: who would go up in smoke first, the farmer or the factory worker? Both were having a hard time adjusting to economic change; both were bewildered and frightened; both suffered blows to their sense of identity and self-respect. The same forces that shattered the security of the farmer turned the proud, independent craftsman into to a mere tool to be used at the whim of his factory boss and of the marketplace.

THE RISE OF INDUSTRIALIZATION

What would surprise a modern visitor to mid-nineteenth-century America was how little industrialization had touched the country. Although by the mid-nineteenth century industrialization was far advanced in Europe, particularly in England, Lincoln's America had not yet fully entered the industrial age, a situation that was to be a considerable problem for the combatants in the Civil War, North and South, who in the early years of the war had to buy much of their armaments from Europe. To be sure, the industrial revolution had made an appearance in the United States in the early 1800s, spurred on by Jefferson's Embargo Act of 1807, which was designed to discourage trade with Europe and thus keep the country out of that continent's interminable wars (unsuccessfully, however, as the War of 1812 proved) and by the protective tariffs later passed by his own party.

The embargo and the war, and later the tariffs, stimulated local manufacturing—the last thing Jefferson had wanted—but its progress was slow, halting, and limited largely to a few parts of Pennsylvania, New York, Connecticut, and Massachusetts. On the eve of the Civil War, "the average American," wrote Bruce Catton, "was in fact what he has been since only in legend, an independent farmer, and in 1860—for the last time in American history—the products of the nation's farms were worth more than the output of its factories."[11] The total national product was four billion dollars that year, and the value of country's agricultural products slightly exceeded the output of its shops, mills, and factories, a sign of agriculture's dominance that was to vanish by the 1870 census.

The image of America as a nation of independent yeomen and shopkeepers beholden to no man seemed so self-evidently true that Abraham Lincoln, in a message to Congress in 1861, could without fear of contradiction describe the United States as a land where most people "work for themselves, on their farms, in their houses, and in their shops, taking the whole product to themselves, and asking no favors of capital on the one hand, nor of hired hands or slaves on the other."[12] To be sure, the four million enslaved blacks, most of whom worked on farms and plantations, could not by any stretch of the imagination be described as independent farmers or self-employed craftsmen, but they nevertheless contributed to the picture of America as a land that was at bottom rural and small town in all things that mattered.

To the jaded modern eye, nineteenth-century life, as portrayed in Currier and Ives prints, seems marvelously attractive—warm, intimate, friendly and, above all, simple. Modern Americans must wonder at Henry Thoreau's advice to his contemporaries to "simplify, simplify." Today, it sounds incongruous; how much simpler could life have been? Though, to be fair, perhaps Thoreau had his friend Ralph Waldo Emerson's coterie of transcendentalists in mind. These idealistic souls, while ostensibly espousing simplicity, pursued a complicated philosophy and an even more complex way of life at Brook Farm, the transcendentalist's dream community, which proved to be a nightmare of communitarian complexity.

In any event, poverty and a primitive technology made simplicity a necessity for all but a few rich families. To the task of working the land, the average farmer could bring only simple agricultural skills and implements: the heavy iron plow, harrow, hoe, pitchfork, knife, sickle, and scythe—all of them familiar to the medieval peasant. To the job of constructing a house and building furniture, the workman, who was often the farmer himself, brought simple techniques tested over generations and tools any ancient carpenter would have recognized: the ax, saw, adz, carpenter's plane, auger, chisel, and hammer. To the problem of assigning tasks, the family brought a simple solution: it divided the labor according to rules sanctioned by centuries of tradition, which apportioned work according to the person's age and sex; some jobs were routinely assigned to men, others to women, still others to children.

Everyone had work to do and, working together, parents and children created a remarkably self-sufficient unit. Almost everything the family ate or wore was made at home. The burden of domestic production and housework fell mostly on the shoulders of women. It was the wife and her daughters who cooked, washed clothes, kept the house clean, churned butter and pressed cheese, made shirts, trousers, and dresses for the family, and labored at a hundred other tasks that kept them busy from early morning until far into the night. Rural women also assisted their menfolk in the field, weeding, hoeing, planting, and picking crops; and not infrequently rural housewives would cultivate a plot near the house on which to grow food for the table or raise a scattering of chickens and ducks, delicacies much prized in a world where shopping for poultry at the local market was out of the question.

Men did the heavy work: clearing and plowing fields, raising fences and maintaining farm buildings, scything hay and planting crops, and carting the harvest to market. In the woodlands, the husband and his sons would hunt for game, deer, turkeys, pheasants; or when the landscape permitted, they fished the streams and lakes for trout and bass. Children were kept busy feeding pigs and milking cows, picking berries and finding eggs in the chicken coop, and doing numerous other chores that left them little time to get into trouble. The fact was that these people needed each other; their survival depended upon everyone pitching in and doing his or her assigned job.

Not everything was homemade, of course. Plows, guns, knives, pewter ware and drinking glasses, nails, hammers, and other tools, a ready-made suit, dress, or pair of shoes for special occasions had to be bought. Money to pay for these purchases came from the sale of wheat, corn, wool, pigs and cows, apples and cherries, and other farm surpluses at market prices. For no matter how independent the small farmer strove to be, he could not shield himself entirely from the vagaries of the market economy. And of course, the large farmer and the one-crop plantation owner, whose products were shipped to distant markets, were intricately tied to the requirements and demands of regional and foreign economies.

Economic, emotional, and physical bonds held rural families together in a way that modern Americans, dismayed at the fragility and disarray that mark so many families today, can only dream about. The physical bonds would probably irk the modern American; yet physical closeness also contributed to the family's enviable solidarity. Family members were in each other's presence almost continuously, sleeping three to a bed as children and sometimes as adults, working cooperatively at spinning thread and threshing wheat, celebrating together such memorable rites of passage as births, weddings, and funerals. This close proximity was caused, in part, by the small size of their houses and by the large size of their households: 35 percent of Americans lived in households of seven or more persons, 66 percent in households of five or more.

But physical closeness also had its costs, because inevitably not every family was happy. Although the idyllic family of America's vanished past projects a heartwarming picture of parents and children living in loving harmony, in fact many families did not fit this idealized model. Nineteenth-century America had its share of troubled families riven with dissension and plagued by, in James Lincoln Collier's words, "brutal fathers, alcoholic mothers, wanton daughters, laggard sons."[13] When intractable differences arose, or when space became unbearably tight and money horribly scant, youngsters could remain and suffer—often the lot of the female—or leave and strike out on their own. Many chose to leave and found work in homes as domestics or as workers in simple industries.

As late as the mid-nineteenth century, much of American industry followed a system known as "putting out." In this system a businessman left orders with various producers throughout the countryside, sometimes supplied them with materials, periodically picked up the finished products, and sold them in local or distant markets. The routine went something as follows. Farmers and cottage weavers brought their cloth, often woven of material they had produced, to the putter-out. After a price was agreed upon, usually at a customary rate, the cloth was then stored in a warehouse. The middlemen came to town periodically to pick up the cloth, usually after having previously placed orders with the putter-out who was in contact with the farmers and weavers. Business canvassing between the various components of the system was infrequent, usually limited to fitful correspondence, and only occasionally accompanied by samples.[14] On the whole the putting out system gave its participants a relatively predictable, minimally competitive life.

Industrialization destroyed the old "putting out" system, with its decentralized production and leisurely way of doing business, and replaced it with a more organized, impersonal, and efficient process that brought together for the first time machine manufacturing and highly competitive marketing methods. The keystone of the new industrial edifice was the factory. By concentrating manufacturing in one place, rather than dispersing it to various households, the factory could use expensive, highly specialized machines, driven by water mill or steam engine, not by the muscle power of oxen, horses, and burly humans. Apart from efficiency, reasons of safety required housing these machines under one roof where they could more conveniently be protected and maintained. In factories manufacturers could produce goods in large quantities and at prices no craftsman working alone or with a few apprentices could meet.

The Civil War, the pivot on which American history turned, gave manufacturing the stimulus it badly needed. "The Civil War," writes Lewis Mumford, "cut a wide gash through the history of the country. . . . When the curtain rose on the post-bellum scene the old America was for all practical purposes demolished; industrialism had entered overnight."[15] Not overnight exactly, as Mumford realized, for the changes embodied in industrialism had been slowly building for several generations. But there is no doubt that the war was a major catalyst to manufacturing. The war demanded huge increases in food, horses, wagons, tents, shoes, uniforms, locomotives, guns, and myriad other materiel; and industry hastily expanded to meet these needs. Large-scale production was profitable because the military gobbled up all that the factories could produce, sometimes at exorbitant prices for goods of shoddy quality, and constantly asked for more. The enormous profits that always accompany frenetic production in wartime gave industry the money it needed to expand production and the incentive to adopt new technologies.

Several important industrial technologies were already at hand when the war began. For instance, as early as 1798, Eli Whitney had standardized the production of muskets, using jigs—metal plates that guided the drilling and cutting of identical units—to mass produce interchangeable parts. Simeon North and Samuel Colt and others improved upon Whitney's method to make revolvers, rifles, ammunition, and many other tools for war. After the war, the same procedures were used to manufacture sewing machines, clocks, farm equipment, and other useful machinery. In time, the mass production of machinery and consumer products composed of interchangeable parts became so identified with the United States that it was known as the "American system of manufactures."[16]

AMERICAN INVENTIVENESS

American inventiveness, coupled with a knack for improving upon devices invented abroad and a talent for finding practical uses for ideas neglected in the countries of their origin, gathered momentum after the war. Americans made advances in iron and steel production, building upon the Besemer process developed in England. They contributed to the development of agricultural machinery, improved flour milling, made strides in the fabrication of steam engines and railroads, introduced the sewing machine and rotary press to eager buyers, made thousands of home-grown inventions for various purposes, and innovatively applied machinery to the manufacturing of many simple products.

An Englishman writing at the time of the Civil War declared: "Mechanical contrivances of every sort are produced to supply the want of human hands. Thus we find America producing a machine to peel apples; another to beat eggs; a third to clean knives; a fourth to wring clothes; in fact there is scarcely a purpose for which human hands have been ordinarily employed, for which some ingenious attempt is not made to find a substitute in a cheap and efficient labor-saving machine."[17] The number of patents granted to ingenious Americans exploded. In the period from 1860 to 1890 the Patent Bureau issued 640,000 patents, and in the first quarter of the twentieth century the total reached 969,428. The average number in any one year during this period exceeded the total number of patents issued in the entire history of the country before the Civil War.

Assisting the growth of manufacturing in the nineteenth century were two epoch-making inventions, one in transportation, the other in communication—the railroad and the telegraph. That the United States badly needed an improved transportation system had long been obvious. Getting around and moving products to markets were intensely frustrating problems. Horse-drawn coaches and wagons crawled along on wretched roads, making travel and commerce expensive, excruciatingly tiring, and unreliable. Travel was impossible on wet spring days and during the stormy winter months, discouraging efforts to seek markets in distant places and diverting trade from its natural channels.

Canals were the exception, it is true, and their construction accelerated the economic development of New York, Pennsylvania, and the Midwest. But traffic on the canal moved at a leisurely pace. The Erie Canal ran 363 miles from Albany to Buffalo, a goodly distance in those days, and it usually took four to six days to make the journey—bargemen who tried to do it in less time were fined $10 for speeding by canal authorities. Moreover, in some parts of the country water-barren terrain limited the use of canals, and winter temperatures often froze them into icy ribbons on which no barge could navigate.

The Civil War presented problems to which the barge and the horse-drawn wagon train offered no efficient solution. Fighting a war in a vast country on several fronts separated by hundreds of miles required moving colossal amounts of supplies and thousands of men over mountain ranges and across swift, tricky streams and rivers. The old transportation system was simply not up to the job. As a result campaigns were sometimes stalled for weeks and months when rain and snow and mud made the roads impassable. Even in the more industrially advanced North the transportation of men and materiel took place on antiquated roads and on overburdened rails. The railroads were sparsely distributed and unreliable; breakdowns were common, schedules erratic, services Spartan. Although the transportation system had improved since the turn of the century—when the cost of moving a ton of goods thirty miles inland equaled the cost of carrying the same goods across the Atlantic, and travel from Cincinnati to New York took three weeks—the movement of people and products by road or rail on the eve of the Civil War was still painfully slow and costly.[18] In the South the transportation system was so bad— many roads were mere rutted dirt paths—that both sides often had to build roads and lay railroad track as they went along.

It was obvious the country had to upgrade its railroad system. Some rail construction occurred before the war, but it was not until the fighting ended that new construction began in earnest. In 1865 there were about 35,000 miles of railroad track in the United States. Within ten years the mileage had doubled, and by 1885 it had nearly doubled again to 128,000 miles. By the end of the century track mileage approximated 190,000 miles, an almost sixfold increase in thirty-five years. Although the rate of growth slowed after this initial burst of activity, it did not stop: by 1930 railroad mileage had grown to 260,000 miles.

The jewel of the new transportation system was the transcontinental railroad, the result of an idea that had been around for some time, but didn't take concrete form until Asa Whitney, a merchant engaged in trade with China, petitioned Congress in 1848 for a charter to extend the existing system from Lake Michigan to north of the Columbia River. Believing, correctly but prematurely, that trade with Asia had a great future, he argued that not only had the time come to build the road but that it could be built cheaply with immigrant labor. Not given to modesty, he asked for a continuous strip of land along the entire road sixty miles deep to defray the cost of building his iron road to the Pacific, though it is unlikely that Congress would have agreed to this enormous giveaway. The eventual builders settled for alternate sections ten miles in depth on each side of the right of way, enough to make the builders seriously rich. In any event, sectional disputes about the route put the idea on hold until 1862, when Congress authorized the Union Pacific Railroad to build a line west from the Missouri river to the western boundary of Nevada and the Central Pacific to build a road from Sacramento to the eastern boundary of California.

The two companies engaged in a spectacular race, since celebrated in countless sketches, stories, and films, to see which line would finish its task first. Using primarily Chinese and Irish immigrants and ex-soldiers of the Civil War, the engineers accomplished marvels of construction, tunneling through mountains and spanning gorges and ravines, all without the aid of modern earth-moving equipment. It was a pick and shovel operation all the way, assisted of course by well-placed explosives. (The engineers had acquired some useful skills from the war; blowing up things that got in the way was one of them.) The race ended in a dramatic union of the two lines at Promontory Point, near Ogden, Utah, in 1869, amid hurrahs and an impressive ceremony called the "wedding of the rails."[19] It now became possible to travel coast to coast by rail, and people soon took advantage of the cuts in cost and time to travel and conduct business. Nationwide commerce and industry flourished as never before.

Improvement in the transportation system had been relatively easy. The builders of the railroads were able to use time-tested technologies, steam engines and iron tracks, both familiar to mid-nineteenth-century Americans. It only needed money and will to improve the movement of people and products. But unfortunately communication was tied to technologies that for centuries had changed little and, though inefficient and expensive, did not seem susceptible of much betterment. Perhaps marginal changes were still possible, but it seemed to many people that the technology of communication had gone about as far as it could go. How much faster could a courier on horseback carry a message?

A small group of brave men tried to find out. Between April 1860 and October 1861 they provided a unique high-speed private mail service, the justifiably famed Pony Express, which covered the 1,966 miles between St. Joseph, Missouri, and Sacramento, California, in just ten days. Changing horses every seventy-five miles, evading hostile Indians, and fighting off bandits, they rode day and night in all kinds of weather—only to be put out of business by a strand of copper wire, the telegraph.

The telegraph (and later the telephone and wireless telegraphy) revolutionized communications and gave economic development in America a giant boost. The revolution began with an invention from a most unlikely source. In 1848 Samuel Morse, a Yankee painter with a flair for mechanics but with no experience in communications, flashed over a wire strung from Washington to Baltimore the first telegraphic message: "What hath God wrought?" Recognizing a business opportunity when it saw it, the Western Union Company in 1856 organized a system of telegraph wires that soon crisscrossed the country, putting everyone in contact with almost everyone else, if they desired. As it turned out many did, and the company prospered mightily.

At the Philadelphia Exposition in 1876, Emperor Dom Pedro of Brazil put a cone-shaped object to his ear and heard Alexander Graham Bell's voice. "My God, it talks," said the startled emperor, and the telephone instantly became the Exposition's stellar attraction.[20] By the end of the century the telephone had become commonplace. Installed in numerous homes and offices, it profoundly affected the social life of the people and quickened the tempo of commerce. Numerous other inventions, not directly tied to communications, also added their stimulus to economic development. For example, the typewriter sharpened business correspondence, the adding machine improved the accuracy of bookkeeping, the cash register speeded retail transactions, and hundreds of other office and business devices lubricated the workings of the industrial machine.

HARD TIME FOR FARMERS

That industrialization would prove hateful to American farmers was not unexpected, but in a way it does seem odd. After all, the industrial system had showered numerous benefits on the farmer. It stimulated inventors, who gave the farmer a cornucopia of new tools—the chilled-iron plow, the twine binder, the combined harvester and thresher, the combined corn picker and shocker—machines that re-

duced toil and increased production. By 1880 machines were capable
of threshing and bagging 450 pounds of grain a minute, a figure
beyond the imagination of an earlier generation of farmers. Besides
the harvesting of cereal crops, new machines improved agricultural
efficiency in a wide variety of areas, from bee culture and flower raising to fruit and vegetable growing, from the fencing of fields and the
planting of trees to the care of livestock.[21]

Dairy farming, to take one more example of a farming activity
greatly influenced by new technology, underwent more changes in
the nineteenth century than at any time in its entire history. For
instance, the dairy centrifuge, a device for separating cream and skim
milk, greatly raised the cream yield of whole milk and increased the
quality of butter and other dairy products. And, as one wit said, the
invention of a machine to measure the fat content of milk not only
revolutionized dairying, it did more to make the dairyman honest
than did the Bible. Numerous examples in other fields could be cited,
but they would all point to the same conclusion: machines industrialized agriculture and enormously increased its output in the last third
of the nineteenth century.

Machines also solved a problem long troublesome to farming in
America—the chronic shortage of labor. Below the Mason-Dixon line
slavery had solved this problem for those who could afford slaves.
Above the line and for the small landholder in the South, labor was
scarce and expensive, as it had been from the very first settlement of
colonists along the coast. For help in planting and harvesting the
farmer had to depend on his wife and children and, when these were
not available or sufficient, on hired hands, if they could be found and
afforded. With the help of machines the farmer became less dependent on others, and he could grow more with less labor.

Improved transportation allowed the midwestern farmer to ship
grain and meat to the east coast, where rapidly growing cities
crammed with hungry mouths offered the possibility of vast sales and
handsome profits. Before the expansion of the rail system the movement of farm products to markets other than local or at best regional
had been expensive, time consuming, and ultimately unprofitable.
Cheap transportation by rail and canal made marketing midwestern
products in eastern cites economically feasible for the first time. Midwestern wheat, pork, and beef could then be transshipped by boat to
western Europe, providing still another highly profitable market. Exports of foodstuffs, valued at 57.5 million dollars in 1866, grew to

537.7 million in 1899, an almost tenfold increase in dollar value despite sharply declining prices. By the end of the nineteenth century the congeries of increased production, cheap transportation, and competitively low prices had made America the granary and abattoir of Europe.[22]

Stimulated by these favorable conditions, American agricultural output increased as never before. In the fifty years from 1860 to 1910 the number of farms trebled, the acreage of land under cultivation more than doubled, and the acreage of improved farm land trebled. The production of wheat rose from 173 million to 635 million bushels, of corn from 838 million to 2,886 million bushels, and of cotton from 3,841,000 to 11,609,000 bales. More land was brought under cultivation in the thirty years after 1860 than in all the previous history of the United States.[23]

Despite increased acreage and production few farmers became rich. To be sure some prospered modestly, but incomes grew slowly. Getting rich quick by cornering a market or speculating on future prices was not the farmer's way—there were no John D. Rockefellers or Jay Goulds in agriculture. Although accurate and generally accepted per capita income figures for farmers during this period elude us, the National Industrial Conference Board estimates total farm income in 1867 at 1,517 million dollars and 2,933 million dollars in 1899, a small increase for a thirty-year period. Another indication of how well the farmer was doing was the value of farm land and buildings, and of all farm implements and machinery. By these measures the record of economic improvement is modest and spotty. The value of land per acre rose from $18.26 in 1870 to $21.32 in 1890 (the depression of the 1890s cut the price of an acre to $19.81), not a dramatic increase in the value of land over a twenty-year period. The increase in the total value of all farm implements and machinery was more substantial; their value grew from 152 million dollars in 1850 to 750 million in 1900.[24]

Despite technological improvement in agriculture and growth in the national economy, the last decades of the nineteenth century were not halcyon years for most farmers. Many found it hard to make ends meet. New, stubborn, and frightening economic difficulties beset them, imposing crushing burdens that were particularly difficult to endure when the industrial sector of the country was visibly growing vastly richer and more powerful. The problem, put simply, was that the prices farmers received for the things they grew did not rise as rapidly as the cost of the things they had to buy. In fact, the prices of many of their products actually fell. Wheat that had sold for two dollars a bushel just after the Civil War fell in a downward spiral to one dollar in the 1870s, until it reached a bottom of 50 cents a bushel in 1895. Corn marketed at 78 cents a bushel in 1867 fell to 31 cents in 1878 and 21 cents in 1896. Cotton declined from 16.5 cents a pound in 1869 to 6.5 cents in 1898. The wholesale price index of farm products dropped from 162 in 1864 to 56 in 1896. On the other hand the prices of the things the farmer bought—machinery, fertilizer, seed, and the goods the family required for everyday living—either increased or remained stable.[25]

It seemed to the farmer that a cabal of evil forces conspired against him: the government, which colluded with the banks to keep money tight, interest rates high, and the greenback tied to gold, in effect denying him the liberal credit he desperately needed to buy equipment, seed, and fertilizer, pay taxes, and get through the bad patches when drought, pests, and crop-failure or personal misfortune exhausted his savings; the railroads, which used their monopoly over transportation to keep the farmer's costs high; the international traders, who manipulated prices to the farmer's disadvantage; the manufacturers, who used their political clout to keep the tariffs on imported goods up and hence the prices of the manufactured goods the farmer needed unreasonably high. They all showed a cold, heartless indifference to the farmer's plight. With his debts mounting and with no money to repay them, many a farmer went under—his mortgage foreclosed, his family dispossessed, his life smashed.

Rural suffering was most acute in the South and the West, for in these sections of the country nature as well as man conspired against the farmer. In 1887 a severe drought withered crops throughout the Plains and pushed many farmers against the wall and some into bankruptcy. To some extent they had only themselves to blame. Ambitious to succeed and optimistic about their prospects, many of them had mortgaged their farms to the hilt. In Kansas, to cite a typical Plains state, there was one mortgage, on the average, to every other adult in the state. In the years 1889 to 1893 over eleven thousand farm mortgages were foreclosed, and in fifteen Kansan counties over three-quarters of the land was owned by mortgage companies. "In God we trusted, in Kansas we busted," scrawled one defeated farmer on his wagon as the family trudged back east.

William Allen White, famed Kansan journalist and editor, poignantly described their condition as they trekked eastward: "These movers from western Kansas . . . after ten years' hard vicious fight, a fight which had left its scars on their faces, had beat their bodies, had taken the elasticity from their steps and left them crippled to enter the battle anew . . . they had such high hopes when they went out there; they are so desolate now."[26] Others stayed, survived, and lived to know better times.

The farmer's mounting fear and anger found expression in new, radical ideologies and organizations. In order to safeguard their interests and improve their economic lot, they formed cooperatives to market their own crops, to buy farm machinery and other manufactured goods, and to agitate on behalf of agricultural research, better schools, and fairer tax laws. Perhaps the earliest and most famous of these cooperatives was the Patrons of Husbandry (or Grange, as it was popularly called), founded in 1867 by Oliver H. Kelley, a postal clerk who wished to broaden the intellectual horizons and brighten the social life of rural citizens. The organization grew rapidly until by 1874 no less than 14,000 local granges were formed.

In 1892 several groups—the Grange, the Farmers' Alliances, the Agricultural Wheel, the Brothers of Freedom—joined the Greenbackers, the Knights of Labor, and the followers of Edward Bellamy and Henry George to form the Populist party, a diverse collection of reformers dedicated to rejuvenating farming and ameliorating the condition of the worker. (The alliance between the farmer and the urban worker soon broke down, as we shall see.) This feisty political party—it was as much a social movement as a political organization—sought stricter public control of the railroads and the business community, tax reform, a more equitable distribution of wealth, and higher farm prices. The method they supported was backing the greenback with silver rather than gold, thus cheapening the currency, raising prices, and making credit easier.

The leaders of this movement knew what they wanted and made no bones about it. There was fiery Mary Lease, who urged farmers to "raise less corn and more hell"; there was Jerry Simpson, who blasted the iniquitous railroads and spread the gospel of single-taxer Henry George; there was "Pitchfork Ben" Tilman, who championed the cause of farmers in South Carolina and became its governor; there was Nebraska's pride, the spell-binding orator William Jennings Bryan, who became the Democratic Party's candidate for the presidency of the United States in 1896. And there were many others who gave to American national politics a more radical and colorful complexion than it has known since. The party they founded died, but populism endures to this day, its hopes and rage and compassion for the common man still deeply rooted in the local politics of the Midwest and rural South.

Futile though the rage of the farmer toward the industrial forces arrayed against him was, and hopeless though his efforts to gain control over his life through political action were (real improvement in the farmer's income occurred eventually but not because of political agitation; rather because of an upswing in the business cycle and the demands of hungry Europeans for American food during World War I), his goals were at least rational. The farmer had a reasonable case against the grain speculators, the stingy banks, and the industrial "trusts" that Teddy Roosevelt so much enjoyed excoriating. But the hatred, anger, and epithets that the farmer flung at urban dwellers were entirely irrational. No economic motive could explain it. City workers were his customers, his natural allies in the fight against Wall Street and corporate monopoly, his peers in poverty. But then, as now, economic deprivation alone cannot explain the fury that seizes a population when it feels abused and ignored. The source of the farmer's anger was as much cultural and psychological as economic.

FACTORY WORKER'S PLIGHT

The farmer was not the only one to feel the sharp edge of industrial change; the artisan was also disoriented and in many cases displaced by the new industrial system. In the industrial system the old independence of the artisan vanished, never to return. Under factory discipline workers operated machines at the direction of management, for stipulated wages and fixed hours, with the product of their labor going to general markets and not to specific customers. Customized work, once the mainstay of the handicraft system, filled only a minor niche in the new industrial system of production. Gradually, self-employed artisans were turned into wage earners who had lost control over their tools, materials, and sales.

On entering the factory the worker became an interchangeable part of an impersonal organization, a faceless object ordered about by strangers, regulated by clocks, and tied to the rhythm of the machine. Decisions the craftsman had once made alone now required the assent of an employer and the marketplace, a rude shock to proudly independent Americans unaccustomed to taking orders from bosses. This was singularly galling in a country whose popular ideology proclaimed the right of everyone to be independent, to enjoy the autonomy that comes from being a self-employed craftsman, shopkeeper, small capitalist, or property owner. To be a wage-earning factory worker dependent on bosses in a country in which everyone was expected ultimately to become economically independent was to many Americans cruelly degrading.

Neither the employer nor the marketplace was especially sensitive to the workers' feelings and to their engrossing need for independence. Since this was intolerable to many workers, they sought to gain some control over their working lives through the formation of labor unions, among them the American Federation of Labor, which had replaced the Knights of Labor as the nation's largest and most militant union. But union activity, though it helped soften the transition to industrialization, did not radically alter the balance of power between workers and owners.

Downturns in the business cycle, to which all industrial economies are subject, sharply acerbated matters. A stagnant economy during the years from 1873 and 1878 and the truly sharp depression of 1893–1894 played havoc with the lives of workers and their families. Unemployment rose, wages dropped, homelessness and hunger spread, and social turmoil ensued. Ragged and hungry bands of men wandered across the countryside, living in hobo camps and eating by camp fires, whose smoke signaled the fury of the dispossessed. Some of this anger was channeled into organized protest, such as Jacob Coxey's "army" of jobless men which marched on Washington in 1894 to plead for public works to provide jobs for the unemployed. Their pleas went unheeded.

Coxey's army was peaceful; some other protests were not. Militant labor organizers, angry strikers, and many normally peaceful rank-and-file workers made desperate by misery and despair took to the streets in violent demonstrations against poor pay, long hours, and bad working conditions. Perhaps the most spectacular of these demonstrations was the Haymarket Riot in Chicago, the culmination, on May 3, 1886, of a long, bitter strike against the McCormick Harvester Company, a riotous tumult during which the police killed and wounded six demonstrators. The next day when the police broke up a mass meeting held to protest the killings, someone threw a bomb into their midst, killing seven persons and injuring over sixty others. The actual bomb thrower was never identified, but this did not prevent a jury from convicting eight anarchists for allegedly inciting the riot by word and deed; they were, according to Judge Joseph E. Gary of the Cook County Criminal Court, responsible for the massacre. One was sentenced to life imprisonment, seven to death. Of these seven, one committed suicide, four were executed, the others had their sentences commuted to life imprisonment, later pardoned by a governor who thought the verdict a miscarriage of justice.[27] The riot and its resultant trial weakened the labor movement and contributed to the growing sense of helplessness among workers entangled in the machinery of industrial change.

INDUSTRIALISM AS A WAY OF LIFE

It took more than inventive mechanics and bold entrepreneurs blessed with business acumen and unafraid to take risks to keep the American industrial machine rolling. It took, in fact, a mix of factors—the vast untapped mineral resources of the West, huge stretches of fertile and virgin soil still awaiting cultivation, an already prosperous middle class eager to become richer, a skilled working class whose ranks were periodically swollen with immigrants unafraid of manual labor and willing to work for low wages, and much foreign capital available and ready to invest in fledgling industries—to propel the United States into the front ranks of manufacturing nations. Working synergistically, these factors produced a burst of economic activity unprecedented in American history to that time, even when contrasted with the bustling period following the War of 1812. A nation that had been at mid-century predominantly agrarian became by the end of the century the world's preeminent manufacturing power.

The statistics documenting America's rise to manufacturing eminence are impressive, even to people who grow restless when statistical overload threatens. It is worthwhile to reflect on these numbers. Between 1850 and 1910 the population of the country quadrupled and the value of its agricultural products trebled. But in the same period the value of manufactured products increased twentyfold; the number of manufacturing establishments more than doubled; the number of workers in manufacturing increased seven times and their wages increased thirteenfold.[28] In 1820 five-sixths of the population was engaged in farming and one-sixth in manufacturing, transportation, trade, and assorted artisan and professional vocations. By 1910 the percentage in agriculture had dropped to one-third and the second group, which includes manufacturing and related occupations, had risen to two-thirds. Where farmhouses once stood, factories now flourished. Where men and women had once toiled in the field, even larger numbers now worked beside machines. A nation once overwhelmingly agrarian had become industrial.

America's manufacturing growth was phenomenal not only when contrasted with its own past but also when compared with other nations. In 1860 the United States ranked fourth among economically advanced nations as a producer of manufactured goods. By World War I it had substantially outdistanced its European rivals. The United States produced in the year before the Great War as much manufactured goods as its three nearest competitors—Great Britain, France, and Germany—combined.

Industrialization in the United States paid its own way from the beginning. With its factories, new technologies, and efficient transportation and communication networks, industrialization was able to create immense wealth in an incredibly short time, a process of growth that is still continuing. The gross national product in the nineteenth century doubled by mid-century and doubled again by the end of the century. By the mid-1960s the average American factory worker produced as much in a half-hour as his British counterpart a century before had made in a whole working day.[29]

Furthermore, improved farming equipment and techniques, based upon devices and knowledge invented and developed in the industrial city, made it possible for whole societies to become urbanized. Before industrialization it took fifty to ninety farmers to produce the surplus needed to enable one person to live in the city; but with the technology created by industrialization, one farmer could feed seven people in 1900, sixteen in 1950, and forty-seven in 1970.[30] The surplus population created by the mechanization of agriculture was eventually absorbed by the industrial city, which needed a huge, cheap labor force to build and run the factories, subways, cars, trucks, and similar contraptions on which the modern city depends.

By the end of the nineteenth century, the typical American could no longer be dismissed as a yokel, naively unfamiliar with the world outside his own family and community. A new American stepped front and center on the world stage. This new actor did not intend to be confined to the role of a farmer with straw stuck in his mouth, a hayseed, friendly and naive, possessing neither intellectual ambitions nor esthetic inclinations. In newly industrialized America, this image did not even remotely fit the facts. It had always been a stereotype, though it had once been thought creditable. With industrialization, for the most part, Americans became what they have since been: skilled mechanics or machine operators, white-collar workers, businessmen, professionals. The new American was educated, read newspapers and kept in touch with national and world affairs, and lived in an industrial city crammed with factories. The industrial city was fast becoming the archetypal American community and industrialism was becoming a way of life.

Industrialism is more than factories belching smoke, more than trains and planes whizzing across the land or through the air, more than gross national product and escalating standards of living. It is also a way of looking at oneself and the world, a way of deciding what deserves to be preserved and enhanced and what needs to be changed, and how to go about doing this. In short, industrialism is a system of values, beliefs, needs, and inclinations, as much as it is a system of production driven by machines.

By the end of the nineteenth century, the First Great Transformation had produced a new character type and a new culture: Darwinian Man and the Refurbished Bourgeois Culture. Both emphasized occupational achievement and success, both celebrated competition and ruthless striving, both created a new set of arrogant winners and angry losers. The cult of success, the preoccupation with winning, the certainty that success signified personal superiority and the suspicion that failure was a mark of personal inferiority—all these contributed to the anxiety of many Americans during the First Great Transformation and have done so again in the Second Great Transformation.

4

Progress and Darwinian Man

Darwinian Man has become so well known that we tend to forget how new he is on the world's scene and how powerful he once was. At the height of his influence his role in society was prodigious and his prestige enormous. For a time his future seemed gloriously limitless. But his role is now much diminished, and a new character type has taken his place. Today, the stage on which Darwinian Man stands is shaky, and the audience he addresses has become increasingly skeptical and hostile. The curtain may be coming down on this once popular performer. Worse yet, the cast that threatens to replace him are hated rivals, old performers who for centuries dominated the play. Their names are fatalism, cynicism, and pessimism. After a long hiatus, they may be making a comeback.

But perhaps it is too soon to count Darwinian Man out. In some circles certain aspects of his character are still admired, some of his values remain embedded in the popular culture, some results of the job he did (and still does) win respect. At the apogee of his power Darwinian Man championed character traits and values that won general admiration—a zest for competition, a passion for success, an exaltation of personal achievement, a willingness to work hard to attain a goal, a firm belief in the inevitability of progress. They were part of a revitalized bourgeois culture promoted by Darwinian Man that enjoyed widespread support. Today these traits and values have come

under attack; a growing number of people believe they are either false
or pernicious.

Many Americans still believe in the old traits and values and are
willing to fight to keep them alive. In order to understand the tenacity
with which people hold on to the old belief system and continue to
admire the traits exemplified by Darwinian Man, we need to examine
their origins in the ideas of personal achievement and of progress.
This is the task of this chapter. Later chapters will analyze why Darwinian Man and the old value system have come under attack and
who their enemies are.

ACHIEVEMENT AND SUCCESS

Foreign observers of American society, from the Frenchman Alexis
de Tocqueville in the 1830s to the Englishmen Geoffrey Gorer and
Dennis Brogan a century or so later, have remarked on the high value
Americans place on achievement and success, especially as expressed
in social mobility.[1] Foreigners are not alone. Native observers have
also shown great interest in success, particularly the exploits of heroes. The media routinely celebrate the achievements of athletes on
the sports field, applaud the successes of entertainers who achieve
celebrity and get invited to the White House, and recount the histories of successful business entrepreneurs who become fabulously
rich, especially if their origins are humble.

The respect accorded the self-made man sets America apart from
much of the world.[2] Americans like to believe that privileged birth
guarantees nothing, and that the will to succeed can overcome most
inherited social handicaps. Accordingly, anyone who achieves success
despite humble beginnings and against the odds wins the keenest admiration of ordinary people in the United States, witness the glori-
fication of the rail-splitter born in a log cabin who became president.

Abraham Lincoln is America's favorite president, the culture hero
who embodies the nation's cardinal virtues. "Even the inevitable
schoolboy knows that Lincoln was thrifty, hard-working, eager for
knowledge, ambitious, devoted to the rights of the average man, and
eminently successful in climbing the ladder of opportunity from the
lowermost rung of laborer to the respectable heights of merchant and
lawyer."[3] If, as it was once said, every sergeant in Napoleon's army
carried a marshal's baton in his knapsack, perhaps unnumbered Amer-

ican youngsters keep (figuratively) a copy of the constitution in their pencil boxes to remind themselves that no one is constitutionally ruled out for the president's job, age and native birth restrictions aside. All it takes is a strong character, hard work, ambition, optimism, and a determination to win, whatever the odds. The right stuff put success within everyone's grasp.

"By the end of the nineteenth century," writes Alan Kraut, "the ideology of success was well ensconced in American mythology."[4] Optimism was part of that ideology, a state of mind that persisted well into the twentieth century. More than an ideology, it became a faith, a firm conviction that, in Neil Sheehan words, "any challenge could be overcome by will and by the disciplined application of intellect, technology, money, and, when necessary, armed force."[5]

Success stories of men (and increasingly of women) who rose from simple origins to positions of prominence and wealth are common. There is, for instance, William Gates, who as a young man and college drop-out founded the immensely successful Microsoft Corporation in a garage. A major stock holder, Gates was estimated to be worth $42 billion in 1998, making him the nation's richest man. And then there is Warren Buffet, the modest Nebraskan from Omaha, still living (only part-time, it is true; he has an expensive apartment elsewhere) in the $31,500 house he bought years ago, whose canny speculations in the stock market have made him the second richest man in America, the possessor of a fortune valued at about $15.3 billion. Any investor smart enough to have given Buffet $1,000 to manage in 1965 would have seen that stake grow to a respectable $2,000,000 in 1996. Gates and Buffet have become heroes to countless young men who would also like to reach the top of the slippery pole, pulling themselves upward and onward with no assets but ambition and guts and brains.

Only industrial societies make culture heroes out of rich entrepreneurs, something that first became noticeable when manufacturing triumphed over agriculture during the First Great Transformation. In sharp contrast to the preindustrial world, the industrial society extols individual achievement, treating it as a major source of the human energy needed to keep the industrial machine humming. Industrial societies press their members to achieve to the limit of their ability, to enter the race for success, and to compete for the prizes that await the winner.

Of course, not everyone enters the race at the same place. Some entrants have a head start, having been placed up front by powerful relatives and friends. Others are burdened by heavy social handicaps— a despised color, a hated religion, an inferior class accent—or discouraged from entering at all. Even so, whatever their starting point most racers are urged to compete for the winner's laurel, and relatively few are given the prize on a silver platter, without effort on their part. Sadly, some racers will stumble and fall along the way, losers in the sprint for success. Still there are many winners. For what sets the industrial society apart from other systems is the unprecedented number and variety of arenas in which one may compete, whether it be the factory floor or the executive suite, the shop or the office building, the field or the laboratory. And from these many competitions emerge a stream of successes, small and large.

The reader may wonder, is there anything new in this? Did not incredible bursts of energy in the arts and sciences, in engineering and technology occur in various places before the advent of industrialization? Were not Periclean Athens, Medician Florence, or Elizabethan London places where personal achievement and robust individualism flourished? The answer must be yes, of course. The extraordinary achievements of those periods were, however, the work of a tiny elite, people of privileged birth or remarkable talent. Granted a midwife's son (Socrates) might become a philosopher, a merchant's son (William Shakespeare) a playwright, a notary's son (Leonardo da Vinci) a painter. Not even the tight hierarchical social systems of their times could suppress their magnificent genius.

Even in those extraordinary times the vast majority of the population was never permitted to enter the big races for wealth, status, or power. The furious and intricate politics of the state and the struggle for money and land were closed affairs and seldom touched the people at large. They stayed in their own circles and left to their betters the big contests for riches and glory. People were expected to accept their station in life, and those who did not, who tried to enter a higher stratum through unseemly striving, evoked the displeasure of the state, the reproaches of the established church, and the envy of their peers.

Pre-industrial societies sought to curb the achiever's acquisitive appetite and to stifle his gnawing hunger to rise above his fellows, by employing a variety of mechanisms. The guild and the merchant league, for example, set standards, controlled prices and wages, and divided up the market in order to discourage competition and ensure a rough equality among people of the same station. Controlling competition seemed the natural and proper thing to do. The feudal mind, for example, thought of society as a complex organism in which each person was a necessary part with important functions and needs. As Richard H. Tawney put it, "Each must receive the means suited to its station, and must claim no more. Within classes there must be equality: if one takes into his hand the living of two, his neighbor will go short."[6] In the medieval view, economic competition and individualism could only lead to the misery of the many for the benefit of the few.

Industrialization challenged and overthrew this perspective; individualism became a fundamental value of the industrial society. But industrialization did more than affirm the importance of the individual; it made the pursuit of profit respectable. Before industrialization the business class could not entirely shake itself free of the feeling that striving for personal gain was somehow reprehensible. Charging interest smacked of usury; reaping profit from simple economic exchange reeked of sharp practice, a case of satisfying one's greed at the expense of the unfortunate buyer and borrower. The pursuit of material success evoked general contempt and censure, especially from the church. However much the Puritan Ethic valued the accumulation of private wealth as a probable sign of God's favor, most people felt that the effort that went into piling up riches was a perversion of talent and character that ought to have been put to better use.

In decisively breaking with the traditional aversion to achievement for mere private gain, industrial capitalism freed the rich from guilt. Unhampered by sumptuary laws or religious scruples, successful industrialists proudly boasted of their success and ostentatiously displayed their wealth without feeling guilty or fearing public reproof and envy. In fact, not only did envy lose its power to inhibit achievement, it became an acceptable tool to spur people on to greater effort, to drive them on to success.

At first the urban masses and the rural poor, still tightly controlled and systematically exploited by the ruling class, hardly entered at all into this new celebration of achievement and success. But in time industrialization encouraged almost everyone to enter the race for success, inviting more people to compete for money and power than any previous society had ever dreamed of doing. What is more, industrial societies began singling out achievers for special treatment, promoting them above their fellow workers and rewarding them with money and acclaim. Worth, not birth, became the socially applauded key to success. More than any other system the industrial society agonized about undeveloped talent and systematically searched for worthy and bright youngsters, plying them with scholarships and tempting them with visions of fame, fortune, and fun, all in the conviction that society prospers when individual achievement is encouraged.

More than in any other kind of society, achievers readily celebrated their success and openly exulted in its rewards. In what other kind of society has this ever happened? None, for not until the advent of industrialization was the broad road to upward mobility opened to the masses. That road now open, many ambitious people ventured upon it, vigorously pursuing success and in many cases achieving it. Small wonder that they came to believe in progress.

THE IDEA OF PROGRESS

Once upon a time, now barely remembered, most Americans at some point in their lives fell in love with the idea of progress, lost their heart to the notion that things were bound, in the long run, to get ever better. This notion gave them the confidence to push into the frontier against the objections of hostile Indians, to build cities in the mountains and deserts and desolate prairies, and to expand the frontiers of science and technology and the economy. Experience justified that confidence, so that in time few dared challenge it. But times have changed, and today questions have arisen—in fact, enough questions to suggest that many Americans have lost their faith in progress.

In order to understand why most Americans once earnestly believed in progress, it is necessary to examine where this idea came from in the first place and what conditions produced it. Only then can we comprehend why it found so congenial a home among Americans, a people who prided themselves in being hardheaded and deeply suspicious of airy notions and high-faluting ideas, particularly those originating in Europe. Only then will we realize how sharp a break with the past the current run of skepticism about progress actually is.

To skeptics the idea of progress seems a loony fantasy. The evidence to support it is at best inconclusive; there is plenty of room for doubt. The conviction that mankind will go on developing and improving into the illimitable future, the belief, in Auguste Comte's words, "that the perfectibility of man is truly indefinite; that the progress of this perfectibility . . . has no other limit than the duration of the globe on which nature has placed us," runs counter to the facts of history and requires a suspension of disbelief, a willingness to ignore cruel reality that seems more appropriate to the theater of the absurd than to the theater of everyday life. Still, notwithstanding experience to the contrary, the idea of progress eventually captured the Western imagination, a conquest that occurred primarily, though perhaps not entirely, in modern times.

Scholars debate learnedly about when this idea first took hold in the Western mind. Some argue that it has been around for a long time. Perhaps the Greeks in Periclean Athens, and the Romans under Augustus and the Antonine emperors came under its influence. Robert Nisbet, a sociologist, believes the idea of progress is clearly evident in the work of Protagoras, Aristotle, and Zeno. But other scholars believe the idea of progress is an entirely modern invention. Thus, Walter Bagehot, historian, journalist, and editor of *The Economist*, maintained that "the ancients had no conception of progress; they did not so much reject the idea; they did not entertain the idea."[7] J. B. Bury, a historian, in his *Idea of Progress*, concurred: the Greeks and Romans gave no thought to the notion of progress; it is a seventeenth century invention reinforced in the eighteenth century.[8]

Why the seventeenth and eighteenth centuries? In part because it was during this period that the effects of technological change, slowly building over previous centuries, spread rapidly across the West, pushing into every aspect of life. New or improved mechanical devices—the cam, crank, gear, cog, flywheel, and triphammer—greatly aided manufacturing. New construction devices—the brace and bit, the truss, to name just a few—made building houses and factories easier and safer. New machines and techniques made weaving and spinning faster and metal founding more efficient. By the time Diderot and D'Alembert published their *Encyclopedia* in the late eighteenth century, they could devote considerable attention to illustrating and describing the construction and uses of an immense treasure of mechanical inventions to which mankind by then had access. Together these innovations laid the groundwork for the industrial revolution of the eighteenth and nineteenth centuries.

Other changes also helped make the idea of progress appear not only logical but inevitable, especially to people with a taste for rationality. Travel and exploration, which flourished in the seventeenth and eighteenth centuries to a degree unparalleled in history, even in the halcyon days of Greece and Rome, opened the eyes and minds of Europeans to the richness and variety of cultures and peoples beyond their own small world. The stumbling of Europeans upon the Americas in 1492 (the Viking landfall on Greenland in 982 and Newfoundland in 1000 having long been forgotten) excited the imagination of philosophers and poets, who projected upon that unknown land their own utopian fantasies of unspoiled societies inhabited by noble savages living together in peace and collectively enjoying nature's bounty.

Adventurers, merchants, and governments, enriched with the gold and silver taken from foreign colonies, provided capital for investment and stimulated economies. More money in private hands and government coffers meant greater support for schools and universities, which grew rapidly in this period. More plentiful and better food, and improvements in medicine and public sanitation, led to better health and lower mortality rates, particularly among the very young, touching off a population explosion that energized economic growth and generated a general sense of excitement and well-being.

Excited by the exuberant growth of science and industry, men like Voltaire and Condorcet, drunk with rationalism and optimism, announced to the world that mankind had begun a march of progress that was both certain and without end. Their optimism was founded on the belief that progress moves in step with the growth of knowledge. Since every generation adds to the store, in part because it is in the nature of knowledge to accumulate, like money growing at compound interest in a safe bank, and in part because man's innate need to enlarge his understanding of the world causes him to continually make new deposits to his account, progress is inevitable. Believers in progress argued that we cannot help knowing more than our ancestors, no matter how bright they may have been. A student today who is skilled in the calculus knows more mathematics than did Euclid or Pythagoras. Progress, not superior intelligence, makes this curious fact possible.

To this chorus of hosannas to progress was added the voices of poets, playwrights and scholars, not all of them devotees of reason, who had grown annoyed by the constant comparison, often invidious, of their work with the masterpieces of ancient Greece and Rome.

Really, it is wearisome, they said, to be constantly told that one's poetry falls far short of the excellence achieved by Homer or Horace, that one's plays compare poorly with the lofty heights scaled by Sophocles or Euripedes, that one's philosophic treatises seem puerile when put up against the works of Plato or Aristotle. More than wearisome, these criticisms are just plain wrong, said Jonathan Swift. For how can we be inferior to the Ancients when we have the benefit of their knowledge? Granted, they were giants, but we can see further than they because we stand on their shoulders. Far from being inferior to the Ancients, we are better—inevitably so—for such is the way progress works.

No one promoted the Idea of Progress with more clarity and determination than did Marie Jean Antoine Nicolas Caritat, the Marquis de Condorcet. A mathematician, philosopher, and revolutionist, Condorcet believed that humanity's future would be better than its past. Seeking to bring about this happy end, Condorcet supported the French Revolution and took part in the Convention, representing the department of Aisne, and wrote influential pamphlets and legislation. But he fell out with his fellow revolutionaries when he opposed the execution of the king, though he favored replacing the monarchy with a republic. Facing arrest for his moderate sentiments, he fled Paris and found refuge in the home of Madame Vernet, the widow of a prominent sculptor.

In her house, an outlaw, fearing betrayal and discovery, neglected by friends he had defended, the guillotine an ever-present prospect, he wrote his masterpiece, a paean to progress, entitled *Esquisse d'un tableau historique des progres de l'espirit humain.* In this book he fleshed out his ideas about progress and his reasons for believing in its inevitable victory. Why inevitable? Because equality of opportunity, the elimination of social classes, and the triumph of liberty and democracy—all elements of progress as he saw it—were rooted in human nature, in man's innate goodness, in his restless curiosity and thirst for knowledge.

Fate cruelly tested Condorcet's faith in man's innate goodness, for, alas, it failed to surface to his benefit during the stressful events of his last days. On the other hand, his hunch about humanity's insatiable curiosity proved all too correct; it was peasant curiosity that proved his undoing. Fearing discovery he slipped away from Madame Vernet's house and sought shelter at the chateau of someone he had befriended, only to be rebuffed. Shelter denied him, he hid for three nights and days in nearby thickets and stone quarries until hunger drove him to enter a tavern and order dinner, an egg omelet. "How many eggs in your omelet?" asked the tavern keeper. "A dozen." "What is your trade?" "A carpenter." To which the skeptical tavern keeper responded that "carpenters have not hands like these and do not ask for a dozen eggs in an omelet." His curiosity and suspicions aroused, he demanded to see Condorcet's papers. Condorcet had none. Whereupon the villagers seized and bound him, and dragged him, feet bleeding and body exhausted from exposure and hunger, on a painful journey to a magistrate in Bourg-la-Reine, where he was cast into a cold damp cell. The next morning he was found dead on the floor, his voice in praise of progress and the common man forever stilled in 1794, the fifty-first year of his life.[9]

PROGRESS AND DARWINIANISM

Despite Condorcet's best efforts, the Idea of Progress would probably not have achieved general popularity had it not married the theory of social evolution. (The marriage took place in England; Herbert Spencer was the best man.) This union would have been unworkable had the theory of social evolution been a biological concept, entirely the work of natural scientists. Charles Darwin, a naturalist to the core, never coupled progress with evolution. In fact, the pairing of progress with evolution offended him and he never accepted it.

To Darwin evolution was a purely biological matter, an impersonal process of natural selection during which some creatures, made fiercely competitive by a constant struggle to gain access to limited resources, adapt and reproduce, transmitting their characteristics to progeny, while those poorly adapted fall by the wayside, losers in the game of life. Darwin never made moral judgments about the ability of a species to survive, nor did he consider survival a sign of some grand design called Progress. Neither did he consider evolutionary survival a mark of Providence's hand in human affairs. Aware of the controversy his work had unleashed, he carefully avoided commenting on the implications of his theory for established religion. The shape of a bird's bill or the color of its plumage might help in the search for food or the evasion of predators, but these were matters of unplanned variation, not the result of a creature's moral stature or of careful planning and intentional change. As Darwin saw it, survival is survival and nothing more.

Herbert Spencer saw things differently. He discerned purpose and direction in the evolutionary process and announced his discovery to enthusiastic audiences in numerous highly popular books, articles, and lectures. In Spencer's hands Darwin's theory underwent transformation. Evolution ceased being solely a biological explanation of how species change; it became a social explanation of how societies change—it became, in short, Social Evolutionary Theory, perhaps the most ambitious and systematic theory of social change ever conceived. For the Social Evolutionist, social change is a movement through stages of development, each stage a different type of society, more complex and differentiated, with more highly specialized parts and functions. The movement gains energy from the conflict between individuals and groups as they struggle to win access to limited resources upon which their survival depends. Spencer looked upon this struggle with approval and called it progress. His critics called it Social Darwinism, and heaped upon it mountains of scorn.

To begin with, they rejected the Social Evolutionist's comparison of society to a biological organism, a living creature like an orange or an orangutan, moving through predictable developmental stages. Nothing in this idea would explain, the critics argued, why some societies never seem to change, hanging on to things as they are well past their prime. Nor does it explain why other societies, to the dismay of enemies and the delight of friends, suddenly throw off the burdens of time and display new bursts of energy and creativity. Also, the critics complained of social evolution's prejudices, its elitism, its indifference to the plight of lesser breeds, its appeal to bigots and racists; and for these sins they cast it into the outer darkness of political incorrectness.[10] Only belatedly did they notice that social evolution was much more than a new theory of social change; it was a new ideology, the offspring of the union between Progress and Evolution, and that it had become in the hands of Spencer's followers a new religion.

To the embarrassment of its adherents, who much preferred to think of their creed as scientific fact, Social Darwinism bears many of the marks of a religion. It is based upon a sacred text, the works of Herbert Spencer, and in Spencer it has a prophet, a charismatic leader beyond comparison and above reproach, the carrier of a special message. When Spencer visited the United States in 1882, his followers treated him as though he were a messiah come to save mankind.[11] Whether this reception pleased or embarrassed Spencer was not recorded.

The followers of Spencer were discouraged from tampering with or questioning the word of the master, but, as in all religions, differences in interpretation inevitably crept into the original body of belief. As a result, there soon emerged several types of Social Darwinists, some of whom moved fairly far from the original creed. For example, not all Social Darwinists shared Spencer's cheerful acceptance of the battle for survival and his somewhat ambivalent optimism about the future. They saw social evolution as a grim struggle, whose unpleasant side effects humanity must stoically accept, leading to a future not everyone would find enjoyable.

Nevertheless, despite doctrinal disagreements, Social Darwinism performed many of the unifying functions of a religion. It provided a vision of an orderly and purposeful scheme of things that was attractive and reassuring in a world plagued by widespread doubt and skepticism. To restless and dissatisfied people who felt that life was meaningless, without purpose or plan, who had lost confidence in the benevolence of Providence's guiding hand and whose faith in conventional religion had been undermined by science and the materialistic ethos of industrialism, Social Darwinism offered a way out of confusion and anxiety.

In the place of God's mysterious inscrutable will, Social Darwinism put the invisible hand of evolution, ever busy separating the fit from the unfit, imposing order on social chaos, moving society toward ever higher levels of complexity and material well-being. But this new order would not be a hedonistic, amoral world devoid of spiritual values, where only sensual appetites mattered; it would be a moral order because only the best people (the fit) would survive. The dross of social selection would be eliminated. In the end, things would be for the best—the universal promise of all religions. In effect, Spencer had created a new religion, albeit without a divinity.[12]

This is ironic, because nothing could have been farther from Spencer's mind when he first set out to instruct the public in the implications of evolutionary theory than the creation of a new religion. Philosopher, journalist, biologist, engineer, psychologist, and sociologist, he was above all a rationalist, a devout believer in science, and an individualist. His distrust of government was monumental. He never tired of castigating governmental interference in private affairs. He opposed state-financed education; he objected to governmental protection of the gullible from the skullduggery of the crooked; at one time he even argued for the private management of war. The government's clumsiness in conducting public affairs appalled him. Will Durant writes: "He carried his manuscripts to the printer himself, having too little confidence in a government institution to entrust them to the Post Office . . . He was a man of intense individuality, irritably insistent on being left alone; and every new act of legislation seemed to him an invasion of his personal liberty . . . When people insisted on coming to see him he inserted stopping into his ear and listened placidly."[13]

He was most certainly not a man of deep religious conviction and enthusiasm. And yet, ironically, it was his lectures and books on the value and implications of evolution that created Social Darwinism. Moreover, it made him famous. For it was Spencer who introduced the phrase "survival of the fittest" into popular speech. And it was Spencer who turned a value-free idea—the survival of the best adapted—into a moral indictment of failure. Failure became the mark of the unfit and unworthy—a highly popular idea then as it is today. In the opinion of the Social Darwinist, the evolutionary process, if left to its own devices, unfettered by governmental restrictions and unmitigated by private benevolence, would unsentimentally select only the most deserving for survival. Only they would get to pass on their physical characteristics, cultural values, and psychological traits to their progeny. But here we come to a perennial and vexing problem: who are the deserving, who the undeserving, and who is to decide their fate?

Social Darwinism had the answer to this problem and therein lies much of its attraction; it would replace natural selection with social selection. No longer would an impersonal force called nature (Darwin's God) make the decision; that power would be in the hands of society, its surrogates and guardians. And who are these guardians? The fit, of course. The question answers itself; only the fit are competent to judge the fitness of others. Who, after all, is better suited to pass judgment on the suitability of others to stay in the race of life, to compete for its prizes, and to pass on their winning skills to future generations than the survivors of evolution's most rigorous tests?

DARWINIAN MAN: A CULTURE HERO

Some ideas, like well packaged and skillfully touted wines, travel well, retaining their pungency and punch even when transported over mountains and across seas. Social Darwinism is one such idea. This product of the industrial revolution, matured in England, wrapped in Herbert Spencer's weighty tomes, popularized by the press, and then shipped across the Atlantic, arrived in excellent condition in the late nineteenth century on American shores, where it found eager and appreciative buyers. The timing could not have been more opportune. Americans in the Gilded Age of national prosperity and international muscle flexing thirsted for ideas that would explain to the world the nation they were building, that would sanction their sometimes brutal mastery over nature, and that would justify their domination of weaker neighbors. Social Darwinism was for them the right idea, in the right place, at the right time.

Social Darwinism arrived in the United States at a time of rapid economic change, growing wealth, rampant materialism, and reckless display—in short, at the peak of the First Great Transformation. Manufacturing was triumphant, markets had become regional and international, and fierce competition in the marketplace forced producers to pay greater attention to efficiency. Hiring and retaining incompetent or lazy workers for sentimental reasons, such as family loyalty, pity, sympathy, or a sense of *noblesse oblige* for the less fortunate, was a luxury few employers could afford if they wanted to stay in business. Manufacturers regarded individual performance as the main criterion for distributing valued resources—money, prestige and power—at least ideally and increasingly in practice.

Specialization, the keystone around which the industrial structure is built, had increased prodigiously. The costly, complex, and energy-guzzling machines that drive the industrial economy require the services of specialists in order to function properly—scientists, engineers, and technicians to invent, improve, and maintain the machines; skilled workers to operate them; and armies of merchants and salespeople to distribute and sell the flood of products the machines produce. Consequently, the industrial society built schools to train the citizenry to take its place in the new industrial order, including the masses from which skilled workers were drawn. This is something new under the sun, Ecclesiastes to the contrary notwithstanding, for never before had any society attempted to provide lengthy formal education to so large a portion of the population.

The newly educated specialists did not lack for work. But this is not to say that everyone found a suitable job without delay or suffered no periods of painful unemployment. After all the industrial system invented the business cycle, and people suffered then, as now, from periodic plunges of the economy into depression, or panic as it was called in the nineteenth century. Nevertheless, the industrial system generated enough jobs to provide work for most people, including the millions of immigrants who came to the United States in the late nineteenth century in search of a better life.

Specialists and achievers come into their own in an economy that pays attention to performance on the job. The industrial system needs energetic, self-disciplined, sober, prudent, industrious workers, and it gives unprecedented importance to excellence in work. For, as John W. Osborne noted, "Until the eighteenth century, the sole concern was that a job be done; the expense and complexity of the industrial system meant that for the first time, how the job was done must be considered."[14] And, to a greater degree than ever before, the industrial system gives achievers their just rewards. They come to be seen as the salt of the earth, workers who bring to their jobs the drive, discipline, and competitiveness upon which the system depends, who parlay energy and skill into money and status.

Whether they are aware of it or not, achievers are a product of a process in which, as Max Weber put it, society "educates and selects the economic subjects which it needs through a process of natural selection."[15] The process employs two basic procedures, selection and adaptation, which in the main operate to give society the kind of people it needs.

The first procedure, social selection, assumes that unplanned, random variation exists within every society and that the task of society is to select out the persons who possess the qualities best suited to its needs. Since individuals vary in every society—ambition, a determination to work long and hard to achieve success, a commitment to excellence, and a willingness to delay immediate gratification in order to ensure future gains can sometimes be found in the unlikeliest of places—a dynamo of energy and ambition may appear in a family of sluggards. The industrial society sends out its agents—teachers, personnel recruiters, entrepreneurs, foundation officials—to find this dynamo (and others like him), select him for training, and put him to work maintaining the system. This he will probably agree to do since his needs and those of society are highly complementary.

The second procedure, adaptation, assumes, reasonably enough, that people will try their best to ensure their own survival in even the most unfriendly environment. Since the repertoire of possible responses to the environment is usually large, they must experiment to see what works best for them, what is most likely to ensure prosperity, and what will lead to disappointment and ruin. As a rule, society encourages adaptive choices and tries to extinguish nonadaptive ones.

In creating the individualistic achiever, the industrial system accomplished an extraordinary feat of psychological engineering; it produced the character type it needed to make the system work—Darwinian Man. A complex bundle of character traits and values, Darwinian Man was a new actor on the social scene, not particularly lovable or universally admired, but admirably suited to the needs of the system and at home in it. In an industrial system that thrives on energetic and unremitting competition, Darwinian Man was preeminently well adapted. He viewed economic life as a war for survival in which only the fit emerged victorious. He believed that winning was its own justification. His determination to come out on top, to do whatever was needed to survive and prosper, and his ruthlessness and calculating shrewdness gave him the force to transform an agricultural economy into an industrial giant.

Darwinian Man saw in his success visible proof of his superiority. He made no attempt to hide his contempt for life's losers, the inferior people who clogged the system and burdened the successful with high taxes, useless philanthropies, and unwanted children. Nor did he try to hide his satisfaction in triumphing over rivals. Contemplating their failure was pleasurable, and trumpeting his own success entirely delicious. The most successful of Darwinian Men, the possessors of great fortunes, many newly made in railroad building, oil and mineral exploitation, banking and stock market speculation, did not hesitate to flaunt their wealth. They built grand houses in Manhattan and Newport, indulged in gaudy extravagances and gave breathtakingly lavish parties and balls. A ball given by Bradley Martin in 1897 at the Waldorf-Astoria, whose ballroom was transformed into a replica of Versailles, required guests to come attired in the costumes of the time. One guest appeared in a suit of armor inlaid with gold valued at the time at ten thousand dollars.[16]

It happened that Herbert Spencer took part in one of these grotesque affairs. At an entertainment given in his honor at Delmonico's, guests were given cigarettes wrapped in hundred dollar bills. The guests lit their cigarettes with a studied indifference to cost that only the very rich can achieve. Whether Spencer, whose austere, parsimonious way of life was well known in London, joined in this display of conspicuous consumption is not recorded. But Spencer's presence at one of these tawdry festivities seems incongruous. Surely the progenitor of Social Evolution needed no grandiose display of wealth to prove his fitness to survive.

In the United States no one epitomized the Darwinian Man better than William Graham Sumner. The son of humble parents, a graduate of Yale in 1863, a clergyman for several years, and a professor and holder of a Chair of Sociology at Yale University for thirty-odd years, Sumner passed every test for fitness and became in the late nineteenth century (he died in 1910) a national figure, America's foremost spokesman for Social Darwinism. His path to success was not easy. It was marked by struggle (as befits the life of an exponent of social evolution) by hard work and by prodigious productivity. In a slew of lectures, papers, and books (his most important scholarly work, *Folkways*, became a classic) he spread the gospel of Social Darwinism. His work, unlike most publications by today's scholars, won a popular audience eager to hear a message that sanctified their success.

As Sumner saw it, the fit are the benefactors of humanity. For it is their hard work, their willingness to plan and defer gratification, their dogged determination to get ahead that provide the human capital on which progress depends. And let there be no confusion as to who is fit; in the final analysis fitness is measured by material success. The fit, the elect of the new religion, are those who have prospered in the competitive struggle for survival.

But they are not merely richer than the common run of humanity; they are morally superior as well. The good man, that is, the fit man in Social Darwinist theology, Robert Green McCloskey writes, "was chaste, frugal, industrious, and devoted to duty; he walked alone, secure in the certitude of rectitude, and mended his own fences. There was no humor about this paragon, no frivolity, very little charity."[17] The good man—fit, elite, and elect—lived in a natural order, followed a rational law of development, and worked toward benevolent ends made possible only by his material success. The unfit—failures and wastrels—are marked by moral inferiority. "No man in this land," preached Henry Ward Beecher, "suffers from poverty unless it be his fault—unless it be his sin."[18]

How pleasing it must have been to the ears of the businessman, weary of being made to feel guilty of avarice when he energetically pursued profits and wealth, to be told that material success is nothing to be ashamed of; rather, it is a mark of moral superiority. How soothing to the sensibilities of the ambitious youth, wounded by accusations of less ambitious peers, who see in his yearnings for success the mark of moral degeneracy and the root cause of unseemly aggressiveness, to be told that ambition is, to use Joseph Epstein's words, "the fuel of achievement and achievement the motor of progress."[19] Such balm to the spirit had been noticeably absent in the past.

The last decades of the nineteenth century were great years for Darwinian Men. They found resources no one knew were there—oil, lead, copper, silver, and gold in rocks and mud. They developed new ways of growing, shipping, and selling the staples of life—meat, fruit and grain. They found ways to make travel easier and cheaper, on the railroads, steamships, and automobiles of their own manufacture. They transformed communication from an exercise between people in close physical proximity into an exchange over great distances through wires. They fabricated machines to make life easier—home appliances to lighten woman's chores, electric lamps to brighten the night, colorful attire to attractively cover comical human nakedness. They produced phonographs, plays, circuses, vaudeville, and movies to entertain and chase away the tedium of everyday life. They worked hard, built factories and created cities in improbable places. They were boosters, believers in progress, worshippers of the bitch-goddess success. Some became successful, famous and rich; others lived in obscurity and earned only a modest living—nonetheless, a living substantially better than that which their parents and grandparents had known. They were winners.

AMERICAN NERVOUSNESS

But, as already noted, the First Great Transformation had its costs, because deep and enveloping social change, even when it brings economic progress, comes with a scary price tag. Invariably, rapid, substantial change stuns some people and shatters their lives, leaving them bewildered and bitter. For the losers the economic toll alone was horrendous—lost farms, lost wealth, lost jobs. But there was another loss, in some ways more painful than any other—the loss of self-esteem. All too often, the First Great Transformation robbed the losers of respect for themselves.

The belief that work and merit ultimately win out lies deep in the American psyche. It is a comforting notion, but it has its dark side. For it can result in failure being charged to defects of character rather than to capricious luck or blind social forces. And when failure comes to be seen as a personal flaw its impact on self-respect can be devastating. This is especially true in the United States, where many people tend to assess their own worth in terms of dollars accumulated, houses occupied, promotions attained, offices held, academic degrees and other credentials harvested—all stigmata with which America marks its members. Without the cover of achievement many Americans feel naked and unrecognized, devoid of memorable individuality, lacking in the patina of merit and importance. So much store has been put in achievement and success that their loss or absence erodes the individual's belief in his or her own personal worth.

This may have been partly responsible for what observers reported seeing among Americans in the midst of the First Great Transformation—that is, pervasive anxiety. Unfortunately, no systematic record of the American state of mind exists for this period, no public opinion polls, no foundation-sponsored psychiatric inventories. But we are not entirely without information. Occasional snapshots of Americans captured by writers and journalists and physicians give us a sense of how people looked and felt. Various writers thought Americans were depressed. To these observers, the typical American appeared anxious, troubled by chronic disappointment and a nagging sense of worthlessness, plagued by irrational fears, and worried about the future, given to chronic insomnia, to inner tenseness and public jumpiness.[20]

The most common explanation for this condition was fatigue. Matthew Arnold, the British writer, believed Americans were "extremely nervous because of worry and overwork," an assessment that agreed with an earlier report in the *Transactions* of the Medical Society of the State of New York, which described Americans as anxious and careworn.[21] While these reports did not single out the losers, it seems reasonable to assume that this particular group was especially prone to anxiety, a condition that could only have been exacerbated by doubts about self-worth. But it was not the losers alone who were anxious; paradoxically, many of the winners also appeared afflicted with anxiety.

George M. Beard, a physician, has given us a lengthy analysis of American nervousness, as he called it, in the late nineteenth century. Beard was a neurologist, a Fellow of the New York Academy of Medicine and a member of other worthy scientific organizations. Writing in 1881, he expressed alarm at the steep rise in the amount of sick headache, hypochondria, nervous exhaustion, insomnia, hysteria, nervous dyspepsia, and other symptoms of the neurasthenia he was witnessing among people in the upper strata of society. He attributed these emotional ailments to industrialization or, as he put it, to modern civilization.

The pace of modern life, he concluded, is too hectic for the emotional well-being of Americans. They have become addicted to work; they are compulsive watchers of clocks and slaves to punctuality— and "punctuality is the thief of nervous force."[22] The cause of this nervousness was not hard to find, he believed. One need look no further than the modern city, which shuts people up in crowded streets and neighborhoods, pummels them with incessant noise, subjects them to intense competition, and afflicts them with information overload.

Beard singled out the telegraph as a major cause of emotional distress. Telegraphy puts people under constant strain, swiftly transmitting news that once took weeks to travel, bombarding them with more information than they can handle, creating confusion and anxiety. Business men were the telegraph's most pathetic victims. It transmitted the prices of goods immediately across the globe, requiring responses to information before it could be digested and reflected upon, and kept the merchant in a constant state of apprehension. "This continual fluctuation of values, and the knowledge of those fluctuations in every part of the world, are the scourges of business men, the tyrants of trade—every cut in prices in wholesale lines in the smallest of any of the Western cities, becomes known in less than an hour all over the Union; thus competition is both diffused and intensified."[23]

Beard was among the first to recognize the effects of ferocious competition and improved technology on the emotional state of people. He was no Luddite. He never talked about turning the clock back, but he was clearly concerned about the impact of too much information on people's peace of mind. What he would think of today's information society (to say nothing of the computer and the Internet), we cannot know. But were he alive today he would certainly study it closely—which is something I propose to do in the balance of this book.

PART III

THE SECOND GREAT TRANSFORMATION

5

The New Elite

Every social order contains the seeds of its own destruction, to paraphrase Karl Marx, who borrowed the notion from Gottfried Leibnitz. (Revolutionary fervor, not philosophic originality, was Marx's strong suite.) The old order is always pregnant with the new. So it was with the manufacturing system. For even as manufacturing was reaching its pinnacle of power and influence—that is, during World War II, when every sinew was strained to harness the nation's resources to the war effort, when, as Franklin Delano Roosevelt put it, Dr. Win-The-War was prescribing the country's medicine—the service sector was emerging as the economy's preeminent force: about as many people were employed in providing services as in manufacturing.[1]

Manufacturing's dominion in America was short. Agriculture had ruled the economy for centuries, manufacturing only decades. From 1870, when for the first time the output of America's mills and factories exceeded the value of goods produced on the farm, to the period following World War II, when the United States became the world's first service economy, less than a century had elapsed. And yet in that brief period a social revolution had taken place—the Second Great Transformation—and the techno-service sector became society's economic mainstay. The scepter of economic majesty passed from hands making tangible goods to those providing services, immaterial products that cannot be driven or worn, put in crates and trucked to distant markets, handled and fondled or smashed to smithereens.

By 1950 the Second Great Transformation had decisively demoted manufacturing to second place. The service sector became society's principal employer; more than half of the labor force (54 percent) was working in the service economy. That figure climbed to 58 percent in 1960; to 62 percent in 1970; to 67 percent in 1980; and to 78 percent in 1994, approximately where it presently is. The share that services contribute to the gross domestic product has increased roughly proportionately; it is now 72 percent, whereas manufacturing has fallen to only 23 percent. The United States has become increasingly dependent on the service sector not only to provide work for its people but also to keep its international trade in balance.[2] In 1993, service exports generated a $67 billion trade surplus, whereas merchandise exports were $115 billion in the red.[3]

After the end of World War II, when agricultural employment declined precipitously and manufacturing, formerly the most robust part of the economy, grew sluggishly at first and then also declined, the service sector flourished. Thus agricultural employment fell gradually after World War I and then plunged after 1950 when the world no longer had to depend upon the American farmer for food. In 1950 farmers made up 11.9 percent of the workforce; today less than 1 percent are full-time farmers. Not since the presidency of Millard Fillmore have farmers been fewer in absolute numbers. Manufacturing's employment record is almost as dismal. Between 1955 and 1980 the economy added some 40 million jobs, but only one out of ten were in manufacturing. In 1970, 27 percent of American workers were in manufacturing; by 1993 the figure had fallen to 16 percent, about where it is now.[4]

The decline in manufacturing employment is expected to continue. The Bureau of Labor Statistics forecasts that by the year 2005 manufacturers will employ only 12 percent of American workers. By comparison, the health sector, only one of many areas in which service workers find employment, added as many jobs as all of manufacturing combined. Education created even more jobs than health. Only 3 million of the 70 million jobs added to the economy since 1950 have been in manufacturing. All the jobs added between 1975 and 1980, about 12 million, were in services.[5]

The growth of the service sector shows no sign of slackening. Social pressures will not permit it. Population trends and social policies increasingly pose problems that more often call for services than for goods, and vast bureaucracies have developed in government and in the health, education, and amenities industries to provide these services. The poor and the disadvantaged, the sick and the aged, the job-shy and the redundant, the retired and the footloose more often need the help of teachers and social workers, nurses and physicians, travel agents and hotel keepers than of welders, millwrights, and machine operators.

The relationship of the service economy to industry is frequently misunderstood. The techno-service economy is not, as some believe, a post-industrial phenomenon. Rather, it is industrialization's most recent stage of development and its leading edge of change. Technological innovation and specialization occur as readily in a service as in a goods-producing industry. "The process of industrialization is underway in every branch of service activity," writes George Gilder, "as plastic cards revolutionize the extension of credit, television transforms the productivity of the entertainer, word processors exalt the efficiency of secretaries, and beepers make firemen and doctors more immediately available."[6]

It is not only the individual consumer who needs services; the goods producing industries are themselves major consumers of services. Manufacturers have come to rely on services to create and sell their products. Computers, tractors, airplanes, radios, and cars are not merely fabricated; they are marketed and advertised as well, and services add a significant and rising part to the cost of manufacturing. More and more, industry finds it needs agents to handle real estate, insurance, and advertising; it needs consultants to work on old problems and introduce new ideas; it needs lobbyists and public relations firms to protect its interests in state houses and in the national capital. Together, manufacturing and the service sector have created a new system—the techno-service economy.

The noisy, whirling, humming, vastly efficient machines of the techno-service system produce a cornucopia of goods, and the bustling city provides an eager, easily accessible market in which to sell them. Economies of supply and distribution have created unprecedented private wealth and general prosperity—washing machines and refrigerators for the homemaker, tractors and combines for the farmer, dresses and skirts for shop girls that are indistinguishable from the *haute couture* apparel worn by affluent debutantes, a car or two in every garage. But all of this requires skilled minds to sort out the inevitable problems of finance, security, distribution, advertising, and sales; and it is to the techno-service specialist that society has turned for help.

So rapid was manufacturing's fall from eminence that the nature of the new order that has taken its place has not yet been fully recognized by the general public. The techno-service economy that ended the reign of manufacturing is an immensely complicated wonder. It is more than a new system of production and distribution, more than a new array of products and services—it is a new social order based on new values and new social relationships, an order run by a New Elite.

The power of the New Elite stems from the unique complementarity between itself and the techno-service society. As knowledge creators and information processors, they possess the talents, skills, values, and traits required for the smooth functioning of a service-oriented, information-based economy—the talent to deal with people, the ability to change as the interpersonal situation changes, the skill to absorb information and apply it. In turn, the techno-service society satisfies the needs and desires of the new breed—its hunger for recognition and wealth, its frantic pursuit of pleasure and success, its inchoate yearning for meaning in life.

Techno-service work encompasses a hugely diverse group, people who fall along a long continuum of skill and training. At one end are routine service workers whose jobs require little schooling. At the other end are highly skilled information specialists—the New Elite—who need long and complex training in order to do their jobs. In between these extremes are many other service occupations with splendidly different degrees of specialization and skill. Policemen, plumbers, and prostitutes; bankers, bookies, and beauticians; computer consultants, caddies, and cashiers; teachers, tax accountants, and tennis instructors—all are part of the service sector. What, if anything, do they have in common? Obviously they are doing different kinds of work, performing tasks that require different skills and temperaments, servicing different kinds of needs. Why, then, are they all called service workers?

They are called service workers because notwithstanding their differences, they have several characteristics in common. First, their services are intangible. For example, technical advice on computer programming, instruction in golfing, medical diagnosis of hyperten-

sion, advice on the vagaries of the stock market, a sales pitch promoting exotic perfumes—to list only a few of the myriad services
performed in a modern economy—all are immaterial and are consumed on the spot.

Also, service work usually involves physical closeness between the
giver of services and the consumer. A claims adjuster ordinarily meets
a claimant face-to-face; a doctor talks to a troubled patient at close
range; a teacher must face students at reasonably close quarters in an
office or classroom; a sales clerk deals with a purchaser across a narrow counter; a waitress serves a customer only inches away. In contrast, a worker in a factory seldom encounters the consumer of his
labor; his product is corporeal, storable, impersonal, and usually used
by someone he will never know.

Finally, because a smiling and friendly mien helps in the delivery
of services, the service worker seeks to create rapport between himself
and the client. If the relationship is to work at all, it must appear to
be based on mutual respect. It follows then that to do their job properly service workers must possess certain personal qualities that contribute to good relations. They must be able to deal with people,
must be sensitive to the cues and subtle signals that reveal the client's
feelings and needs, and must know how to act on this knowledge.
Needless to say not all service workers possess these skills. As in any
field of work there are some misfits, but most service workers have
the requisite skills and do what is expected of them even when their
performance falls short of the ideal.

Although the triumph of the techno-service sector is new, service
work, of course, is not. In fact, service work antedates manufacturing
by many centuries. Knowledge specialists and skilled personal service
workers have long been in demand; servants, nurses, teachers, priests,
clerks, soldiers, and minstrels have been with us since the dawn of
civilization. Even in America their number has long been impressive.
As far back as 1840, the earliest year for which useful figures are
available, service workers made up 21 percent of the labor force. More
than one million persons worked in services, producing a value-added
measure of output in excess of 500 million dollars. During the rest
of the century the percentage of service workers in the labor force
steadily increased as industrialization took hold, until by the turn of
the century 33 percent of all workers were engaged in the service
sector.[7]

Throughout the nineteenth century the vast majority of service

workers were providers of routine personal services—bellhops, por-
ters, waitresses, cooks and maids in restaurants, hotels, and boarding
houses; attendants and orderlies in hospitals; and domestic servants
in private homes. In fact, servants made up a large part of the labor
force. Americans today would be amazed, perhaps envious, at how
commonplace it was a century ago for middle-class families to employ
one or more servants, mostly young women fresh from the farm or
recent immigrants from Europe, principally Ireland, to clean house,
cook, wash clothes, and care for the children. Up to World War II,
middle-class families typically had a servant to help around the house.
In 1940 the Bureau of Labor Statistics counted 2.6 million domestics,
almost one job in twenty.[8] Middle-class households today seldom
have more than a baby-sitter and someone to mow the lawn. Even
the terribly rich, who a century ago employed scads of servants, must
settle for far fewer. The pool of cheap domestics has dried up, and
with their disappearance the nature of the service force has changed
radically.

The service economy today is not composed entirely of low-skilled,
poorly paid, dead-end jobs, as its detractors maintain. Bed pan emptying is service work, but so is investment banking. "Many of the
service people . . . have customer contact and this requires judgment,
responsibility, ingenuity," says Audrey Freedman.[9] And we know that
the fastest job growth in the United States has been in the higher
paying service industries. According to Beryl W. Sprinkel, former
chairman of the President's Council of Economic Advisors, more
than 60 percent of the increase in employment since 1982 has been
in the highest paying occupations, most of them in the service sector.
Only 12 percent has been in lowest-paying, low-skill service jobs.[10]

Technology radically changed the nature of personal services and
the character of the people performing them. Work became, in many
fields, more skilled, more capital intensive, more dependent on advanced technology. As a result, routine service workers are no longer
largely unskilled, barely literate, badly paid, and always looked down
upon. Today, many personal service workers require extensive training before they can do their jobs. Becoming a police officer, for example, is no longer merely a matter of pinning on a badge and
strapping on a pistol; it take months of specialized training and years
of experience to make an acceptable officer of the law. Hospital orderlies take time to train, and so do physical therapists, dental hy-
gienists, firefighters, flight attendants, and many other providers of

personal services. All of this involves costs previous centuries were spared.

Many service workers need expensive, complicated equipment in order to do their jobs properly. It is no longer sufficient to equip a secretary with a pad and pencil, a typewriter and telephone, relatively simple equipment that almost anyone can quickly learn to use. Now this often distracted, always overburdened (so we are told) creature must master the inscrutable computer, or at least its word-processing function, become the comfortable ally of the facsimile machine, tease out the significance and mysteries of sundry devices for taking and answering messages, and know the ins and outs of temperamental photocopiers. Even the domestic servant must learn to use expensive, easily breakable machines—vacuum cleaners, dishwashers, floor polishers, clothes washers and dryers, garbage disposers. Despite the wails and fury of contemporary anti-technology fanatics, no one escapes the clutch of the machine in the machine age.

An increasing proportion of service workers are highly educated, and industries that require educated employees have been the fastest growing. In the 1980s the biggest rise in service sector employment was in finance, insurance, property and business service; and in 1987 (the latest year for which figures are available) 30 percent of Americans in such jobs had been to a university, as compared with 18 percent in manufacturing.[11] Among the most educated people in society today are the service workers who operate and control the information economy. They are the vital center of the Techno-Service Society.

Because information is critical for the efficient functioning of a techno-service system, the size of the information sector has grown rapidly. Drawing upon Bureau of Labor Statistics data, Daniel Bell concluded that from 1900 to 1980 the information sector grew by almost 400 percent, while the routine personal service sector remained virtually unchanged. As a result, the number of persons working in the information sector became much larger than those employed in the personal service area. Thus, in 1900 workers in the information sector made up 12.6 percent of the experienced civilian labor force; by 1980 that percentage had grown to 46.6 percent. In contrast, workers in the personal sector were 25.1 percent of the labor force in 1900, a figure that grew only slightly by 1980, increasing to 28.8 percent.[12]

THE INFORMATION PROCESSING ELITE

The New Elitists of the techno-service economy are skilled in processing complex information; their skills have made them the mandarins of the Information Society. Information covers a lot of ground, of course, and using it is commonplace. Many different kinds of people earn their living processing information, which, as Arno Penzias, Nobel Laureate and research scientist for Bell Laboratories points out, is simply "the manipulation of symbols—particles of thought, like numbers, words, and pictures—that are subject to the rules of logic."[13] A brain surgeon, an air traffic controller, a police detective, a stock broker, a librarian, a hotel clerk, a race track bookie—all process information for a living. But not all of them belong to the New Elite.

Elite information processors, highly-educated specialists and manipulators of symbols, have mastered the art of creating, collecting, and processing the data that shape the perception of reality, expand the range of options, assist in the evaluation of choices, and reduce uncertainty. It is this ability to manipulate symbols and use information that has given the New Elite its extraordinary influence and power. As Daniel Bell observed: "Information is power . . . what counts is not raw muscle power, or energy, but information."[14]

New Elitists control and operate the financial, news and entertainment, publishing, health, and education industries. They are masters at creating and merchandising ideas. They interpret events and history, set the standards for fashion and beauty, and disseminate dreams and fantasies. Included in this group are professors in elite universities, creative designers of consumer products, innovative wizards of the new computer technologies based on digital compression and high speed data transmission; well-placed public-relations experts, consultants, and problem-solvers in finance, business, and government; influential writers, journalists and editors, artists and creative people in publishing, television, motion pictures and the theater. This list is not meant to be exhaustive. It simply illustrates the range of jobs held by the New Elite.

New Elitists are among the best paid and most cosseted people in society. They are highly rewarded because their ideas may lead to new and more efficient, perhaps more enjoyable, ways of doing things. Drawing upon their fund of knowledge and using state-of-the-art techniques, they allocate resources in ways that save time and energy. They innovatively develop ideas or techniques that reorder how people work, how they think about the world and themselves, how they pursue and achieve pleasure. For good or ill, the cars we buy, the food we eat, the clothes we wear and for what effect, the movies we see and the tunes we dance to—all are influenced by the work of New Elitists, who cleverly weave together fabric and fashion, metal and machines, ideas and skills to produce new goods and services that give concrete form to our fantasies and hopes and dreams.

Estimates of their number vary widely. Using data taken from the *Yearbook of Labour Statistics*, published by the International Labour Office, Herbert Dordick and Georgette Wang estimate that workers in the information sector in the United States made up 56.7 percent of the labor force in 1987.[15] Robert B. Reich is more modest: he estimates that symbol analysts (his term for information specialists) make up about 20 percent of the workforce.[16] A more conservative estimate puts their number at roughly 12.5 million, people with household incomes in the top 5 percent of the population.[17] Whatever the exact number, it is clear that the New Elite constitutes a substantial and growing section of the working population.

Building and servicing the technology the New Elite uses has become a major component of the economy. Investment in information technology currently accounts for 52 percent of all capital spending. Three semiconductor plants costing $1 billion or more are now in operation, and sites for ten more have been announced. "In terms of size, growth and importance to our economic future, information technology is now clearly the basic industry of America," said Stephen S. Roach, the chief economist of Morgan Stanley & Company. Investment in computers and software for the telecommunications industry now outstrips the money spent on capital goods in steel mills.[18]

Corporate executives spend huge sums on telecommunication because it makes their work more efficient. They can conduct operations in sites scattered across the world, directing operations and fashioning plans with splendid ease and speed never possible before the electronic revolution. Instead of traveling to distant locations for on-site inspection and consultation, arriving jet-lagged, tired, and out of sorts, managers can confer at their convenience with other personnel by conference telephone or e-mail and exchange documents by computer or facsimile machine, enormously speeding up the process of making decisions. Arriving at a correct decision may still be difficult, of course, but at least the mechanics of exchanging information has been greatly simplified.

Consider, for instance, the shoe industry. Shoes made in Rio de Janeiro may have been designed in Milan, shipped to wholesalers in Chicago, sold to customers in Toronto, and charged to credit cards processed in Dublin, using software written in Bombay. The entire process is coordinated by one company with headquarters in Buenos Aires, which keeps its money safely banked in Zurich. Multinational corporations are nothing new, of course, but in the past the coordination of many diverse activities over many far-flung sites was often too difficult to be profitable.

Working at the leading edge of the techno-service society, the information specialists who control the intricate telecommunications and data transmission system of the techno-service economy sit in the catbird seat. Nowhere is this more apparent than in international finance. Positioned before computer terminals, they bind the world of finance together in an electronic network that transcends national boundaries and parochial interests. A few taps on a computer keyboard can send millions of dollars, marks, pounds, francs, and yen streaming around the globe. The global currency markets trade about one trillion dollars worth of currency each day. Buying and selling stocks, bonds, and currencies, twenty-five-year-old bond traders with nerves of steel and ice water in their veins operate beyond the control of governments, evaluating economic performance, depressing or elevating the value of national bank notes at international currency exchanges in Tokyo, Frankfurt, London, and New York, and putting to naught the efforts of central bankers to control the value of the world's money. In the course of their work, currency traders loosen or tighten the flow of money available for investment, and ultimately they touch the lives of almost everyone.

Vast sums are made and lost in a few minutes on bets made by speculators located in cities thousands of miles apart. Take for instance the celebrated case of George Soros and the Quantum Fund. Soros, a refugee whose family fled Hungary penniless in 1947 to escape Soviet domination, founded in 1969 the Quantum Fund, a private partnership geared to wealthy investors that attempts to achieve quick, large profits by making highly leveraged bets. He has been, on average, spectacularly successful. An investor who was lucky or canny enough to give Soros $10,000 in 1969 would have more than $2,000,000 today.[19] In 1992 Soros took part in a massive speculator's

raid against the British pound. Using the most sophisticated techniques of electronic currency trading, he bet the ranch, about ten
billion dollars, most of which he borrowed, that the Bank of England
would not be able to maintain the pound's value in the European
Rate Mechanism. The Bank tried and failed; the currency was devalued. Soros' bet paid off handsomely; he is said to have garnered a
profit of about two billion dollars.[20]

Of course there are losers as well as winners in the electronic speculation game. In early 1995, Nicholas Leeson, a 28-year-old stock
trader with the Singapore branch of Barings Bank, speculated heavily
in the Tokyo stock market. Using state-of-the-art electronic gad-
getry, he bet heavily that the market would rise. When the Nikkei
Index dropped 1000 points after the Kobe earthquake, he doubled
his bets in an attempt to recoup his losses. Leeson reputedly lost
nearly 1.38 billion dollars, and the venerable bank (it had helped finance England's war with Napoleon) went bankrupt. Only its purchase by a Dutch firm saved the bank from utter dissolution. Leeson
fled to Germany where he was jailed for six and a half months before
being extradited to Singapore. Plea bargaining reduced the charges
against him to two counts of fraud and forgery, and he was sentenced
to six and a half years in prison.

PROFILE OF THE NEW ELITIST

Although they have impressive influence, the New Elitists have as
yet been only sketchily described. Their being a diverse group hasn't
helped matters, but enough is known to permit a tentative description
of some characteristics common to most of them. This is possible
because they tend to come from similar backgrounds and, working in
similar areas of the information system, tend to develop similar traits,
skills, and values.

Most Elitists work at much the same central task—identifying and
solving problems—work that is anything but routine and repetitive.
Organizing and manipulating data, they create ideas and images, re-
arrange words, sound bites, and pictures to inform, influence, and
amuse selected audiences. They use a complex panoply of knowledge
and skills, frequently employing tools difficult for the layman to
grasp—technical jargon, scientific, financial, and legal expertise, complex mathematics—that vary with the problem. They show us how

to get the job done—how to make more money, run a business more efficiently, lose weight and make love, live longer and more successfully, and have more fun. All this despite the world's best efforts to frustrate our legitimate right to live well at small expense and with minimum effort. Sometimes they are successful; nearly always, successful or not, they are well paid for their efforts.

They usually come from modest middle-class families. Their parents were competitive, deeply concerned with their children's development and eager for them to succeed. When possible they opened doors for their offspring; they tried to push them along, urging them on to greater effort. Elitists like to believe they have gotten ahead on their own, by dint of hard work, furious striving, relentless ambition, which accounts for the emphasis they place on merit and the need for society to keep the system open to ambitious and talented youngsters. Merit does in fact figure significantly in their good fortune. They are competitive and not afraid of success, highly intelligent and articulate, good at using numbers, words, and images to convey information and ideas.

They work hard. A survey of the Harvard Class of 1969, which no doubt included many information processors, found that of the 45 percent who responded to the questionnaire 69 percent worked 45 hours or more per week; 88 percent had postgraduate degrees; 16 percent were in medicine, 18 percent in law. (Perhaps they pay a price in family instability for their long hours at work; 47 percent of the women and 34 percent of the men have been divorced.) They earned, most of them, a fairly large amount of money. Their median family income was $135,000; their median net worth was $500,000. The Class of 1970 did even better; those who responded to an anonymous survey for their twenty-fifth reunion reported a net worth of $1 million or more.[21]

Over the course of their lives, Elitists are tested, evaluated, and separated from the chaff that could not meet the group's standards. Selection began early. As children and youths they were subjected to a series of psychological tests, IQ tests, and SATs to determine their fitness for college. Having passed the tests, they went on to graduate from a four-year college, usually from a prestigious school whose diploma carries significant cachet. Often they move on to obtain advanced degrees. In time they become credentialed by professional societies, legal institutions, and their peers.

They sometimes work alone, sometimes in teams, sometimes in

temporary groups that meet to tackle a certain problem and then disperse. The ability to work with others figures importantly in their knapsack of skills. For though their stock-in-trade is knowledge, it will not count for much unless it can be communicated; and for this to happen in situations where information is transmitted as advice rather than as an order, as is often the case, Elitists must be able to deal with people, must appear friendly, open to the give and take of sharing information, and sensitive to the reactions of others in the group. For they know that information obtusely presented may be stillborn, ignored and unused even by clients who would have welcomed help had it been offered in an acceptable way.

They have enemies, which is not surprising—bright and successful people usually attract hostility, even in a success-oriented society. What is surprising is that their most vocal critics are people like themselves, other Elitists who for a variety of reasons, often political, despise their peers. Critics describe the Elitist in terms tinged with derision, anger, and fear. Michael Lind, a writer and social critic, calls the New Elitists arrogant (he says they constitute an "overclass"), unfeeling, shallow, and exploitative, indifferent to the plight of inner-city blacks and unemployed workers, impatient with failure and without compassion for losers.[22] Stephen Kleinberg, a sociologist, agrees: Elitists are baffled by losers, especially those in the working class. "What's wrong with them?" asks the Elitist. "Why can't they go back to school?"[23]

Christopher Lasch weighs in with even more damning indictments. He calls Elitists hypocritical and hollow, without steadfast principles, willing to twist and turn where the winds of opinion blow, motivated only by self interest. He says they are not true egalitarians. If they are egalitarian at all, it is only in the sense that they applaud social mobility and want to keep the system open to anyone with the necessary qualifications to enter their ranks. He maintains that their claim to compassion is a pose, a sham. For in truth they despise the untalented and uncredentialed fellow who cannot make it in a competitive economy. Despite their rhetoric of compassion, deep down they feel no obligation to help the weak. If they favor programs to aid the losers, it is only to lift the financial burden of caring for life's failures from their own shoulders onto the backs of the lower-middle and working classes.[24]

Critics ridicule the Elitists' manners and style—their way of speaking; their obsession with self-improvement; their fixation with appearances, with being lean and trim; their determination to stay eternally young and sexually attractive; their preoccupation with the latest nutritionally-approved foods and the latest designer-labeled apparel; their passion to be on top of the latest fashions in art and music, to appear learned about esthetics. All this may seem risible, but they are no joke to critics who think Elitists are perverse bundles of contradictions—liberal on social issues, yet economically conservative; pro-choice on abortion, tolerant of moderate drug use, and accepting of homosexuality; but favoring low taxes and balanced budgets, and increasingly reluctant to spend public moneys on social programs. Increasingly letting their pocketbooks influence their politics, they are slipping into the ranks of conservative political parties. Often the children of liberal Democrats, some of them have begun to vote Republican.

But the critics who mock the New Elite, dismissing its life-style with a smirk and a knowing wink, fail to understand the logic behind this behavior. The esoteric things Elitists eat, drink, and wear, the far-out ways they sometimes spend their leisure time, though laughable to their critics, make economic sense. The techno-service system is a consumer society. Every day it creates tons of goods and services that must be sold at a profit. Elitists are consummate consumers, with educated tastes, insatiable appetites, and full pocketbooks, just what the system needs. How else would those mountains of goods be reduced? Imagine what would happen if the New Elite set an example for the rest of society by adopting Spartan habits of consumption. The economy would go into a tailspin, that's what.

Whether the New Elite presently constitutes a fully formed social class is doubtful, but it may be on the way to becoming one. Elitist information processors occupy similar if not identical positions in the occupational structure; they attended similar if not the same schools; they tend to marry other information processors; they understand the importance of networking and try to keep in touch with others of their ilk, though they are far too numerous to make contact with more than a tiny fraction of the group feasible. Most important of all, they have begun to create a common culture and a common social character, and this is making it possible for them to develop common codes of behavior and symbols of recognition. They have also begun to develop a community of interests and a shared ideology—a passion for self-realization and egalitarianism—as an ideal, if not a practice.

A true social class may be a generation or more away, but the process of forming one seems well underway.

To men like Lind and Lasch and to others of a similar political bent, usually of the left, this new class is anathema, phony and manipulative, morally obtuse, socially irresponsible, politically reactionary. There may be some truth to their accusations, but they have left out an important part in their critique and analysis. What is missing is an understanding of why New Elitists think and behave the way they do. It is not enough simply to castigate Elitists for the way they act and for their failure to live up to their ideals; it is necessary to know where these actions and ideals come from, and to understand why Elitists still pursue them even as the gap between the ideal and the real lengthens.

The answer is complicated, and much of the following chapters go into documenting it. In brief, New Elitists behave as they do and yearn for a certain kind of new world because (in large part) the techno-service society wants it that way. And in the long run society will get, for the most part, the kinds of people it needs. How else will it function and survive? It badly needs, certainly not less than the manufacturing-dominated society which preceded it, hardworking, conscientious, intelligent, talented, ambitious, competitive workers. But unlike its predecessor it does not require most people to do simple, repetitive, standardized things, in a relatively fixed pattern. The information system puts a premium on constantly innovative work practices, on new products and markets. It needs workers who can change as the situation requires. Commitment to tradition, to practices handed down from previous generations, only gets in the way. Change, innovate, and grow—or die! That is the order of the new order.

The New Elite is establishing a new social order, as it must if the changes it wants are to endure. Yet the work it does and the very traits that make it valuable to society also make its members exceptionally vulnerable to anxiety. As most of them will be quick to tell you, New Elitists tend to work under great pressure. Their work is excruciatingly demanding, requiring more than mere technical skill and knowledge; it also requires interpersonal skills of very high order. The process of exchanging information is often a game between people; and if the process is to succeed, if it is to have its intended effect, it is essential that the players know how the game works. For this to happen, the successful player must understand the other players, must sense their needs and values, must adapt to them or at least conceal disagreement, and must have enough insight to hide any personal quirk that can damage the relationship.

To be successful at their trade, elite information processors must be consummate actors and dissemblers. They must appear helpful even when they feel out-of-sorts; courteous even when provoked by a client's nastiness; able to make others feel at ease even when circumstances make them nervous and frightened; friendly and at the same time detached emotionally and uninvolved in the lives of their clients. They must be individualistic yet cooperative, approachable yet distant, open and friendly yet impersonal. In short they must be masters of deception, appearing to be what they sometimes are not, manipulating others in what is supposed to be everyone's best interest. Managing impressions is their forte, and only when they do this well will they perform their job properly.

Above all, New Elitists must be able to change with the system. They must be flexible, able to break away from established habits and the ties of family and community, capable of adopting new procedures, ready to change direction when the need arises. They must be skilled at recognizing the direction of change and willing to fit into each new situation as it develops, unburdened by fixed principles and a permanent identity. Call this trait chameleonism, if you like, but it is highly adaptive in an information society.

The problem is that being a chameleon can be cruelly taxing and disorienting. In managing impressions, in having to assume attitudes and adopt manners that may be alien to their true natures, Elitists may lose sight of who they really are. The public role, initially assumed purely for pragmatic purposes, may override the private inner identity. The result is confusion about who one is and what one truly believes. In short, one may fall victim to the Chameleon Complex. But more about this in future chapters.

6

The Chameleon
Personality of Our Time

Elite information processors have inherited the world but they are not satisfied—not with themselves, not with society. For despite its importance and affluence, all is not well in the knowledge community. Many of its members appear to be discontented, worried about their future, and confused about the direction the country is taking. Strange to say, anxiety has found a capacious home among service-land's wealthiest workers: the well-educated, exceptionally intelligent, skilled manipulators of knowledge, the information specialists upon whom society has smiled most benignly. What is going on here? Why are so many of fortune's favorites discontented?

Discontent is idiosyncratic; each one of us achieves it in his own way. Generalizations about its causes must, therefore, be treated with caution. This caveat granted, I will nevertheless argue that elite information processors tend to develop a character structure that causes them to feel dissatisfied, betrayed by a world which fails to serve them as they believe they deserve. Not all of them feel this way, of course; no category of people is entirely homogeneous; we are dealing with central tendencies. But there are enough similarities in the work they do and in their childhood experiences to induce in many of them a character structure I call the Chameleon Complex. This complex is ultimately harmful; it is a major contributor to contemporary discontent.

The Chameleon Complex can be found among people in every sector of society. It is, however, especially pronounced among the New Elite, which uses it as a defense against anxiety, showing that anxiety can be prevalent among winners as well as losers. Anxiety also points up the remarkable similarity between the First and Second Great Transformations. Not only were both transformations times of rapid business expansion and improvements in the technology of communication, both were characterized by intense personal competition. Were he alive today, George M. Beard, the eminent nineteenth-century New York psychiatrist, would surely be struck by the almost unbridled competitiveness of life in today's America and the anxiety it creates. And given his predilection to link anxiety to the rapidity with which communication occurs (as noted, he blamed the telegraph for much of the anxiety prevalent in his day), he would no doubt see a connection between the computer, fax machine, and cellular telephone and the anxiety among the New Elite. Whether he would recognize the role of the Chameleon Complex in all of this we don't know, but I would like to think that he would.

What exactly is the Chameleon Complex and how does it help people cope with anxiety? Or to put it differently; what is troubling the New Elite? What has society done (or failed to do) that so upsets it? What expectations of itself does it have that it fails to meet, and what is the source of these expectations? These questions can best be answered if we understand the conditions that generated the Chameleon Complex in the first place.

A collection of situational pressures make the New Elitists especially vulnerable to disappointment and anxiety. They work in an exacting ambience, doing things governed by high standards and that offer little room for error. A mistake that might be bearable in some other kind of work can be ruinous in the fast-moving, high-risk environment of speculative finance and cutthroat capitalism, or in the creative world of fashion design, theatrical production, publishing, and advertising. Elitists can expect almost no tolerance for failure— and they know it. They know there is no market for a new Edsel car, few viewers for a new Heavensgate motion picture, and even fewer buyers for a new Nehru jacket. A misjudgment of public tastes, a slackening of creativity, a slowness in decision making will cost them (or their employers) a fabulous amount of money and every scrap of personal influence and power.

Age and seniority offer no protection. Indeed, work in an information-oriented, high-tech economy tends to be a young person's game. Advancing age, it is thought, causes one to fall behind in the race to keep up with new developments at the leading edge of technological change and dulls the zest for the competitive fray, both fatal flaws in an arena where the scramble for success is furious and unending. Winning isn't just important to the ambitious elite information processor; winning is just about everything.

This is understandable because the rewards for success can be enormous; the rise to great power and wealth can be breathtakingly rapid. The market showers successful information specialists with big bonuses, praise, adulation, vacation apartments in Europe and the Caribbean, planes to jet here and there, and warrants to buy expensive stock at low prices. But it also coolly and without ceremony buries them in contempt, speedily stops all benefits, and shows the poor miscreants the door when they fail to deliver the goods.

To protect themselves against failure, to prevent the emotional damage that a fall from grace into obscurity and penury inevitably brings, New Elitists tend to develop defensive psychological armor designed to fend off competitors and safeguard self-esteem. This armor is the Chameleon Complex, a mostly unconscious component of personality acquired in childhood and reinforced in adulthood. It is composed of four parts: chameleonism (the core trait), narcissism, hedonism, and perfectionism. Each is analytically different, but all serve a common purpose—to shelter the individual from attack and safeguard self-esteem.

Together they provide solace when things go wrong and help shield the elite information specialist against the ever-present possibility of losing out in the merciless struggle for success. Let us look at each of these parts separately, disentangling one from the other, even as we recognize that in the mind of the Elitist they fit neatly together. We begin with the core of the Chameleon Complex, chameleonism.

CHAMELEONISM: SHELTER IN A HOSTILE WORLD

Because they work in a fiercely competitive world, elite information processors become adept at recognizing any danger of attack from any quarter. They keep their antennas raised at all times to pick up signals of trouble ahead. Watching the horizon for the smallest cloud and scanning people's faces for the slightest variation in mood, they become skilled at quickly recognizing changes in the expectations of others and learn to adapt smoothly to changing conditions.

Like their namesake, human chameleons assume a facade whenever they find themselves in a hostile environment. They try to please, to be liked by whomever they are with, to lose themselves in the group. This ability to take on an outward appearance congenial to others, much as a ship (to change our metaphor) hoists acceptable colors in order to attach itself to a convoy navigating dangerous waters, helps assure survival in a unfriendly world. Much depends, obviously, on choosing the right convoy, on identifying the winning side.

The chameleon should not be confused with the other-directed personality of David Riesman's typology.[1] True, Riesman's other-directed personality, like the chameleon, constantly orients himself toward others, but this is because he lacks a core of convictions. He wants to know what to believe; he is seeking direction. Chameleons, on the other hand, are seeking protection. They do not necessarily lack convictions; they may, in fact hold strong opinions, but—knowing when it is not expedient to express them—they go along in order to get along.

Being a successful chameleon is not easy. It takes concentration and luck, for the chameleon's path is strewn with mines. One misstep and the game is up. The chameleon lives, therefore, in constant fear of being found out and unmasked. Yet unmasking a chameleon is not as easy as most people think. They imagine they can spot a chameleon at a glance, and sometimes they may be right, though often they are wrong. For chameleonism well done is difficult to discern; even chameleons are often deceived by their own facade—they begin by fooling others and end up fooling themselves. Nevertheless, discovery of the fraud they are visiting upon others is an ever-present possibility, and with detection comes rejection and disgrace. Chameleons must, therefore, keep their guard up at all times, must never become absent-minded, must never forget to keep their antennas extended and their receivers well tuned.

Sensitivity to environmental signals may become an obsession with the opinions of others. Readily shifting their positions to align them with the strongest signal and waffling when no signal dominates the screen, chameleons sometimes appear indecisive and insincere. Sensitivity to the opinions of others may also develop into an insatiable need for approval, and self-esteem comes to be hinged entirely on what other people think. It is to others that chameleons turn, automatically and almost indiscriminately, for validation of their success, attractiveness, sexual appeal, intelligence, and moral stature. Elite chameleons are especially proud of their high moral stature, for they are convinced that they are working in the best interests of others. Unfortunately, a high opinion of oneself all too easily slips into self-righteousness, the conviction that one not only is brighter than others but also knows what is best for them. Eventually, intellectual arrogance and claims to moral superiority cause resentment and lead inevitably to alienating others.

In pursuing acceptance chameleons develop traits that eventually make foes, endangering the safety they so desperately seek. Interpersonal skill and high intelligence, the very things that make them successful chameleons, may eventually boomerang against them, for these qualities may come across as manipulative arrogance. Skill at impression management and handling people all too easily becomes cynical finagling for personal aggrandizement. The need to control the perceptions of others becomes an obsession to dominate them. From domination to exploitation is an easy step, and not surprisingly the chameleon tends to use people.

Chameleon Elitists are often pulled in different directions. They treasure independence but seek to merge into the group; they privately cultivate self-detachment but seek to convey an impression of genial collegiality. They present an inviting facade but are at heart reluctant to establish enduring relationships with others. What they truly want is to be free to break old ties and make new ones whenever their interests require. Consequently, they avoid true intimacy as a trap and resist commitment to anyone or anything that would inhibit unlimited freedom of action and hinder their chances to get ahead.

When they are aware of what they are doing, human chameleons know they are acting in ways deeply at odds with what they really believe. For example, a white liberal living among racists, whose acceptance for some reason he must have, may resort to chameleonism, voicing stereotypic slanders on blacks and acting as offensively as he dares, actions that as a liberal he would instantly damn in others. He will also find himself endorsing the hostile stereotypes that racists have about white liberals—their soft-headed, bleeding-heart mentality, and their unwillingness to take a hardheaded stance on the issues of law and order.

To be sure, the human mind can hold absurdly contradictory points of view at the same time, and it is not uncommon to observe people acting in ways distinctly opposed to their private views. Various psychological defenses—compartmentalization, denial, cognitive dissonance reduction—help keep the chameleon unaware of, or indifferent to, personal inconsistencies.[2] But to believe that contradictory attitudes and behavior can be permanently sealed in neat compartments without causing confusion and anxiety is to expect too much of human nature. Inevitably the chameleon pays a price for acceptance bought with counterfeit coins, for safety obtained under false pretenses. The price is a profound confusion about one's identity and a pervasive anxiety about what to believe and whom to trust.

It is easy to view chameleonism with distaste, and this would be warranted if chameleonism were entirely calculated, a devious ploy steeped in insincerity, basically manipulative, designed to deceive others for personal gain. In fact it often is not. It begins, true enough, as a response to danger, as a deliberate practice to be used and dropped when the occasion requires. But in time, after repeated use, it tends to become a deeply embedded habit, the existence of which the chameleon is unaware and would deny having if accused, not wanting to be thought two-faced, underhanded, and dishonest. But there is another, more complex and subtle reason. The fact is that chameleonism is far more than the concealment of who one truly is and the pragmatic assumption of a useful disguise; it is a deep-seated personality trait to which the individual has become strongly and stubbornly attached. Even though it is a costly practice, human chameleons are usually ignorant of its price. It is a practice they will not easily abandon.

As noted, chameleons can be found in every sector of society. No social class, no racial or ethnic group, no occupational category has a monopoly on the ability to disguise its intentions and actions. Perhaps everyone at some time or other has played the chameleon. It is a price we pay for getting along with others. But many elite information specialists have chameleonism deeply built into their character, for it is integral to the work they do. Schooled in impression management and constantly facing situations that demand dissimulation, they easily become astute chameleons. Moreover, chameleonism has its advantages. As chameleons, they can move easily in and out of relationships as their situations require, and this gives them a significant advantage over people who lack this flexibility.

NARCISSISM

Chameleon Elitists are intelligent, skillful, and resourceful, and, not surprisingly, with these admirable qualities to their credit, they tend to have a high opinion of themselves. They become enamored by their own brilliance and charm, their ability to take other people in, to create a fictional character good enough to fool a gullible public. In short, they tend to be narcissists, narcissism being another component of the Chameleon Complex. Blatant narcissism offends everyone, of course, and smart Elitists try to conceal it. But it is a difficult matter to hide, in part because they have no control over it, in part because they are unaware of its existence, and in part because they cannot bear to part with it.

The original narcissist was a handsome youth named Narcissus, in Greek mythology, who, upon seeing a reflection of himself in a pond and not recognizing himself in the image became enamored with its beauty. Bending over to kiss it, he fell in and promptly drowned—a fitting punishment, the ancient Greeks thought, for self-infatuation.[3] Modern opinion is more tolerant of self-love. Today it is thought to be healthy to have a good opinion of oneself, and there is concern when some people develop low self-esteem, particularly members of disadvantaged minorities. Indeed, programs have been instituted, at government expense, to promote healthy self-esteem in vulnerable creatures, such as minority youngsters, women, and others said to suffer from low self-regard. Only when self-love becomes excessive, based on illusion, is it deemed pathological.[4]

The narcissist's wildly inflated self-esteem is mostly based upon illusion. Narcissists imagine themselves to be far more clever in social affairs, more resourceful in emergencies, more attractive and sexually irresistible, more upright and deserving of respect and deference than any objective evaluation would justify. Paradoxically, this unrealistically high self-evaluation coexists with deep-seated doubts about true worth, a nagging suspicion that the real self and the imagined self are worlds apart. But then self-doubt is unavoidable, because narcissism is based upon an objectively false image of oneself, on expectations so out of touch with reality they cannot possibly be satisfied. Narcissists want to be accepted on their own terms and demand that an often coldly indifferent world acknowledge their superiority. Needless to say such demands will inevitably be rejected. The reaction to this rejection is rage, contempt, and hatred, directed against both oneself and society.

HEDONISM

Hedonistic self-gratification, a third component of the Chameleon Complex, is a logical ancillary to narcissism. Narcissistic hedonists see nothing wrong with treating themselves to a good time. For the well-heeled Elitist caught up in the Chameleon Complex the pursuit of pleasure in a consumer society is easy, entirely acceptable, indeed almost obligatory. The media constantly hammer away at the idea that self-indulgence makes sense. Advertisements promise easy beauty and ever-lasting sex appeal through the faithful application of skin creams and hair lotions. Tantalizing commercials hold out the prospect of improving one's status by being seen in an expensive car. Consumers are exhorted to take costly vacations, to fly now and pay later, to believe that new experiences in exotic lands will change their lives. What is wrong, thinks the hedonist, with changing one's life and enjoying oneself?

Hedonists dismiss self-denial and frugality as silly holdovers from an earlier period when America was a society of scarcity. As believers in the contemporary fun culture, they scoff at self-control and at the blue-nose puritanism of earlier times. Appealing to Keynsian economic theory, the hedonist claims that self-denial and thrift are not even in the economy's best interest. Where would the country be if we all pinched our pennies? Buying would decline, shops would cut purchases, and factories would shut down. To be sure, with more savings more money would be available for investment, but to what end if buying becomes unpopular and the economy goes into a tailspin? Therefore, sensible people take their pleasure whenever possible. If that is self-indulgence, so be it.

But calling hedonism mere self-indulgence or economic necessity misses the point; hedonism has become a religion and material enjoyment its road to salvation. Seen as religious practice, the pursuit of pleasure gives focus to life and the attainment of pleasure becomes an important component of self-esteem. Hedonists pride themselves on living well, convinced that joy is strength, that the road to fun leads to self-fulfillment, that having a ball is an essential part of what life is all about.

But are they not just fooling themselves? There are good reasons for doubting that hedonism is a good guide to a full life. Consider that hearty eating and drinking can be hard on the digestion and liver, that constant partying can lead to sleeplessness or pregnancy. And medical or moral considerations aside, there is still the problem of satiation. Surfeit is the Achilles heel of hedonism. Double dips of ice cream, trips to Paris, cashmere sweaters, constant partying, unlimited sex—all grow boring beyond a certain point, though it is true that not everyone gets to reach that point. The untrammeled pursuit of pleasure becomes a treadmill, wearying and endless, when each new thrill must be surpassed by one even more ecstatic. If the pursuit of pleasure becomes frantic, the end result can only be disappointment and exhaustion. In the long run, hedonism turns out to be a fragile foundation on which to build self-esteem, as hedonists graying at the temple eventually find out.[5]

THE PERFECT SELF

If chameleonism, narcissism, and hedonism are flawed defense mechanisms, causing more distress than they relieve, what else can Elitists do to protect themselves against harm? They can become perfect people. Perfection, the fourth component of the Chameleon Complex, puts them beyond the reach of envious competitors; perfection armors them against backbiting criticism; perfection stills self-doubt and smoothes over the jagged edges of failure. And so, unconsciously, the attainment of a perfect self—that mysterious amalgam of self-image, self-esteem, and ego skills that develops out of efforts to cope with the world—becomes the all-encompassing preoccupation of Chameleon Elitists, their means of finding personal salvation, their Holy Grail.

The need to protect the self and to actualize its inherent potentials, to become perfect, coupled with defensive self-righteousness rationalized as loyalty to one's true self, guide their thoughts and actions. They believe that the self's potentials are rooted in the organism, a genetic blueprint that must be followed if happiness is ever to be attained. And in their search for self-fulfillment, they tend to become totally absorbed with themselves, with their own needs and wishes, with their appearance and manners, with their power and status.

Psychologically sophisticated Elitists justify their determination to attain self-fulfillment, which often appears to others as mere selfish-ness, by pointing to the theories of self-fulfillment psychologists such as Abraham Maslow, Erich Fromm, and Carl Rogers.[6] These theorists reject the idea that life must be a continual struggle for instinctual satisfaction. Self-fulfillment psychologists grant the importance of the instincts, cede to the unconscious a major role in shaping human behavior, and recognize the role which conflict plays in human affairs. But they also believe the social environment plays a far greater part in the formation of personality than orthodox Freudians are willing to concede. True, our efforts to adapt to an often unfriendly envi-ronment—the ego doing its job—can make us into the selfish crea-tures we all too often become. True also, humanity's innate need for sexual pleasure and its tendency toward aggression can lead to socially undesirable consequences.[7] But they give to these instincts a far smaller role in everyday life than did Freud. They believe there is more to human nature than lust and venom, more to life than fighting and fornicating.

Self-fulfillment psychologists reject the notion that human beings are instinctively competitive and aggressive. On the contrary, man's true nature, they say, is benign, predisposed to friendship and coop-eration if only society would permit them to behave that way. Given the right circumstances, people would lead orderly, constructive, moral lives without needing to be held in check by guilt, shame, and the police. It is society, with its obsessive need for order, its emphasis on competition and material possessions, that pits humans against each other. Cut out the malignancy of savage competition for material advantage, and people would be healthy and cooperative, eager to live in peace with their neighbors and themselves. Self-fulfillment psy-chologists sometimes wax lyrical about the human capacity for co-operative living. Fromm believed that given the right conditions people would naturally live in small cooperative communities founded on brotherly love, mutuality, generosity, and respect.[8]

Elite information specialists take to self-fulfillment psychology like ducks to water. They find it a friendly pond on which to paddle single-mindedly toward happiness, a buoyant body of ideas that sup-ports an intense preoccupation with the self. Such preoccupation appears justified to them, for only through self-understanding can one acquire the skill to impart knowledge to others—their main task. The popularity of self-fulfillment psychology also reflects a unique con-juncture of forces in the 1960s and 1970s, a time when utopian frenzy seized the minds of young people, especially the children of affluent parents. As part of a huge demographic cohort, large numbers of Elitists-to-be went to college and took a variety of courses in the social sciences, some of them in self-fulfillment psychology. They loved it, for it sanctioned unlimited self-absorption and adolescent acting-out, both of which they found congenial. Turning off the demands of the establishment and tuning in to their own desires was deliciously attractive. It held out the prospect of their taking charge of their lives, of becoming friendly, carefree, cooperative people, unthreatening and easy to get along with—if only the shackles of the old tyranny could be overthrown. Rebellion was in the air and rebellion, any rebellion, was to their taste.

But when they graduated from college and went to work they discovered that revolution had gone out of fashion. Survival, not revolution, would become their major preoccupation. They found themselves in a Darwinian world in which competition continuously culls the weak from the strong. The unremitting competition for wealth, status, and power in a winner-takes-all environment inevitably generates deep insecurity. The loser is vulnerable to serious psychic hurt, the pain of feeling rejected and inadequate. Elitists who work in hideously unpredictable, capricious, and frightening environments, and who have taken refuge in the Chameleon Complex, always feel vulnerable to betrayal and punishment. Feeling endangered by a world that is out to abuse, cheat, and humiliate them, they tend to fall victim to grave anxiety. In extreme cases, they come to believe that their world is on the verge of collapsing on their heads.

Continuous insecurity imperils self-esteem, because it is hard to feel good about oneself when the signals all about one threaten punishment and possible expulsion if expectations are not met, expectations that are usually exacting and hard to satisfy. Only an exceptionally strong ego can operate in this kind of environment without becoming vulnerable to psychic damage. Something must be done. A wound to self-esteem demands attention, and serious remedies must be applied. Too much is invested in developing and maintaining a satisfying self-regard to let an injury fester under trivial treatment. A simple poultice to reduce the pain will not suffice. Consequently, when confronted with danger, Elitists will move heaven and earth to change things. They will try desperately to find a way to protect themselves and safeguard their self-regard.

Drastic surgery is called for. The old self, mutilated by trauma, must be cut out and replaced by a new self, one that is proof against criticism and other kinds of grievous mistreatment, a self so armored against enmity and envy that it repels the calumny and the treachery of wily competitors, some of whom work in offices down the hall.

And so, entirely unconsciously, irrationally, and narcissistically, the emotionally beleaguered Elitist sets about creating a self with which he or she can live comfortably—a perfect self, both flattering and reassuring, that gives meaning and purpose to life. This bright, fresh self is delightfully attractive (at least to its owner) because it has been purged of all unwelcome elements and now contains only those flattering to the injured ego. It no longer reflects experiences in the real world; it is a phantasm of wishes and dreams, a beautified image of the kind of person the injured person admires and wants to be. Once in place, the perfect self becomes an object of veneration, not open to inspection and correction. It must be protected by all possible means, and all the energy once devoted to actualizing the old self is now focused on the new perfect self.

Three entrancing ideals go into forming the Elitists' notion of a perfect image: compassion, equality, and social justice. They think of themselves, and would like others to see them, as caring persons, sincerely committed to fair treatment for all and devoted to breaking down every barrier to social equality. Prejudice and discrimination of any kind, including value judgments that imply invidious comparisons, the suggestion that some things are better (or worse) than others, infuriate them. They are enraged at the neglect of the poor and the weak, and appalled by gross inequalities of wealth and power. Righteous rage makes them feel good; it is a mark of their superiority. They are themselves without prejudice, altogether wonderful people who feel other people's pain. Of all this they are quite aware. What they are not aware of is their monumental passion for their perfect self. Unfortunately, this passion is not rewarded, for the pursuit of the perfect self condemns them to constant disappointment. Elitists in thrall to the Chameleon Complex have abandoned rationality; they have begun a quest that will never leave them in peace.

In fashioning the perfect self they will, of necessity, draw upon materials at hand, which vary with the circles in which they move and the kind of work they do; but it will always contain, because they work in a world saturated with the language of excellence, elements fused with the imagery of excellence. In fact, they are less infatuated with excellence than with success, though they would indignantly deny this. Success for its own sake, they maintain, is gross and empty. It is the search for excellence—the flawless computer program, the sales pitch no consumer can resist, the leveraged buy-out to end all buy-outs—that lashes them on to ceaseless effort, or so they believe.

Actually it is not excellence or even success, but perfection that they seek. It is perfectionism that drives them on, that keeps them perpetually dissatisfied. Perfectionism is key to understanding their character, and perfectionism is precisely their problem. Perfectionism makes them cruelly unforgiving toward any flaw in themselves and the world. Perfectionism causes them to flagellate themselves for any personal imperfection. Perfectionism impels them to pour scorn and hatred on society for failing to live up to their expectation that the world be perfect. And it is perfectionism that creates a pit of guilt into which they are prone to fall.[9]

Now, perfection in some activities, such as bowling, taking multiple-choice examinations, and pistol shooting, may be possible, though unlikely; but perfection in life, never. It eludes each and every one of us, even the most diligent and worthy. Personal flaws, the stupidity and malevolence of one's fellows, the blows of existential catastrophe, and brute chance—all these and more will in the end defeat every drive for perfection. Only the perfectionist blinded by hubris will fail to see this.

The great playwrights of tragedy, Sophocles and Euripedes and Aeschylus, understood the hubris of perfectionists. So did Shakespeare and Balzac and Tennessee Williams and many others. And so do most people today, when they stop and think about it. The perfect person without a characterological flaw, the perfect society without crime, violence, deprivation, and injustice is the stuff of dreams, a will-o'-the-wisp forever beyond reach, the fantasy of utopians. Rational people understand this and settle for less. But the pursuit of perfection is not rational, but an unconscious desire hidden in some deep corner of the mind. Irrational and obsessive, doomed to failure, the pursuit of perfection is the cause of much misery.

Since the quest for perfection must fail, why does it survive the challenges of reality, the stubborn and grudging refusal of the world to accept perfectionists on their own terms? The answer, simply put, is that they do not notice the evidence that contradicts their ideal self-image. They screen out information that doesn't fit and admit only supporting evidence. Moreover, notwithstanding its long term costs, the ideal self works for them, at least initially: it soothes hurt feelings, and legitimates the search for a perfect society. Also they are unaware of the ideal self's psychic price. They do not connect it with the disappointment and anger they feel about themselves and the world.

No one has reasoned more cogently about perfectionism than Karen Horney, a psychiatrist and keen observer of American society. Horney came to the United States from Germany in 1931, after having broken with Freud over his explanation of neurosis in women. She believed Freud gave too much weight to biological factors and not enough to the social environment in which women lived. It is not, she maintained, genital inferiority, expressed in penis envy, but their demeaning social role, their relegation to church, nursery, and kitchen that undermines the mental health of women. But psychoanalysis (and Germany) was not ready for the new feminism, and her views were harshly rejected. Not willing to abandon her viewpoint, she broke with the psychoanalytic group with which she was associated and sought more congenial surroundings in the United States. For a time she worked in Chicago and then moved to New York, where she founded the American Institute of Psychoanalysis, which she headed until her death in 1952.

Soon after her arrival in the United States, Horney was struck by how different Americans were from Germans. Not merely the visible differences in dress and diet; these were surface matters, interesting to tourists and authors of travel books but not necessarily important. The important differences were in national character, in the moods and views of the people, in their aspirations and ambitions, in the loose way Americans were tied to their traditions and to one another. As Horney saw it, the Germans, like other Europeans, lived in a far more psychologically stable society than Americans, and enjoyed a more leisurely way of living than the one she encountered in the United States. Americans, she felt, were on the whole more isolated, more insecure, and far more competitive than Germans.

She was struck by the peculiar hurry-hurry gait of Americans; their hang-ups about time, punctuality, appointments, and meetings; their obsession with getting ahead, with winning, with becoming successful. She thought this a result of America's competitive commercial culture, its ethos of success, and the precariousness of everyone's position in the social order. Nothing is fixed for Americans. They have constantly to prove themselves, to struggle to hold on to what they own and to grab even more. Naturally, this puts them in competition with others who feel the same way—hence, the deep fear of losing status and falling behind that she observed in many Americans.[10]

A fiercely competitive struggle for survival and success invariably produces anxiety, particularly among the upwardly mobile professional class, emerging just then as the vanguard of the New Elite. Since this anxiety must somehow be controlled and if at all possible reduced, she observed that some Americans were unconsciously resorting to perfectionism and the pursuit of an ideal self as a way of solving their problems. Then, as now, perfectionism helped in the short run but only at a terrible price. The price was pervasive anxiety about self-worth, not unlike the anxiety many members of the New Elite suffer from today.

To be sure, New Elitists are not the only people in America in thrall to anxiety and the Chameleon Complex. Indeed, they may not be most afflicted, though without adequate comparative statistics we do not know who holds this dubious distinction. But that their level of discontent and anxiety is high seems entirely likely. And that they tend to make perfectionism the centerpiece of their lives seems equally true. Importantly, their state of mind enormously affects society. For this phalanx of scribblers, impression managers, problem solvers, illusionists, and idea peddlers has the skill to put its disgruntlement into words and pictures. And in books, films, editorials, essays, television scripts, newspaper reports, and lectures, they have let loose a howl of anguish that reverberates across the land, setting the nation's nerves on edge and upsetting people's composure.

They have convinced themselves that terrible crimes have been committed against them, not only to their detriment but to society's as well. Moreover, because they have the power far in excess of their numbers to give voice to their anguish, they can spread their message to the remotest corners of the nation. No one should doubt their influence. As the premier source of ideas, as masters of the mass media, they do more to form opinion and establish the national mood than any other group in the country.

7

The Roots of the Chameleon Complex

Chameleons are made, not born. No one comes into the world fully equipped with the ability to blend into the social background whenever danger arises. No one has located a gene predisposing people to seek shelter in protective social coloration. Whatever the biological predisposition to chameleonism may be, if it exists at all, it has so far defied detection. It seems reasonable, therefore, until we learn otherwise, to assume that the chameleon's skill at adopting any fashionable manner the situation requires is learned. Therefore, the search for the origins of chameleonism must begin with the experiences people have coping with everyday life, learning painfully through trial and error to survive.

The previous chapter examined the development of chameleonism among adults whose stressful work life caused them to seek refuge from danger by donning a chameleon's mask. But it would be a mistake to assume that chameleonism begins in adulthood. More likely, its foundation is laid in childhood, when a harrying and unpredictable environment causes children to seek safety in dissemblance and disguise, in feigning attitudes they do not really hold, in behaving in ways alien to their true inclinations, acquiring in this way habits of concealment that carry into adulthood. The exact origins of this strategy of dissimulation have never been mapped; but a tentative description, with some shadings and qualifications removed for clarity's sake, of how it is learned seems useful at this point.

As already noted, chameleonism is a response to perceived danger, to the fear of attack, to the anticipation of rejection and expulsion, to the threat that love will be denied or withdrawn. To ward off this calamity children assume a protective identity, take on an acceptable coloration, and seek to blend safely into the environment—they become chameleons. The question is, what frightened them and why did they adopt chameleonism as protection against danger? The answer, I believe, can be found, in most cases, in their early experiences with parents and peers.

THE NEW TECHNO-SERVICE FAMILY

The search for the roots of chameleonism begins with an examination of the family. Fortunately, we know a lot about the family; unfortunately, much of what we know is distressing. With few exceptions, scholarly research and the popular media paint a picture of the American family that is alarming and depressing. It is now common to hear experts assert that the American family is alone in a heedless world, that it has become weak and unstable, that it damages children and leaves them on their own, lonely and unprotected.[1]

Judging from reports, the family seems in danger of falling apart: divorce rates are at an all-time high; single-parent homes threaten to become the norm; births out of wedlock outnumber legitimate births in some communities; spousal violence has become so common that newspapers seldom bother mentioning it.[2] To be sure not every family is torn by conflict or reduced to pathetic apathy; many appear to be doing their job quite well, even under adverse conditions. Yet one can hardly deny that many families are in trouble. The family's tragic fragility and instability and turbulence in a society that neglects it shamefully—notwithstanding the ritualized clamor in the mass media and by politicians on the campaign trail about the importance of family values—has made it a poor setting in which to raise emotionally secure, anxiety-free children. For many children the American family has become a hazardous habitat in which to grow up, a boiling cauldron in which they can get badly scalded.

In this anxiety-creating milieu all kinds of defensive behaviors develop and flourish. Not all are effective, of course; some are grossly self-destructive. One temporarily effective mechanism, though in fact harmful in the long run, is chameleonism. It is not surprising that some children seek refuge from uncertainty and harm in chameleonism. A troubled household, with tired, worried parents who feel useless and ignored and who sometimes take out their frustrations on their children, is precisely the environment in which chameleonism can flourish. Fending off danger by dissimulation, pretending to be what they are not, children find shelter from unbearable threat and possible harm.

Without a doubt the techno-service economy has contributed to this alarming situation.[3] Though enriching society over the long haul, it has also created a host of problems for the family in the short run. For instance, economic downturns put great pressure on family finances and heighten tensions between husbands and wives, who may quarrel over how money should be spent. Far more serious, the new economy dramatically altered the relationships between husbands and wives, and between parents and children. It did this in a number of ways: it helped isolate the nuclear family from the kinship system; it infused the family with competition and anomie, generating new tensions between parents and children; it robbed the family of many of its functions; it undermined parental authority.

First, building upon changes wrought by earlier stages of industrialization, the techno-service economy further weakened the traditional family network. The tempo of industrial life, its impersonality and competitiveness, seeped into the family and loosened the special closeness once characteristic of familial relationships. The rich diversity of modern life—its excitement, the wide range of cultures, the multiple opportunities to meet strangers and hence to develop emotional attachments outside the family—enticed people to look elsewhere for intimacy and stimulation and support.

Three-generational households have become increasingly uncommon. As recently as 1952, 38 percent of people over 65 were living with children; by 1995 the figure had dropped to 20 percent. The ties of the nuclear family to the extended kinship system—grandparents, uncles, aunts, cousins—became much looser, in part because declining fertility made the extended system logically impossible. The extended family needs a plenteous infusion of new members to survive. Where are these new members to come from when with every generation fewer children are added to the family pool? It is true that some forms of the old system survive among certain groups, particularly recent immigrants from Latin and Asian countries, but it is now more often a curiosity that the vibrant entity it was in the past.

At first the effect of these changes on children was liberating. They no longer had to live under the constant surveillance of numerous relatives, who monitored their behavior and reported infractions to parents or themselves chastised miscreants. But there is a price for this freedom. Because the nuclear family tends to be small and relatively isolated from the extended system, numerous children are alone and lonely much of the time. They miss their parents' touch, and yet when they eventually capture parental notice, the effect may be overwhelming. Having only a few children to nurture, the loving parent tends to pour an avalanche of concern called quality time on the hapless child. It is nice to be in the spotlight of attention, of course; but the bright glare can bewilder and unsettle a young inexperienced mind.

To further complicate matters, the techno-service economy has drawn vast numbers of women into the labor force, taking wives and mothers from the home and siphoning off some of the time and energy once devoted almost exclusively to satisfying the claims of husbands and children for attention and care. The result may be a wife/mother, the traditional keystone of the family, who does not have the physical and emotional strength to help keep the family in as good repair as may have once been the case. With both parents working and tired, with no parent at home during the day to look after the kids, including even the preschoolers, the child can easily come to feel alone and neglected.

Of course, it should be noted, many families are still remarkably cohesive. Even though the techno-service economy, by frequently shifting workers from place to place, dispersing families across the vast distances of a continent-sized country, has made physical contact between adult family members time-consuming and expensive, many family members still maintain contact with each other. For the new economy, while fragmenting the family, has also given family members the means to keep in touch through the telephone, e-mail, and snail mail. One recent survey found that 70 percent of all respondents talk to their mothers at least once a week.[4] Moreover, in a prosperous industrial society many parents have the emotional and intellectual and material wherewithal to respond to their children's cries for help, appeals for affection, and strivings for independence, in this way helping to keep the ties within the family reasonably strong.

Second, on the whole, the techno-service economy has changed the family game—and not in ways that everyone understands. Often, family members no longer play by the same rules, no longer move in concert, no longer seek the same ends. The surface may seem unchanged but the internal organization has been drastically altered. What has happened is that the family's job and the relationships between its members have undergone serious alteration. The new economy has hastened the family's loss of many of its functions. For some time now the family has ceased to be an important economic unit; most production occurs outside the home. Nor is the child's education primarily entrusted to the family; the school long ago replaced the home as the principal locus of formal teaching, except for a small number of parents who distrust the public school system and prefer to educate their children themselves. Medical care, physical protection, and spiritual guidance, all important family functions in earlier eras, have increasingly passed into the hands of professionals—teachers, physicians, policemen, social workers, clergymen. While these changes were well underway before the advent of the techno-service society, the family's loss of functions has become more pronounced in recent times.

An institution whose usefulness has been severely curtailed will turn its attention to the few things society still asks it to do. This is what has happened to the American family: many parents focus on the one job society thinks them best at—rearing children. Since families today tend to be small, some parents shower obsessive attention on their children, who become the target of continuous concern and scrutiny, worry and alarm. These parents shower their children with suggestions for improvement, with ecstatic approval and affection when things turn out well, and with painful reproof when they don't. Such attention is inevitable, for these children are the precious vessels of parental hopes and dreams.

Though no doubt well intended, these hopes and expectations are sometimes too heavy a responsibility for some children to manage. They feel suffocated by their parents' concern, overwhelmed by their fears and wishes. As a result, they may become resentful, even as they bask in the warmth of parental approval. To compound their problems, inordinate parental interest may cause some children to believe that they are extraordinary beings. Why else would parents lavish so much attention on them? But as they will soon learn, not everyone shares their parents' point of view. Caught in this muddle of conflicting evaluations, pummeled by unrealistic expectations, frightened by predictions of dire things to come if warnings are ignored, loaded down with excessive emotional freight, the parents' attention eventually becomes more than they can bear. Desperate for relief, they may seek refuge in dissimulation as a way of appeasing what appears to them to be the unreasonable hopes and dreams of foolish adults. They pretend to follow directions, to aspire to the things the parents desire, though in fact they have no interest in them at all. They have become chameleons.

THE DECLINE OF PARENTAL AUTHORITY

It could be argued (as I am inclined to do) that there is a bright side to the changes the techno-service economy has brought to the family. For instance, children today have more room to maneuver than in the past. Under the influence of the new order, the family has become less restrictive and authoritarian, less controlled by hoary tradition. Parents and children talk more easily to one another, express their feelings more freely, show hostility as well as affection more openly. In this more expansive atmosphere the child has more freedom of choice.

The reason for this can be found, at least in part, in the needs of the new economy. The techno-service system has less need for the strictly authoritarian ethos of the past, the submissive, robot-like obedience that was once the rule. Such behavior often prevents the work from being done swiftly and efficiently. The new economy needs workers who can work independently, who can on occasion take the initiative and solve a problem on their own without calling on a boss for help. For what matters to the techno-service economy is not mere submission to authority but that the work be done ably and willingly. One consequence of this is that many parents, following the economy's lead, have taken the ethic of the workplace into the home and are rearing their children more permissively.

The techno-service economy, by substantially enhancing the power of women, also has given the child more breathing room. Women encounter fewer barriers to employment in the service economy, and the economic independence they gain through working outside the home gives them the leverage to challenge arbitrary patriarchal authority. As power becomes less linked to gender, personal qualities rise to the forefront. Skill, guile, determination and strength of will, a hunger to control others, an ability to get things done and to make money—all begin to play important roles in deciding who will make decisions in the family and how resources will be distributed. No longer can the husband expect to dominate his family simply because tradition once so ordained.

The wife/mother, her position bolstered by the money she brings to the family coffer—chips she can use to improve her hand in the game of family bargaining—may, if she desires, interpose herself between the father and the child in order to negotiate in her children's behalf, to gain for them greater freedom in matters where once the father's will was absolute. With power more equally divided between husband and wife, parental authority becomes less concentrated and hence more easily contested, even though the contestant be only a child.

This increase in family egalitarianism is no small achievement. It represents a decisive break with the past. In the traditional family of the past (and in some cases, of the present) the family was authoritarian; parents commanded and children obeyed—or at least were expected to. In this system no one wielded greater power, commanded more respect and inspired more fear than the patriarchal father. Usually, children found their efforts to become independent thwarted by their father, who regarded the child's wish to be independent as a wicked scheme to rob him of the authority he believed rightly belonged to him and to him alone. Not prepared to share power, viewing the child's move toward independence as a threat to parental hegemony, as a flagrant act of rebellion, he sought to crush it, often successfully. The child could expect little support from others, in or outside the family. Rebellion against parental authority was a heinous crime in the past, and neither his relatives nor the community would lend assistance to anyone engaged in such wicked behavior.

Granted the authoritarian family does not present an altogether attractive picture of parent-child relations, at least to the modern observer accustomed to an equalitarian system; but it has its compensations. A firm, stable, orderly, albeit authoritarian family, perhaps softened by a mite of affection and concern for the child's welfare, gives children a predictable and realistic environment in which to grow up. Children learn that authority can be forceful and unbending, not overly concerned with their wishes, and determined to get a day's work for a day's pay—a not unrealistic picture of the world the child will someday enter. Assuming the parents are not brutal or completely neglectful of their responsibilities, the child will enjoy a degree of stability sadly lacking in many modern egalitarian families.

Indeed, the problem for most children in the techno-service society is not authoritarian parents; the problem is parents who have lost much of their authority. When children lack stable and respected authority figures at home, they may become anxious and vulnerable to chameleonism. Without consistent guidance from strong reliable parents, without a firm standard to rally around, children feel unprotected, vulnerable to threatening forces that push them now in one direction, now in another. Their parents expect one thing, their relatives another, their teachers something else, their peers something different from them all. Not sure in what direction to go, they may temporize, trying first to please one, then the other, and end up trying to please them all, depending on whose company they are in at the time. In effect the child has learned how to be a chameleon.

The techno-service economy undermines the ground on which parental authority traditionally rests—the belief that submission to authority is the linchpin that holds society together; the belief that authority at every level, the family, the school, the church, the workplace, must be obeyed; the conviction that any questioning of authority will inevitably lead to social chaos. The techno-service society allows—nay, encourages—children to question some previously unchallenged assumptions: that parents know best and that their past is the best guide to the child's future; that their knowledge, skills, beliefs and values are all that children need to learn in order to prepare themselves for the future. Furthermore, children are no longer expected to believe that parental needs should take precedence over those of the child. What are these parental needs? They are the usual ones found everywhere—the need for approval, affection, help. But above all the need for deference, respect and obedience—a need that is simple, direct, urgent, and not to be denied.

Traditionalists think that parents are entitled to deference and obedience because only they can prepare children for adult life. They believe their lives exemplify the future awaiting the child, their roles the roles the child would play as an adult, their skills the skills the child must learn to survive, their values the values the community would support for the foreseeable future. They assume they have the knowledge to continue guiding their children toward traditional goals, using traditional methods to help get them there.

Savvy parents in the techno-service economy know they can make no such assumption. They know they must prepare their children for an unknown future, and that almost nothing can be assumed about tomorrow except that it will be different from today. They have seen ideas that had developed slowly over generations become outmoded with mind-numbing speed. They have observed skills that took years to acquire become obsolete overnight, as new technologies put some trades on the shelf and make previously valued occupations archaic and unwanted. To their horror, they watch helplessly as new ideologies sweep cherished ideas and beliefs into the ash can of history. Deeply prized values that gave meaning to life for one generation are derided by the next as irrelevant and comical.

In these circumstances a strong commitment to an outmoded system of ideas, methods, and goals can be suicidal, particularly for young folk who must make their way in a world far different from the one their parents grew up in. And so, to help their children survive and prosper in a swiftly changing world, parents must focus on the future and try to understand what it will be like. They must be flexible and ready to jettison the past when they believe doing so is in the best interests of the children.

But an orientation toward the future drastically weakens parental authority. It confers a special status on children, who are seen as more in touch with the present and better able to adapt to the future than are their parents. In the future-oriented, child-centered techno-service family the child becomes the central figure in the drama of family life—a far cry from the traditional scene in which children play only supporting roles or wait quietly in the wings while the parents strut on center stage, performing all the major parts, enjoying the spotlight of attention, getting society's rapt attention and receiving most of its rewards.

The techno-service society further diminishes parental authority by restricting the parents' freedom to shape and control their children as they see fit. The police, social workers, and judges may come between parents and their children and attempt to regulate parental behavior, moving against parents who use undue force to extract obedience from their children. The vigorous use of a hand, a cane, a leather strap to chastise an unruly youngster is unacceptable to enlightened opinion and will quickly bring the weight of the state against the offending parent. Such intervention, no matter how well intended, inevitably reduces the authority of parents over children. To the powerful state parents must eventually yield, though they may squirm and weave, futilely seeking to evade its force.

More subtly, the techno-service state weakens parental authority by placing before children nonparental models whose values and behavior run counter to those of the parents. In school the child encounters teachers whose views may differ from those advocated by parents. Or, as often happens, children may come upon in magazines, movies, or on television that ubiquitous modern figure, the expert, whose prestige in advanced technological societies is enormous and whose advice sometimes nullifies parental teachings. In fact, some parents turn voluntarily to the expert for guidance, substituting an expert's judgment for their own, a tactic that makes it difficult for the parent to maintain a posture of omniscient authority. Whatever their point of entry into the family, outsiders are continually generating torrents of counter-ideas and visions that may rudely erode the foundation on which parental authority rests.

THE EXPERIENTIAL CHASM

The technological changes embodied in the techno-service revolution sap parental authority by sowing confusion in minds already disoriented by monumental social change. And, obviously, confusion is not exactly the state of mind authority should present to children if it expects to be obeyed. Technological change confuses people because it tends to occur in quantum jumps, not in small incremental steps to which the hapless target of change can gradually become accustomed. Abruptly, machines require people to work in places and in ways totally alien to their previous experience or inclination. Without warning, they find themselves in briskly automated factories and offices, tied to computers and other arcane devices, and forced to adjust to circumstances they consider neither pleasant nor comprehensible.

Technological change does more than disconcert the parental mind; it also creates an experiential chasm between generations, a gulf between the lives of parents raised in one technological age and those of their children exposed to another.[5] Communication across this chasm can be excruciatingly irksome and difficult. For what can a father who balances his accounts with a simple desk calculator say about work to a son who attacks a similar project with a multi-gigabyte computer? What can a mother, whose view of the world was derived from limited personal experience, now totally dated, or from books, equally passé, or from amusingly quaint films and television programs now fit only to be smiled at—what can this mother say to a daughter to whom the media present a varied, constantly changing picture of life, one without fixed guidelines or moral prescriptions? Not much. At least not much that is intelligible to the youngster.

The experiential chasm invalidates the pertinence of parental wisdom and insidiously weakens parental authority because, in Philip Slater's words, "parents have not experienced what is of central importance to the child, or at least have not experienced it in the same way, at the same time of life."[6] Having grown up in different worlds, daily moving in separate circles, parents and children may gradually drift apart until the generation gap, imperceptibly small in simpler times, grows into an unbridgeable canyon. Standing on shifting ground, parental authority may lose its balance and fall into the experiential canyon, a victim of unintelligible change.

Describing the painful condition of living in a rapidly changing world, Philip Slater writes, "Parents must face the irrelevance of their knowledge and skills for the world in which their children will mature. And this is an accelerating trend. . . . Parents cannot define the parameters of the future for their children—cannot even establish the terms of possible change or a range of alternative outcomes. They are, therefore, useless and obsolete in a way that rarely befell parents in any previous century."[7] Even when parents presciently grasp what their children need to know and the skills they must have to cope with conditions in a rapidly changing world, they may lack the ability to transmit this knowledge to their progeny. Not many parents can anticipate the future and skillfully transfer their insights to their offspring in an acceptable and understandable way.

To sum up, when parents become uncertain as to how best to prepare their children for the future, when they suspect their own skills and knowledge are no asset to the child—worse, a liability—when experts and state agencies intervene in family affairs, then a serious erosion of parental authority must take place. Baffled by a world they do not understand, bewildered by social change, many parents lose confidence in themselves and become unsure of their ability to guide their children through life's uncharted waters. Consequently, the prestige and power of parents deteriorate and the relative position of the child improves.

Some parents wisely accept the need to change; others change with obvious reluctance, performing their new roles awkwardly, ill at ease in the new family; still others resist change fiercely and denounce the new world they never wanted and cannot accept. This resistance is understandable: change does not come easy to most people. Consider what a battle it is to be an old-fashioned parent in a new-fashioned society that extols individual autonomy, equality and individualism, even for relatively young children. Consider what a burden it is to assume family obligations, when meeting family expectations hinders the more valued pursuit of private satisfaction. To a growing number of people in the techno-service society, authority itself has become anathema. Not surprisingly, they have made the authoritarian parent a prime target of their drive for social change.

While it is true that the techno-service economy encourages independence, equality, and achievement and has driven authoritarianism out of the mainstream of everyday life and into its backwaters and eddies, this is by no means an act of altruism. As noted, the techno-service society has good reasons for what it does. It needs self-disciplined, individualistic, independent, achievement-motivated workers and will do what it can to get them. Recognizing that child-rearing practices establish the foundation on which the kind of people it needs can develop, the techno-service system promotes values that urge parents to encourage independence and achievement in their children. It expects that a child reared in this new way will grow up to be the self-reliant, organized, ambitious worker the system requires and thrives upon. These expectations tend to affect how parents rear their children, particularly parents in the technocratic middle class who want their children to be winners in the Second Great Transformation.

In the middle class, the social womb of most New Elitists, parents who accept the techno-service value system try to inculcate in their children the traits they must possess to get ahead in the world: ambition, verbal facility, social empathy and flexibility, orderliness and punctuality, a willingness to work hard, and the gift of self-confidence. Educated and ambitious themselves, these parents know that good school grades and graduation from a prestigious university will open doors to their children, and they urgently push them toward achievement. They encourage their offspring to believe in an open world where anything is possible, if only they work hard enough.

To these parents their children's strivings for autonomy, self-assertion, and achievement seem entirely admirable. For they recognize the important roles that competitiveness, ambition, and a capacity for self-direction play in the struggle for success. Thus each achievement and any sign of precocity in their children are noted and applauded. In order to move the achievement process along, they set high standards and reinforce good performance with praise, smiles, gifts, and treats; they also get visibly upset when their progeny do badly. The effect is to build into the child a strong need to excel, to do well in competition with others, to achieve their goals.[8]

Verbal facility is especially valued. To promote this skill middle class parents make a point of reading to their children during the day or at night, whenever appropriate; and they deliberately use an elaborated mode of speech, emphasizing vocabulary and complex diction, when talking to them, thus subtly imparting the knack of using words.[9] They also deliberately foster those cognitive skills that enhance the children's ability to get along with peers—sensitivity, sympathy, empathy—urging them to try to understand people, to put themselves in other people's shoes, to see the world as others do. Empathic skill, they are told, is a tool necessary for success. Sympathy for others is admirable, of course, and encouraged. But they must understand that without empathy they will not know what is expected of them and will be lost.

In responding to the ethos of the techno-service system, the typical child-centered middle class family has become a marvel of liberal ideology and rational practice. It extols individualism and egalitarianism; it wants to give the child every opportunity to develop its own precious potentials; it encourages the child to be assertive, to challenge authority, even that of its parents, if the child believes itself in the right. While this may sometimes be annoying, parents committed to the ideals of the techno-service society accept it as the price they must pay to promote egalitarianism, though in practice principle may occasionally go by the board when the child goes too far and inflames parental tempers. As rationalists these parents appeal to the child's reason when justifying their expectations and actions. They are blissfully tolerant of filial infractions, gauging their children's behavior not by its consequences but by their motives—a childhood experience which helps explain adult Elitists' confusion when people judge their actions by effects and not by intentions—which they know are noble and beyond criticism.

When punishment must be administered, it is almost never physical. Liberal middle-class parents loathe violence—it strikes at the very foundation of their belief in rationalism, their faith that all disagreements are amenable to negotiation, that all problems can be ultimately solved by good will.[10] Therefore they abjure the slap and the strap, preferring instead to use reasoned argument subtly backed by threats to withdraw love if the child does not behave. As a result, children learn that acceptance and love are never unconditional. They discover that approval is entirely contingent upon meeting the expectations of others, first their parents, then peers, and finally teachers and other important adults. Gripped by a longing for love, they become excruciatingly sensitive to the need to win and keep the approval of the powerful people around them.

If parents follow the script written by the techno-service society, as many of them try to do, they will eventually equip their children with the intellectual and emotional tools they need to prosper in the information age. This is what they had in mind. What they had not intended was to turn their children into chameleons. And yet, in raising their children as they did they made them keenly sensitive to the dangers that await the unwary who ignore the opinions of important people in their group. At the same time they furnished them with the instruments they need to detect what others expect and the skill to conceal their own wishes when to express them would jeopardize their safety. By the time they reach adulthood, the child already has at hand a useful kit of survival tools—he or she is ready to become a chameleon when the need arises.

THE STORY OF WILL

Perhaps the process through which chameleonism develops will come into sharper focus if we examine a specific case to illustrate our argument. Let us call this person Will. Southern born, the product of a middle-class family as that class was defined in his region, he grew up in somewhat difficult surroundings. His mother was a nurse, his stepfather a salesman; money was never plentiful in the family, at times quite scarce, but stark poverty was not an issue. His mother was doting, lively, supportive, and warm; his stepfather was unpredictable, occasionally moody and abusive, a person to be catered to and treated with circumspection. All in all, not a comfortable family to grow up in but not one to arouse much attention in his social milieu.

Will himself did arouse attention—it was soon apparent that he was bright. His skill with words and abstractions, presentiments of later successes, filled his mother with wonder and pride, which she did not seek to hide. At school his intelligence delighted his teachers, who singled him out for attention and praise. Now, in circumstances where adults openly admire a child's skill and applaud his accomplishments, accompanying the applause with affection and reasonable expectations for further achievement, it is easy for him to develop a high opinion of himself. Fussed over by his mother, other adults, and teachers, he naturally comes to consider himself someone special, someone gifted with talents that set him apart and above his fellows.

So far so good. But then problems set in, for sometimes the process goes awry. In some homes, bastions of parental applause, where any evidence of precocity evokes paeans of praise, one or both parents lose their balance and appreciation turns into adulation. The applause is indiscriminate and the expectations unrealistic—a problem in itself. But when the praise and affection and indulgence are withdrawn unexpectedly and for no apparent reason, as sometimes happens, the problem grows out of all proportion to the cause.

Perhaps Will's parents were too busy, too harried by everyday concerns, to always pay him the amount of attention he had come to expect. Perhaps a younger sibling was competing successfully for a larger share of parental affection. Whatever the reason, Will came to feel neglected; he became angry and confused. He wondered what he had done wrong; he wondered whether he was truly loved; he began to question his self-worth. The satisfying image of himself, like a fine statue lovingly constructed from materials given to him by parents and others, excellent in every important way, superior to run-of-the-mill humanity, suddenly seemed fragile, in constant jeopardy of breaking into pieces.

Dismayed by this turn of events, he tried to protect himself by redoubling his efforts to impress and please his parents, only to learn that his problems did not end with the family. He found that he had peers to contend with and to his horror they proved even more troublesome. At school, possibly even earlier, he discovered that the high estimation his parents had of him was not shared by his peers, who considered him just another kid, brighter and more talented perhaps, but withal human and not always likable.

For needless to say, his air of self-importance did not sit well with his schoolmates. They disliked his pretensions to superiority. They resented the attention he received from teachers, the favors, nods of approval, signs of respect, words of encouragement they routinely sent his way. Most of all, they envied the ease with which he mastered school work and obtained good grades. Thoughtlessly, carelessly, he had let them see his report card; perhaps he even boasted of his grades, naively expecting approval and admiration, like the reaction of his parents. What he got surprised and frightened him—not approval but derision, not respect but scorn, not friendship but surly rejection. He was called teacher's pet, a sissy, a grind. This was a lesson in what it means to be different from others, to stand out in a crowd, to be visibly superior to one's mates, to be the object of envy. It is a lesson he will never forget, for he knows that forgetfulness will put him in peril.

Like most children he wanted desperately to be part of the group, and he quickly learned that being popular with teachers is not the way to become popular with classmates. He learned from the jeers and jabs of envious classmates to conceal his achievements, to hide his grades, to downplay his abilities, to denigrate his intelligence, to attribute his successes to chance and luck. He employed subterfuge and deception to disguise his thoughts. He pretended to be uninterested in grades, when he was really eager to do well; he played energetically in schoolyard games and joined enthusiastically in discussions of sports or other aspects of youth culture, when he was really only mildly interested. He sought to placate enemies and fend off foes by flattery and smiles, by offering to share his lunch, by attempting to help the less academically talented with their homework. In short, he tried to be a good sport, but in fact he was becoming a chameleon.

All these developments could not have happened at a worse time. He was now about eight, and even his indulgent mother had begun to be occasionally critical of his behavior and to place restrictions on his freedom. She was less tolerant of his selfishness, which she used to accept but now called childish. His parents demanded more signs of self-discipline, more attention to family rules, and greater respect for the needs of his younger sibling and others. Clothes may not be dropped on the floor for others to pick up; toys may not be snatched from a younger brother at will; his bed must be made and room kept tidy—and so forth.

This change, often abrupt and without explanation, from permissiveness to stricter control, can in a previously indulged, already confused child induce feelings of distrust, weaken his sense of security, undermine his self-confidence, and destroy his belief in a predictable and friendly world. For apart from the inevitable annoyance the new criticisms and restrictions bring, the sudden and inexplicable nature of the change startles and frightens him. What is going on? he wonders. And so must we. Why of all times have his parents (or grandparents) chosen age eight to suddenly begin imposing new limits on what the child may do and say? Why not earlier, or later, or not at all?

No doubt the answer has something to do with the maturational changes that have taken place in most children by age seven or eight. By that time, developmental psychologists say, most children have acquired the cognitive skills needed to distinguish between right and wrong, and parents or their surrogates seize upon this to impose rules based on the moral judgments they assume children can understand.[11] For whatever reason, the imposition of restrictions on the child tends in many places not to occur until age seven or eight. This is certainly the case in Brazil, for example, where many people believe children are heaven-sent bundles of joy, innately incapable of self-control. External control grows stricter only after age seven.[12] In rural Taiwan, according to Margery Wolf, children under seven are thought to have little capacity for understanding instructions; hence parents think it pointless to teach them anything or expect much from them. Only after the child has attained the age of seven or perhaps later will parents begin the painful task of correcting the child's unwanted behavior.[13] In the Okinawan village studied by the Maretskis, the child is thought to be "a helpless, pitiable treasure, incapable of knowing, understanding or learning until he reaches six years of age."[14] In rural Puerto Rico the parents studied by David Landy regard all children as innocent angels who lack innate resources and from whom little can be expected, particularly the boys. But after the age of seven or thereabout control grows tighter.[15]

For most children, the transition from the protected early years to the more demanding time of late childhood, especially the move from the home to the no-nonsense surroundings of the school and the peer group, is a passage fraught with peril. Much harm can come to the child's fragile self-confidence during this period. Fortunately, many children make the trip without excessive damage to their self-esteem. But for Will the transition was more difficult. Restrictions at home and in the classroom, reprimands around the dinner table, and rebuffs in the schoolyard, produced not a grudging acceptance of reality but a sense of bewilderment and rejection. Disappointment at a world suddenly grown cold and demanding turned into unreasoning anxiety and resentment, a consuming suspicion and distrust of the world. He became unsure of where he fitted in, inclined to question his self-worth, eaten by feelings of gnawing rage.

But this rage in most cases could not be expressed openly, for he saw that to do so would be dangerous. His parents no longer indulged his displays of temper; other adults refused to tolerate his whines and complaints. Temper tantrums that were considered cute when he was tiny are rejected as unseemly in a big boy of eight. And schoolmates took a dim view of his aggression. They were not amused; angry words evoked anger in return, and blows brought a punch in the nose.

When a child discovers that showing anger is forbidden, however justifiable and altogether enjoyable its expression would be, he will try to cope with the turmoil in his head, the unvoiced fury eating at him like acid on bare metal, in several ways. He may let out his anger indirectly in numerous, seemingly unrelated ways—in displays of pique like kicking the dog, neglecting his homework, making a rat's warren out of his bedroom, scattering litter around the house, picking on younger siblings. This is satisfying in itself, naturally. But it leaves the problem unresolved. The causes of his misery remain unpunished, and the rage is still there, seething beneath the surface and threatening to erupt at any moment, with possibly disastrous consequences.

He may, therefore, pursue a drastic strategy—the unconscious repression of hurt feelings, the rigid denial of the wrath and hatred that is churning inside him. He rejects the reasonable, if less adorable, picture of himself which everyday experience has fashioned for him. In its place, without his being aware of what is happening, he puts an idealized image of himself, a delightful picture of perfection composed of all the qualities he values in others and which the critical, cold, mean world refuses to recognize in him. This seems to work splendidly, at least at first. The idealized perfect self is flattering and comforting; he can once again feel pleased with himself.

Repression keeps the surface calm; no one is aware of the anger boiling below, not even the boy himself. But peace bought through repression comes at great cost. For one thing, as noted, the perfect self contains aspirations that defy attainment; failure is inevitable. The result is unrelenting self-hatred for failing to live up to one's own ideal. This self-fury, like the murderous anger directed at parents, peers, and the whole cruel world, is not recognized and understood because it is repressed. Nevertheless, it continues to do its deadly work, with ruinous consequences. For, as Freud once pointed out, repressed rage produces disabling self-doubt, a sense of dreary emptiness, and vague feelings of anxiety. Chameleonism covers these feelings; it does not eliminate them.

If the child is father to the man, then it is understandable why the defense the boy constructed to deal with frustration and anxiety would be the one he adopted as an adult. This is not to say that childhood experiences necessarily determine adult character; only that the defenses fashioned early in life lay the groundwork for adult responses to social threat. In some cases, later supportive experiences may well obviate the need for chameleonism; or perhaps other traits may be called into play that work even better than dissimulation and deceit.

Numerous people of Will's generation routinely employ the Chameleon Complex to defend themselves against attack, for they also experienced many of the vicissitudes that marked his childhood. Like him they grew up in interesting times: a time of bewildering social change and the breakdown of conventional standards; a time of decline in parental authority and the elevation of the child to stardom in the family circle; a time when the explosion of communication technologies catapulted the information system into economic prominence and separated the generations into those who adapted well to the new technologies and those who did not. All in all, it is not surprising that other people besides Will, worried by frightening change and intimidated by demanding parents and envious peers, would seek protection in the Chameleon Complex.

It is easy to disparage the Chameleon Complex; it certainly smacks distastefully of insincerity and cunning. But it is important to remember that this complex is no accident. It exists in part because of the turmoil of the times, in part because it serves the needs of the techno-service society, and in part because it is useful to some individuals, especially the New Elite. The Chameleon Complex serves the needs of society by fashioning people whose chameleonism disposes them to be flexible, adaptive to change, and sensitive to the moods of their clients. It produces people whose hedonistic appetites support a consumer economy and whose perfectionism celebrates excellence and achievement, both core values of a techno-service system. It serves the interests of the individual by providing protection from criticism and an escape from crippling self-doubt. In short, notwithstanding the psychological damage it eventually does, the Chameleon Complex can be a valuable asset to people striving to make their way in the intensely competitive culture of the techno-service society.

In the next chapter, I will show that the Chameleon Complex helps the New Elite in its rebellion against the domination of the business class by justifying its efforts to capture the culture and control the Techno-Service Society. For, in addition to its characterological components, the Chameleon Complex contains an ideology that articulates the New Elite's grievances and gives focus to its inchoate yearnings and ambitions.

8

The Ideology of the New Elite

Revolutionaries need an ideology to justify their grab for power. Without an ideology they would look like power-hungry upstarts eager to eat at the nation's nourishing, treasure-filled trough. With the aid of ideology they can drive off competitors, gorge themselves to their heart's content, look like saviors, and feel morally uplifted at the same time—in effect, have their cake and eat it too. For an ideology arms the rebels with the ideas, slogans, dreams, and fantasies that capture the hearts and minds of frightened and angry people who feel at their wits' end. Ideology offers them a glowing vision of the future and a program for a better world. Ideology, in short, has important uses. No group seeking power should be without one.

Although they are in fact a farrago of individuals only loosely allied and sometimes at odds with each other, the revolutionary members of the New Elite have one important thing in common—they tend to have made the Chameleon Complex a part of their personalities. As already noted, chameleonism is attractive to Elitists because it satisfies their need for security. But the New Elite wants more than security; it wants power. It wants to win its war against the business class and thus fulfill its destiny to control the new world created by the Second Great Transformation. To this end the complex is useful, for it contains an adversarial ideology that legitimates the Elite's struggle for power, in part by justifying its hostility toward the business class and in part by providing a program to eject the enemy from the perch of power. The Elitists' ideology expresses their unease with the market economy. They like money, but the market makes them queasy; the term greed comes easily to their lips when describing the messy business of making money. If only life could be less competitive, more egalitarian, and more fair, they would be more content—or so they think.

In the hands of militant Elitists an adversarial ideology is a formidable weapon in their cultural war with the business class. Philosophically it undergirds their struggle to seize control of the culture and define the American identity; practically, it provides them with a vehicle to ride over their opponents, to accuse them of venality and meanness and incompetence. Despite the rumors that the cultural war is over (a rumor spread by New Elitists themselves, who used to deny the cultural war existed), the war is alive and has grown increasingly bitter.[1] It is a conflict in which almost any subterfuge, calumny, or devious maneuver is justified, a take-no-prisoners struggle that is poisoning relationships between racial, ethnic, gender, and other groups, and contributing to doubt and cynicism in contemporary America.

The adversary ideology flows from the character of the New Elitists and the vision of the world they would like to create—a world without flaw or fracture, free of evil people and oppression and invidious distinctions. The adversarial ideology proclaims the right of everyone to pursue his or her own path to personal liberation and self-actualization, the right, indeed the obligation, to enjoy life. It extols compassion for the weak and disadvantaged; it professes to link merit to reward but would make exceptions for women, people of color, and other minorities.

Above all, the ideology extols egalitarianism. To the Elitist all persons and cultures are inherently equal and all deserve equal respect. Paradoxically and despite their own special talents and attainments, nothing offends a dedicated Elitist more than the judgment that some person or group or culture is inferior to any other. Judgmentalism is a cardinal sin and inequality an abomination. In essence the adversarial ideology, tempered in the crucible of the 1960s, reformulated in the 1980s, and brought up to date in the 1990s, is late eighteenth-century egalitarianism gussied up in newfangled clothes.

As a rule, ideologies rarely attract followers for more than a short time, and without dedicated followers they soon end up in history's dustbin of unloved and forgotten ideas. But the adversarial ideology of the New Elite is different. It continually attracts supporters because it taps into a powerful grievance—the sense that society wickedly withholds the power and status that aggrieved Elitists believe is their just due. It thrives because it analyzes the cause of this grievance and then suggests how things can be made better.

Everyone has a grievance or two, of course. Some people have many—they collect grievances the way a magnet attracts iron filings. Some grievances are petty, some comical, some serious. Perhaps the most serious and deeply rooted is the complaint that authority behaves badly. This grievance is intensely felt because it is rooted in the frustrations of early childhood. A child denied a mother's kiss, a youngster punished by a father for an infraction not adequately explained, a pupil humiliated by a teacher before classmates—these and other frustrations may create a lifelong festering resentment against authority. This resentment gains strength and focus in later life when encounters with employers, the police and the courts, the military and arrogant government bureaucrats demonstrate to people how limited their autonomy and choices really are.

No group feels its grievance against authority more keenly than the New Elite. Elitists tingle with pleasure when they remember their youthful defiance of authority. And though they are now adults, authority still tends to rub them the wrong way. Almost reflexively, they stand ready to challenge the authority of most institutions, and they will usually justify their defiance as socially necessary. They are especially skeptical of the authority of the business establishment, whose selfish obstinacy—as they see it—stands in the way of social progress. Elitists charge that the business class is indifferent to the plight of the poor and the weak—women, homosexuals, blacks and other people of color—and that it resists every effort to promote equality and social justice. The adversary ideology embedded in the Chameleon Complex wins the hearts of Elitists by offering them a vision of a just society freed from the authoritarian oppression of the business establishment.

Not incidentally, the adversary ideology wins the hearts of Elitists by sanctioning pleasure as an acceptable way to attain that quintessential Elitist goal—the fully realized self. By siding with the Dionysian Spirit, which exalts sensual release and abandon, and opposing the Apollonian Spirit, which emphasizes self-control and rationality, the adversary ideology legitimates the pursuit of unfettered pleasure and condemns dreary self-denial. This inevitably enchants Elitists.

Their narcissistic souls revel in the idea that not only is fun accept-able, it is also therapeutically necessary.

Elitists tend to see themselves as victims of conventional morality, prisoners of an oppressive system that restricts pleasure and stifles creativity. Their targeted enemy is the traditional middle class (es-pecially its business component), which emphasizes discipline and self-denial, and tends to associate the pursuit of self-realization with selfishness. Most Elitists consider the middle class a collection of blue-nosed spoil-sports who use over-zealous policemen to frustrate the pursuit of pleasure. Elitists yearn to break out of the constricted existence in which middle-class society seeks to confine them. As they see it, only by shaking off bothersome social restraints can they be free to achieve true happiness.

To rebellious Elitists freedom means the right to live without hin-drance or guilt, the right to choose a sexual partner of any race or sex; the right to ignore rules about commitment and marriage when they stand in the way of pleasure; the right to use drugs, to have an abortion, to work, dress, play, speak as one wants—in short, the right to live pretty much as one pleases without suffering public censure or private remorse. By supporting these fantasies and wishes, the ad-versary ideology articulates the Elitist's longing for untrammeled freedom, for pleasure without cost, for ecstasy without letdown, for acting out wishes without social restraint and punishment. Small won-der the adversary ideology quickly won the affection of many New Elitists.

It would be a mistake to dismiss these warriors as mere dreamers, fanatics, and, in some cases, show-offs. True, among the Elitists are some feminists or gays who, in John Leo's words, "chant daily to Mother Earth about their menstrual cycle or march naked up Fifth Avenue proudly displaying their genitals."[2] These noisy, colorful, highly publicized performers are a boon to television news reporters, but they should not be taken as typical of the Elites presently at war with the business class. The most important combatants, the leaders and most ferocious fighters, are less colorful but not less serious. They know they are engaged in a deadly long-term war, and they mean to win it.

This war is being waged by a mutinous crew determined to take charge of the ship of state—disaffected academics, left-wing intellec-tuals, radicalized feminists, politicized homosexuals, certain angry leaders of racial and ethnic minorities and their allies in the media.

The feminists want to reduce the power of men by downgrading the male contribution to high culture, while elevating the work of women. The homosexuals want to gain acceptance by drawing attention to their condition and its vicissitudes. Trendy academics and intellectuals want to dethrone the Europe-based canon and de-emphasize the idea of rational causation. Afrocentric blacks and some spokesmen for other racial or ethnic groups want to replace the dominant white culture with one that gives their own group more importance and visibility.

As different as they appear to be from each other, they all march to the same drummer and sing the same tune. In unison, they proclaim the glory of egalitarianism and pluralism, and they ululate hosannas to sensitivity and tolerance. But drums and chants, catchy slogans and stirring pronouncements are not enough to win a war. Although a song may stir up enthusiasm and help keep the troops moving, more is needed than enthusiasm and fervent declarations of faith. What is needed is a coherent program, and troops to intimidate resisters. Fortunately for the insurgents, their ideology outlines a program and energizes a cadre of highly motivated program directors and energetic militant enforcers.

THE ROOTS OF THE ADVERSARIAL IDEOLOGY

Like many modern ideologies, the adversary ideology encapsulated in the Chameleon Complex originated in the philosophy of the Enlightenment and in the slogans of the Revolution of 1789. But its more proximate roots are in the rhetoric of the Parisian Bohemians of the early nineteenth century and in the modernist literary-artistic esthetics of the late nineteenth and early twentieth centuries. Perhaps linking eighteenth-century European philosophy, nineteenth-century Parisian Bohemia, and modernist esthetics with twentieth-century American cultural war seems a bit farfetched. After all, tumultuous changes spread over two centuries separate these wonders; they grew out of sharply different times and national cultures. What could they possibly have in common? What, for instance, does Norman Mailer, a hipster who adores the underclass and admires its addiction to violence, or Jack Kerouac, the celebrant of the open road and the working class, have in common with Gustave Flaubert, a staunch defender of the old order, who loathed the lower class and feared its penchant for anarchy? Not much, it would seem on first inspection, not even writing skill: Mailer and Kerouac are not in Flaubert's league.[3]

And yet the link between Flaubert and Kerouac and Mailer, and the movements they represent, is strong. For the clownish antics of the Bohemians in the 1820s, the feverish capers of hipsters, beatniks, and dropouts and student radicals in the 1950s and 1960s, and the strident demonstrations of the speech controllers and diversity police in the 1990s are closely connected. All are part of a cultural war against the hegemony of the business class. Still, travelers on the trail of this rebellion as it evolved across the decades frequently get lost. This is understandable, for the protagonists, the labels they used to describe themselves, the issues they raised, and the tactics they employed to win their battles with the establishment have changed over the years. But getting lost is not inevitable; we need only follow the bright markers the rebels left of their progress.

The first of these markers is a radical movement in the arts and letters known as Bohemianism. The Bohemians were artistic rebels against authority and conventional standards, but it is important to remember that the literary-artistic elites have not always been rebellious; more often they were fervent supporters of the establishment. Until well into the eighteenth century the literary elite and the ruling aristocracy had enjoyed a mutually rewarding relationship. An educated, esthetically-inclined aristocrat (always a tiny minority; most nobles were indifferent to the arts and letters, preferring to spend their time hunting, intriguing, and wenching) might sponsor an artist or writer, support his work with a modest stipend, and protect him from pestiferous government censors. In return for this minor outlay of money and time the aristocrat, as a patron of talent, received the pleasure of the artist's or writer's company, an occasional dedication in a poem or play, and the chance to display his talented client to a salon of other titled dilettantes.

Most writers and artists treasured their association with the nobility. They felt a certain kinship with the aristocrat, for after all, were not artists and writers aristocrats themselves, not of birth perhaps, but surely of intellectual and esthetic attainment. As to the hierarchical world of titled gradations, the literary-artistic elites felt at home in it. Theirs, too, was a graded world, albeit of talent and creative excellence. That the aristocrat's titles and offices carried more prestige and weight and power than the creations of the talented artist and writer—this the literary-artistic elites understood and accepted.

They were men of the world. Power and wealth cannot be ignored, and their possessor must be deferred to, especially when position is sanctioned by centuries of privilege. But the aristocrat-patron was more than a powerful and rich person, more than a protector and moneybags; he was a connoisseur, a cultivated person sensitive to artistic talent, someone who understood and appreciated the creative spirit—or so the writer and artist liked to believe.

There was never, however, any question of equality between the aristocrat-patron and his commoner-client. Writers and painters, no matter how eminent in their fields, were sometimes required to enter the noble's domicile through the servant's entrance, and impertinent assertions of equality met with cold reproof or worse. The Chevalier de Rohan, feeling himself insulted by Voltaire, who dared to assert his equality during a disagreement, had his servants cane the impudent young writer, while the Chevalier coolly stood by. Out of such experiences revolutionaries are made. But most writers were not revolutionaries; like other members of the literary-artistic elites, they were enthusiastic supporters of the aristocratic order.

The French Revolution of 1789 put an end to arrogant aristocrats beating insolent writers who dared to bandy insults with their titled superiors. It did this, of course, by putting an end to the aristocracy. And though the old aristocracy was restored for a time, following the final defeat of Napoleon when a Bourbon king once again sat on the throne, its power had effectively ended with the fall of the Bastille. But much before that dramatic event a new dominant class had appeared on the scene—the bourgeoisie. The bourgeoisie began to develop real power in the seventeenth and eighteenth centuries, when international commerce started to flourish. Slowly, throughout western Europe, the middle class—merchants, bankers, professionals, higher civil servants, prosperous manufacturers—grew rich and powerful, in fact if not in the outward signs of formal status. Their assumption of formal power was relatively peaceful in England, bloody in France, and though slower and less spectacular elsewhere, always relentless, ever grasping, culminating in impressive wealth and power.

As the industrial revolution progressed, the business class (as we now call the bourgeoisie) gathered numbers and grew strong by participating exuberantly in the growth of commerce and promoting a market system which unabashedly supported trade for profit. By the middle of the nineteenth century the bourgeoisie was in effective control of most of western Europe, and the aristocratic structure of power, erected during the Middle Ages, lay in ruins—elegant and genteel ruins perhaps, but ruins nonetheless.

With the collapse of the aristocratic edifice the literary-artistic elites suffered a hateful blow to their personal security and self-esteem. The destruction of the old order left them reeling and disoriented, feeling unappreciated and vulnerable. Without warning they were cast adrift in the cold, rough commercial seas of the industrial system, bouncing about like flotsam in a storm, without familiar landmarks, on their own, and with no assurance of rescue. Gone was the familiar, comfortable world of the patron-client relationship. In its place was the impersonal market of buyers and sellers; the anonymous public, unknown and unknowable to writers and artists, became the arbiter of their fate. This many of them could not understand and would not accept.

Who was this anonymous public? The bourgeoisie, of course. Only the bourgeoisie had the money and time to purchase and consume the enormous number of books, pictures, plays, operas, and statues the ambitious, money-hungry, fabulously energetic creative elites produced. The paying public was large, its appetite for cultural uplift and entertainment was insatiable, and for the first time the creative elites could grow rich on the sale of their work. But first their work had to catch on—that was the rub. Excellence was not always recognized; some of Stendahl's novels sold fewer than 400 copies, and Baudelaire fared even worse. As the creative elites soon learned, the public was fickle. Its tastes were untutored, its preferences unfathomable; today's favorite could become tomorrow's nonentity.

Perhaps most distressing of all, success, when it came, carried the imprint of the bourgeoisie's approval. This was galling, because for centuries the bourgeoisie had been ridiculed and scorned by the aristocracy as beneath contempt, had been flayed with every epithet and insult at the aristocrat's disposal, had been dismissed as vulgar, pretentious, cowardly, mean-spirited, an excrescence unworthy of serious attention. The literary-artistic elites—aristocrats themselves, as they understood the term—were only too glad to join in the attack. They had mocked the bourgeoisie's awkward imitation of aristocratic manners and rejected bourgeois culture as irremediably inferior.

But now the businessman was in the driver's seat, directing the great carriage of culture, holding the reins of power and deciding who would receive the moneys from the private and public purses upon which the artist and writer had come to depend. This new dependency affected writers and artists differently, of course. Some accepted the dominance and tastes of the bourgeoisie, albeit reluctantly, and rode on to personal profit and glory. For instance, the Dumas family, father and son, became rich and famous by satisfying the popular craving for tales of derring-do, swashbuckling adventure novels that had enormous appeal to readers of all ages.

Others found the ride intolerable and got off. They could not endure the uncertainties of the marketplace; it made them anxious and resentful. They could not pander to the wishes of a bourgeois audience, whose sensibilities, as they saw it, were crude and probably beyond improvement, and still keep their self-respect. To lower their standards to please unrefined clods, no matter how rich and influential, was unthinkable. And to become the equals of the bourgeoisie, or worse, their inferiors—to be mere entertainers—was humiliating. If such was the price of success, then success was demeaning, not worth the effort. Success, they thought, ought not to require any price other than good work and a devotion to excellence, and these the literary-artistic elites believed they possessed in abundance. The superiority of their work placed them far above the parvenus of trade, the makers of carpets and coats, the bankers and money-lenders, the exporters and speculators, the new men of business who controlled the new world.

In this new world the merchant and manufacturer had become rich and influential, whereas most artists and writers remained poor and ignored. Surely a just world would grant creative artists their just due—respect and position and money and power, far more than bourgeois society was prepared to give. How could they be part of an unjust society and still remain true to themselves? They could not. They would not be part of a world they loathed. Estranged and alienated, bitterly hostile toward the ruling bourgeoisie, some of them withdrew, physically and spiritually, into their own world—Bohemia, a community of like-minded free spirits, where they could associate only with people who understood and appreciated them.[4]

In private and in public the Bohemian challenged bourgeois ways of speaking, grooming, and behaving. Usually young, always infatuated with self-expression, exhilarated by rebellion, Bohemians showed their contempt for sober, rational, boring, joyless bourgeois society by openly embracing romantic irrationality. If the bourgeois advised moderation in drink and dress, then they would drink to get drunk and dress in raffish costumes—in colorful gypsy attire; or in expensive garments, lace, high cravat, tight trousers, short velvet waistcoat; or in the rude, tattered clothes of the working-class, all certain to be offensive to prim middle-class sensibilities. If the bourgeoisie counseled caution, cleanliness, and a prudent concern for health, then they would take drugs, be sexually promiscuous, refuse to bathe or cut their hair, grow a long beard and a ferocious mustache, glorify violence and sometimes commit it, and flirt with suicide, often disastrously: the suicide rate among young Bohemians was high.

Sometimes they showed their contempt for the bourgeoisie by behaving like madmen and buffoons, seeking in this way to puncture the smug, materialistic complacency of a soulless middle-class world— in public for all the world to see. The painter Emile Pelletier went on walks accompanied by his pet jackal. Gerard de Nerval, a poet, took a lobster on a leash through the Tuilleries Gardens. "It does not bark," he said, "and knows the secrets of the deep."[5] Eccentricity of dress and demeanor was a way of thumbing one's nose at middle-class pomposity.

Were these simply the affectations of rebellious, overprivileged youths, the high-spirited capers of self-willed youngsters flaunting their rejection of bourgeois normality for the sheer pleasure of upsetting their elders? To some extent, yes. But other Bohemians had serious objectives. They wanted to make an important point: that, in Cesar Graña's words, "the bourgeoisie represented ambition without passion, possessiveness without desire, power without grandeur, everything that was spiritually paltry and anti-vital, everything that was inadequate and pettily protective, in a psychological and even a biological way."[6] In brief, they wanted to dismantle, or at least tarnish, the grandiose house of middle-class morality and pretension. And to a remarkable degree they succeeded.

THE MODERNIST ROOTS OF
BUSINESS HATRED

The Bohemians of the 1820s and 1830s were the vanguard of a momentous ideological movement that would change the social and cultural life of western Europe and eventually touch much of the world. From its nucleus in Paris, romantic irrationalism metastasized and grew into a rebellion that spread across Europe. It became modernism, our second marker.

Modernism in the arts and letters should not be confused with modernism in the economy. Economic modernization refers to the process by which agrarian societies become industrialized and acquire the characteristics of technologically advanced nations. In contrast, literary and artistic modernism (hereafter, simply modernism) refers to changes in the form and content of literature, painting, music, and sculpture that began to emerge in the middle to late nineteenth century.[7]

Taking their cue from Baudelaire, an avatar of modernism whose erotic poetry extolling unfettered emotionality shocked the stodgy burghers of France, a few young artists and writers broke with the past and began exploring new avenues of creativity. Today we find what they did quite conventional, but at the time their innovations aroused a storm of criticism and alarm. In painting they experimented with colors and textures that gave their pictures new depth and feeling and chose topics seldom considered by classical artists. Bored with classical themes—heroes making war, gods and goddesses prancing about in elegant gardens, aristocrats cavorting in bedrooms—they turned for inspiration to the everyday life of ordinary people. From their palettes came a stream of pictures about simple people at home, at work, or at play that eventually breached the levees of the classical canon the classicists had erected against change.

Although modernism began as a rebellion by young artists and writers against the cold, formal, arid, passionless portrayal of life that had characterized much of eighteenth-century writing and painting, it developed into a passionate rejection of industrialism. Far from being advocates of change, many modernists in the arts and letters were hostile to technology, with the possible exception of the Italian Futurists, who found machinery an exciting subject for their pictures. On the whole, modernists denounced industrialization as a curse and an abomination, a point of view they transmitted to later generations of artists and intellectuals. They believed that an industrial society was hostile to artistic genius and that technology was destroying the mind and spirit of the people. Machines were at the root of the problem. Machines deformed workers, shriveled their brains, and numbed their senses with their infernal racket. "What a din has industry brought into the world. What a noisy thing the machine is," Gustave Flaubert exclaimed in exasperation to friends one day. He also accused the machine of spawning countless "idiotic occupations" leading to "mass stupidity."[8] Stendahl (Marie Henri Beyle) and Charles

Baudelaire were also vehement enemies of industrialization in early nineteenth-century France.

This theme was picked up by later generations in other countries. Almost a century later, in England not long after World War I, D. H. Lawrence blamed the devastation he observed in villages adjacent to coal mines in the midlands on industrialization, a monstrous juggernaut that treads men down in "the rush of mechanized greed or of greedy mechanism." Speaking through the voice of Lady Chatterley's lover, Oliver Mellors, Lawrence went on to say, "[I]t's a shame, what has been done to people these last three hundred years; men turned into nothing but labour-insects, and all their manhood taken away, and all their real life. I'd wipe the machines off the face of the earth, and end the industrial epoch absolutely."[9]

Writers were not alone in their hostility to the machine. Many painters also found machines frightening and infuriating; the machine mimicked nature and defiled it. The painter Ferdinand Victor Delacroix, while visiting the International Exposition of 1834 in Paris, witnessed artificial flowers being made to bloom at the turn of a crank. He left deeply disturbed that a mysterious natural event had been copied mechanically. That this process could be repeated endlessly and at will troubled him even more.

To the intellectual-artistic elite, the machine was a misbegotten offspring of materialism and reason, which could not help being evil because reason and materialism were themselves false gods. Reason robs life of spontaneity, mystery, and ecstasy—reducing it to a cold, predictable, calculated, shriveled movement through carefully apportioned time, a joyless existence devoid of passion and excitement and adventure. Technology makes man a slave of the machine. It twists and bends his body to fit the contour of the machine, invades and molds his mind to fit the needs of the machine. Eventually, drained of all vitality and independent volition, man becomes a machine himself.

As for materialism, what had it given humanity but a vulgar contentment, a mean-spirited, crass, stodgy life, essentially trivial and inhumane, without greatness and grandeur? Even John Stuart Mill, English philosopher and consummate rationalist, described the materialist view of life as "pinched, hidebound and narrow."[10] At the heart of materialism was an insane obsession with work. And work is not only tiring, it is boring—the refuge, as Oscar Wilde put it, of people who have nothing better to do. Stendahl moaned that work and life bored him, and Baudelaire thought boredom so terrifying that it would lead mankind in its despair to reduce the world to rubble.

No one exemplified the terrible effects of overwork and boredom on life better than the bourgeoisie. The bourgeoisie, Baudelaire thought, were "cold, reasonable, and vulgar," mechanical people, imprisoned within the stifling confines of a tidy existence, who speak of "nothing but virtue and economy, robbed of vitality and sexual passion by dull, endless work."[11] As for himself, Baudelaire believed he celebrated in his own person and poetry the apotheosis of non-utility—the Dandy, idle, vain, pleasure-loving, and adverse to work of any sort. He attacked materialism as loathsome and poor-spirited. What, he asked, had industrial materialism given to mankind but oppressive machinery and debilitating work, the exploitation of workers and their children, the rise of large-scale prostitution, and the proliferation of noisome slums?

The hatred modernists felt for industrialism and the business class was genuine enough, but the reasons they gave for their disaffection were somewhat disingenuous. To be sure, they worried about the decline of traditional high culture and in a general way railed against the impact of machines on the general populace, including the working class. But since they believed the lower class made no contribution to high culture, they actually gave little attention to the grave situation of the working man. In fact, many writers, composers, and painters were reactionaries, nostalgic for an idealized past, virulent haters of democracy and equality, timid esthetes terrified of a lower class whose growing frustration would, they feared, explode at any moment into bloody violence. In short, it was not the sorry condition of the factory worker in a machine civilization, but the jeopardy in which industrialization had placed them that infuriated the literary-artistic elites to the point of splenetic frenzy.

In time the modernists reduced the barriers to artistic change to rubble. In their pictures cubists ridiculed the notion that art should imitate life with *tromp l'oeil* exactness. Abstract expressionists abandoned any pretense at portraying life with photographic reality, and the surrealists and dadaists seemed amused or horrified at the very notion of reality. The fauvists thought bright, colorful, raw sensation more important than careful drawing and painted as they pleased. Modernism was not restricted to painting; it pervaded all the arts. It could be found in solipsistic poetry, in stream of consciousness novels, in atonal music, in non-representational sculpture. This turning away from time-honored precepts and interests caught on. With astonishing speed an almost unnoticed movement initiated by a daring few became by the early twentieth century the expected style of the many.

So varied are the elements of modernism that it is difficult for the uninitiated to identify what modernism's many manifestations have in common. Fortunately, anyone who wishes to understand the modernists (and the post-modernists, whose mixture of modern and traditional elements leave all but the cognoscenti confused) can turn to the work of learned scholars, literary critics, and other savants for guidance.[12]

If you are puzzled by some piece of modern painting, music, sculpture, or writing, if you are unable to fathom its meaning or recognize its content, be not surprised. The artist intended it that way; he meant to be difficult. The modernist deliberately seeks to be opaque; he consciously works with strange forms or with familiar objects in unfamiliar settings in order to challenge the audience's expectations. He delights in leaving the audience in the dark, puzzled and confused, at a loss as to what the artist is saying and what he wants to accomplish. Lucidity is not a modernist virtue.

And if you find yourself becoming exasperated as you stand bewildered before a wildly imaginative inexplicable modernist picture or statue, or catch yourself wincing at the strange jarring notes of atonal music, or hear yourself muttering darkly at a reading of a particularly opaque piece of modern poetry—do not be embarrassed; this too is intended. The modernist "seeks deliberately to disturb the audience— to shock it, shake it up, even to transform it as if in a religious conversion."[13] Like a therapist who uses electric shock to treat a patient suffering from depression, the modernist seeks to jolt the audience out of its cultural apathy with an esthetic shock, the "shock of the new," to use Robert Hughes' apt expression.[14]

It is important to understand that the artistic and intellectual elites who shape the culture take themselves quite seriously. To the general public they may appear to be mere daubers of paint, molders of clay and stone, tunesmiths, scribblers of books—refugees from reality who operate in rarefied spheres of little practical importance. But the elites demur; they believe they have an important mission: to instruct the public, to refine its tastes and sensibilities, and to raise its moral level.

Instruction is the elites' least controversial mission. Many artists and writers, holding up in their work a mirror to reality, attempt to show the public how human nature and society work. Dickens, Flaubert, and Tolstoi never hesitated to use their novels to illuminate the inner workings of the mind and society, and to unmask the hypocrisy with which people conceal their true designs. They hoped in this way to increase their reader's self-understanding and to provide a guide to effective living. The renown with which they were rewarded shows how eager the public was for instruction.

On the other hand, improving the public's esthetic standards and uplifting the moral order has proved difficult—and nearly always controversial. In the past the literary elites were disarmingly open about this goal. Moliere thought it his duty to "correct men while diverting them," and Rene Le Bossu wanted to give moral instruction to the public under the guise of entertaining allegory.[15] But today writers pursuing these ambitious, not to say presumptuous, goals, which not incidentally justify their existence as redeemers of society through their art, frequently run into resistance. Few people take kindly to the suggestion that their tastes are vulgar and their behavior morally deplorable.

Not to be outdone, painters have also gotten into this act; they too want to edify the public. For instance, according to Robert Hughes, "the Dadaists believed, as many artists of the time did, in the power of art to save mankind from political abominations; the central myth of the avant-garde that by changing the order of language, art could reform the order of experience and so alter the conditions of social life had not yet collapsed."[16] This ambitious objective has never been accepted by the entire public nor by all artists, some of whom believe in art for its own sake and see no need to justify their work as social uplift.

But whatever resistance the artistic-literary elite's efforts to inform and uplift the public may have met, it pales into insignificance when contrasted with the reception their drive to control the culture and shape the national identity encounters. Trying to accomplish this mission the elite lit a fire storm of controversy, partly because some of their methods shock and offend conventional tastes and intimidate the public, and partly because their casual dismissal of traditional standards challenges popular opinion. But more than that, their attempts to gain control of the culture constitute a distinct threat to the established order.

But neither intentional obscurity nor deliberate provocation is the most significant characteristic of modernism. Had modernism been nothing more than an exuberant rebellion against the prevailing conventions of artistic expression, it would today be just another period in the history of art, comparable perhaps to the Baroque or Rococo eras, a subject for critics and art historians to debate, a body of work for collectors and museums to fight over. But in fact the significance of modernism extends far beyond its artistic contributions. For at some point in the late nineteenth century modernism became more than a point of view on esthetics; it became a social movement and a political philosophy.

At the core of modernism is an intense hatred of the business class. The modernists, despite their up-to-date sounding name, were much like their predecessors of an earlier generation, the Bohemians, who, as we have seen, also loathed the bourgeoisie and the industrial system—its machines, factories, and the myriad devices of the new technologies. Auguste Renoir, a pioneer modernist in painting, is a somewhat extreme, though not entirely unfaithful, example of modernism's hostility to industrial change. He objected to virtually everything modern. He "adamantly opposed the income tax, lending at interest, banks, railroads, electricity, sulfur matches, formal education, and even the new science of dentistry."[17] Such consistency is hard to beat.

POLITICIZATION OF THE ADVERSARY IDEOLOGY

The appeal of modernism was not limited to sensitive, esthetically attuned artists; it also attracted the attention of hard-headed politicians and political activists—the third marker. For modernism's attack on industrial capitalism made it a useful tool with which political activists could belabor the ruling bourgeoisie. That much is well-known. What is not generally recognized is that the ideology of modernism appealed to both the ultraconservative right and the radical left.

On the right, the savants of conservatism, such as the American ideologue Russell Kirk, the French writer Edmond de Goncourt, the German philosopher (and Nazi sympathizer) Martin Heidegger, repeatedly voiced a visceral hatred of industrial capitalism. Modern industry, scientific, mechanized, aseptic, and corporate, horrified them. Heidegger, for example, advocated a return to a simpler time when cows were milked by hand and cream skimmed with a ladle, when the soil was turned with a simple plow drawn by horses, and crops planted and harvested with simple implements in the hands of simple peasants. Oddly enough, his nostalgic yearnings for a simpler past coincided with a time when Germany was using its advanced technology to build rockets, tanks, and airplanes. But then, Heidegger had no objection to using modern technology to win the war. Making food was something else; he didn't want to eat butter churned by machines.

The conservatives' complaints reflected their conviction that industrial capitalism had destroyed the traditional order they loved. They believed that industrialization, with it exaltation of science and technology, its delight in rationalism, and its praise of pragmatic utility, was inherently lethal to traditional life. They accused industrialization of insidiously eroding the people's faith in religion, the ancient mainstay of the old order, and undermining a time-honored hierarchical system in which everyone knew and accepted his or her place in life. Echoing the complaints of the Bohemians (who, by the way, had shown almost no interest in politics), the conservatives charged that industrialization had put in place a new system, a pinched, petty, sterile way of life, joyless and meaningless, dominated by machines. For when machines replaced people, human relationships shriveled and grew fretful, leaving the individual alone and impotent in a world devoid of the warmth and security the old order had provided.

But there was more to the conservatives' anger than a hatred of machines. They were furious at having been robbed of a golden era when status and privilege was based on land tenure, when lineage mattered more than money, a past which resembled to a stunning degree their idealized picture of feudal society. It was a fantasy, of course, a dream world that had never existed. But no matter. Industrialization may have killed their dream world, but it would never kill their dream.

In contrast, the radical left cared nothing for the past and precious little for esthetics. The brouhaha among artists and writers over artistic standards left most radical leftists cold. Though radical in politics, they were seldom radical in artistic preferences. If anything their tastes in art, literature, and music tended to be conventional, which explains why modern art suffered as much under Stalin as it did under Hitler. As for industrialization, the left, in a break with artistic modernism, openly favored it. Industrialization produced the wealth needed to improve the lot of the common people, and for this it was to be applauded. In fact, the appeal of modernism for the left was political. Reasoning that their common enemy was capitalism, the left embraced modernism, then gobbled it up, and eventually regurgitated it in a new form—a politicized adversary ideology.

The political left tacked on to early modernism several elements that would have been of little interest to the modernists of a century ago. To the modernist's contempt for bourgeois society, the left added its own commitment to social equality, its concern for the condition of racial minorities, and an infatuation with governmental control of the economy. Like the esthetic elite, it was driven by a hatred for the business class. Just how intense this hatred can be is abundantly evident in the following comment by Theodore Roszak, an avowed leftist and a guru to the flower children and student radicals of the 1960s. According to Roszak the business class "is obsessed by greed; its sex life is insipid and prudish; its family patterns are debased; its slavish conformities of dress and grooming are degrading; its mercenary routinization of life is intolerable."[18] Incorporated into the adversary ideology, this rage became a cudgel with which to pound the ruling business class.

In the adversary ideology the New Elite found the framework in which to organize their diffuse anger, inchoate yearnings and muddled ideas into a politically focused program with definite goals. One of these goals is to tame the excesses of industrial capitalism. What constitutes excess will vary somewhat from group to group within the New Elite. Take, for example, the environmentalists. (Not all Elitists are fanatic environmentalists, though most favor protecting the environment.) As protectors of the earth they worry about the effects of science and industry on the habitat. Speaking to a group of students at Cornell University, Ramona Africa, a member of MOVE, called for the end of all modern industry, charging it with "polluting our air, our water, our soil." Environmental pollution, she went on to say, has "depleted" the nutritional content of all food. Her speech drew a standing ovation from an enthusiastic crowd of about three hundred and fifty.[19]

Environmentalists protest the incursions of developers on scenic and unspoiled locations, the turning of pristine beaches and forests into anthills of humanity, crowded places unfit for backpackers and campers. They demand a halt to industry's despoliation of wildernesses and other natural resources. They brood about the population bomb, the rampant mechanization of work, the impersonalization of life, the decline of community. All this they blame on science and industrialization. They think industrial capitalism inherently evil, a heartless system to which mankind will be forever ill-adapted. They wish industrialization would just go away, though who would manufacture their backpacks, sleeping bags, walking shoes, canoes, and survival equipment is unclear.

This hostility to industrialism and the business class has spread across the Western world. In England, to cite one country, it has become common for young writers and artists, as historian J. D. Plumb points out, to believe that society is antipathetic to artists, and that they must live beyond the shallow and restrictive conventions of ordinary life in order to fulfill their mission, the pursuit of truth and beauty.[20] They agree with Shelly, Byron, Godwin, and other romantics, who maintained that society, in its determination to exact conformity to its rules, inevitably stifles the creative spirit and smothers the spark of genius.

Artistic grievances against society are nothing new, of course; in almost every society some elements of the literary elite have always been at odds with established authority. In ancient Athens intellectuals routinely challenged orthodox opinion; no belief or idea was taken as self-evidently true: "every conception and every institution sooner or later came under attack—religious beliefs, ethical values, political systems, aspects of the economy, even such bedrock institutions as the family and private property."[21] Even a state crisis could not silence dissent. Aristophanes, for instance, was openly critical of the war with Sparta and in his play *The Acharnians* has an old Athenian farmer make a private peace with Sparta—a bit of literary license that in similar circumstances today might well put a playwright in prison for sedition.

In Renaissance Italy artists took issue with the judgments of their "dull, ungrateful and capricious masters," as Luigi Barzini put it.[22] Thus Michelangelo Buonarroti quarreled with Pope Julius the Second and Leonardo da Vinci argued with the authorities of the several cities in which he resided during his lifetime—not a safe thing to do, as he discovered. Even in Spain, a land much less tolerant of dissent than Italy, Miguel de Cervantes mocked the pathetic chivalry and frayed gentility of the impoverished nobility, and cautiously exposed the hypocrisies embedded in Spanish society. In the United States a string of writers, from Henry Thoreau and Henry Adams to Theodore Dreiser and Sinclair Lewis, expressed alarm at the corrupting influence of commercial civilization on American character and institutions. Commercialism, they all agreed, impoverished the nation's spirit, encouraged crude hedonism, infantalized the emotions, and produced a dreary race for success that distorted the lives of countless Americans.

Still, if criticism of a society by its creative elites is not new, the outright rejection of an entire civilization most certainly is. Radical elements of the New Elite, enamored of the adversary ideology embedded in the Chameleon Complex, wish to destroy the established order, root and branch. To acomplish this goal, they denigrate the bourgeoisie's past achievements and spurn its values and standards as mere tricks to hold on to power. This attack has sparked a lively debate among intellectuals, a noisy squabble some people dismiss as interesting to insiders who enjoy a good fight over ideas but of no practical importance. In point of fact, it is important to everyone. For it is a fight over who will control the creators and transmitters of culture, and as Antonio Gramsci, political theorist and a founder of the Italian Communist Party, once noted, whoever controls the culture controls the country. In his *Letters From Prison* he argued that to change society one must first change people; and to change people one must first control the intellectuals and the teachers, the schools and the universities, the churches and the media of mass communication.[23]

The ideology of the New Elite is a crucial part of a struggle now going on for control of the culture and the definition of America's identity and future. In this battle all sides have sought the support of diverse groups—ethnic and racial minorities, the young and old, men and women. Perhaps no group is more courted, and no group more entangled in the adversary ideology and the Chameleon Complex, than successful women—the latest addition to the ranks of the New Elite. And perhaps no group has suffered more from chameleonism and the effects of participating in the competitive, nerve-frazzling economy of the techno-service society. In the next chapter we will examine what this society has done to and for women.

PART IV

WINNERS AND LOSERS

9

Women as Winners

Who would have predicted that middle-class women would be major winners in the Second Great Transformation! That middle-class men would profit from the changes the transformation produced was obvious. It needed no *pontifex maximus* reading the entrails of the emerging techno-service economy to predict that businessmen would do well: they had always shown themselves adept at adapting to social change. But middle-class women? Nothing seemed less likely. Mind you, these were the privileged wives and daughters of industrialists, merchants, and professionals, women who had shuddered at the thought of working for pay. Occupational success seemed hardly in the cards for them.

And yet in the past few decades, to almost everyone's surprise, women as well as men, women have achieved remarkable successes in the field of paid employment. This upset in conventional expectations was mostly made possible by the growth of the techno-service economy. The vast changes in the structure of the economy, particularly in the service sector and the triumph of the information society, opened up new jobs to women, changed attitudes, and lifted the hopes of countless women who had never imagined that success awaited them in the occupational world. Many of them have made the most of their new opportunities and have become outstanding in their fields.

What would have certainly surprised most people in the early nineteenth century is that manufacturing and its successor, the techno-
service economy, would make winners out of women—surprised
because when the first feminists, true daughters of the industrial revolution, urged women to become co-equal workers with men in the
labor market, middle-class women paid them no heed. They were not
interested; smelly factories and dreary offices were not for them. And
yet before the nineteenth century was out, they had entered the labor
force in large numbers. A movement that began as a trickle in the
last century became a torrent in this one.

No longer content to stay at home, impatient with ties that bound
them to the kitchen and the nursery, many women exchanged the
apron and the baby carriage for the business suit and the computer,
and sought new experiences and rewards in paid employment outside
the home. But women have done more than join the labor force; they
have changed it. Many of them have become part of the New Elite.

WOMEN ON THE MOVE

To a degree unparalleled in history, women have achieved lucrative
and important jobs in government, in the skilled professions, and in
science and business, irreversibly changing the sexual composition of
the work force, a revolutionary break with the past that is changing
women and society, a surprise to almost everyone. In truth, the movement of women into the upper reaches of the corporate structure,
into the lofty hierarchies of the universities, and even into the tight
little world of the arts and sciences, startled a lot of people, women
as well as men. Who would have thought so many women would
achieve so much in so short a time?

This chapter focuses on women winners, in large part because they
show the way the Second Great Transformation creates problems for
winners as well as for losers. Although women tend to view the
achievements of women with understandable pride, some with exul-
tant triumphalism, they slowly have come to recognize the price
women pay for their victory: growing tensions between men and
women competing for the same jobs; increasing physical and emotional exhaustion; and mounting disappointment and anger among
women who have not found in work the release from enervating de-

pression that they had expected. Anguished cries of disillusionment and frustration are beginning to fill the air.

This should not surprise anyone. Success as sudden and profound as that which women have experienced in recent decades was bound to cause resentment, envy, and fatigue—resentment and envy among women left behind by their successful sisters; fatigue among women holding down two jobs, homemaker and career-maker. This discomfiture reflects the feeling that something has gone awry, that unjustified inequalities have developed among women, and that unexpected burdens have been dumped upon an already overburdened sex. To the surprise of some women, success invariably comes with a price tag.

But why the surprise? Wasn't it well known that hard work and the success it sometimes brings takes a toll on people? And wasn't it apparent that on the job women were performing at least as well as men and that they would succeed in what they wanted to do? And wasn't this exactly what society wanted? Had it not been doing its best, working through the family and the school, to see that so far as work was concerned the differences between males and females would be eliminated? Indeed it had, and for this reason most of the differences between the sexes in their work-related attitudes and values have all but disappeared. The evidence for this conclusion can be found in the workplace and in a growing body of research.

Consider, for instance, my study of adolescents conducted in three American cities in the late 1970s, and later replicated in seven English cities and two Italian cities. This research shows how successful industrial societies have been in reducing centuries-old attitudinal and behavioral differences between the sexes. Judging from the responses of approximately 3200 adolescents (many of whom have no doubt grown to become part of today's knowledge-processing elite) to questions put to them, the gap between girls and boys in certain attitudes, values, and behavior commonly believed conducive to success in work has been markedly reduced.[1]

For example, on average, girls and boys were found to be equally intelligent, as measured by IQ tests, achievement tests, or teacher assessments. Girls perform as well as boys in school and engage in many of the same activities. Girls and boys hold similar values; both sexes applaud independence, self-reliance, and achievement. Girls enjoy levels of self-esteem on a par with those of boys, and respond to threats to their interests with equal degrees of hostility. These girls, now women in their thirties, are part of a cohort that is making a mark for itself in the workforce. All this being the case, could it not have been foreseen that once the social and cultural barriers to female achievement had been dismantled and economic forces given free play, that the pent-up needs and desires and abilities of women would explode in a burst of energy that would propel them into every part of the occupational structure? Indeed it was foreseen; this is precisely what the early feminists predicted would occur.

Women now work in all sectors of the economy and compete with men, often successfully, for advancement in fields long dominated by men. Women now hold positions of managerial responsibility in companies across the country, including many in the *Fortune* 500 category. According to 1994 Department of Labor data, 43 percent of all business managers are women. In some fields, such as insurance and nonprofit social services, more than half of the managers are women. They are also doing well in high-growth businesses like biotechnology and health care.[2] But the most dramatic changes have come in the ranks of the professions. "We're penetrating professions we were not in before," exulted Lenora Cole Alexander, former director of the Federal Women's Bureau.[3] She could not have been more right about the trend. The percentage of women in the legal profession rose from 3 percent in 1971 to 23 percent in 1995. It is expected to reach 40 percent by 2010.

It is true that some women view these numbers with open skepticism. What the numbers do not reveal, they say, is the stubborn and shameful gap between the wages of men and women. Except in jobs at the highest educational level, women tend to earn less than men. In 1995, the average earnings of women who worked full-time were 72 percent that of men, up from 62 percent in 1972, a significant improvement but not the parity women seek.[4] As for the argument that women have brought this misfortune upon themselves by choosing to work in traditionally low-paying "pink-collar" jobs and by dropping out of the labor force from time to time to care for their children—this cuts no ice with angry women's advocates. To these women, the explanation for why women choose these jobs is obvious. Women suffer the indignity of rotten jobs and poor pay because males, determined to protect their privileged positions, put them there.

Nonetheless, the gap between women's and men's pay scales, particularly in the professions, has steadily declined. A decade ago, Janet Norwood, the Commissioner of Labor Statistics, noted that pay discrepancies between men and women had "nearly disappeared when each occupation was broken down into its component levels based on skill and experience."[5] In 1995, according to June Eleanor O'Neil, Director of the Congressional Budget Office, among young, educated workers the gulf is close to disappearing. Among those age 27 to 33 who have never had a child, women's earnings approach 98 percent of men's. Today young women in university teaching or in medical and legal practice earn as much as their male peers.

Perhaps most significantly, women have broken through the glass ceiling that was said to keep them out of top managerial positions. For example, in 1995 Ann M. Fudge, a 44-year-old black woman, ran a $1.4 billion business as president of Maxwell House Coffee Company. Carolyn M. Ticknor was general manager of Laser Jet Printer Group at Hewlett-Packard, overseeing an estimated $5 billion operation. Brenda Barnes managed a $6 billion business as chief operating officer of Pepsi-Cola North America. And these are only a few of the stars that dot a constellation crowded with achieving women.

Looking at salaried work alone misses a big part of what is happening to women; they have become a dynamic part of the business world. According to the Census Bureau, the number of businesses owned by women increased 40 percent between 1987 and 1992, to 6.4 million, one third of the total. A recent study by the National Foundation for Women Business Owners estimates that almost 8 million businesses are now owned by women, employing 18.5 million people, or one out of four workers. More female achievers are in the making, for the enrollment of women in law, medical, engineering, and business schools has more than doubled in the last decade. Women make up about a third of students at business schools, 40 percent at medical schools, and just under half at law schools. Clearly, still more female luminaries loom on the horizon.[6]

WOMEN AND INDUSTRIALIZATION

Fashionable opinion gives to the Women's Movement most of the credit for bringing women into the labor force, keeping them there, and promoting their interests. No doubt much of this credit is deserved. First as a few isolated voices, then as scattered inspirited small groups, and finally as a powerful, organized social movement, women attacked the barriers erected over the centuries to deny them economic and social justice. As fighters and revolutionaries they have been remarkably successful. One by one the legal barriers to the movement of women in the labor market fell before the assaults of militant women, who then put in place affirmative action programs designed to help women enter fields once closed to them.

But women were not alone in their battle for economic equality; they had powerful allies—industrialization and the techno-service economy. Without the aid of industrialization the movement of women in the labor market and the success of their struggle for economic equality would have been at the very least much delayed or at the worst aborted. In the nineteenth century, manufacturing began to make it possible for poor women to escape the drudgery of domestic work and to earn a living in factories. Then in the twentieth century, the techno-service economy lured middle-class women out of their safe and comfortable homes and persuaded them to take their place in the workplace.

The welcome manufacturers gave to women was not an act of altruism. An industrial economy needs women. Machines must be tended, sales made, claims adjusted, grievances handled, credits and debits entered into the computer, clients and patients helped—and women have shown they can do these things as well as men, sometimes better, and often more cheaply. That much had been long apparent. Early on, industrialists recognized the advantages of hiring women, and with a canny eye to profit and labor peace they invited women into their factories to spin thread, weave cloth, make shoes, roll cigars, decorate hats. They saw that women constituted a vast reservoir of eager, hard-working, docile, cheap labor and did not long hesitate to tap it.

When industrialization separated the workplace from the homeplace, and cottage industry gave way to the factory system, changing forever the way goods would be produced, the factory became a powerful magnet to women in need of money. Factories gave jobs to women who had left home to find work when family distress or size began to press the limits of sustenance on the farm. And the factory provided work for the hordes of penniless immigrant women who flocked to American shores. Upon these women many families depended for their very survival. In most cases they were the daughters of farmers or artisans, unmarried girls who sought in factory work the means to help their families, to acquire a dowry, to escape from domestic drudgery. In the past young women in the paid labor force had typically been employed in domestic service. By one estimate, of the single women in the labor force in 1840, 70 percent had hired themselves out as servants.

In the first quarter of the nineteenth century the industrial system began to expand in New England, New York, and Pennsylvania, and women flocked to the newly established textile mills. Factory girls became a common sight on the floors of mills and on the streets of all manufacturing towns—a fact not lost on puritanical busybodies, who worried about the effect of factory work and dormitory life on the morals of unchaperoned young women. In 1821 the mills of Waltham, Massachusetts, employed 4.5 times as many women as men. By 1860 women made up 53.4 percent of the workforce in the textile industry, 45 percent in clothing, and 27.3 percent in paper and printing. In some New England mill towns women made up 65 percent of all industrial workers and 90 percent of those working in millinery shops and textile mills. By the end of the nineteenth century women constituted a significant part of the labor force, a share that continued to grow throughout the twentieth century.[7]

Consider the record. In 1870, the first year in which reliable national data on working women were collected, women made up 14.1 percent of the labor force. Each decennial census thereafter reported a steady, though modest, increase in the female component of the work force. Thus from 1880 to 1900 women's share of the workforce increased from 14.5 percent to 17.7 percent, a 1 or 2 percent increase per decade. As a result, by 1920 the percentage of women in the labor force had grown to 20.2 percent, and by 1940 women made up a quarter of the paid working population.

When in the twentieth century the service sector burgeoned, employers recruited even more women, this time not merely because of their availability but also because women were thought to possess personal qualities that made them ideally suited to service work. From 1940 to 1990, each decennial census revealed an increase of 4 to 6 percent in the female component of the labor force. By 1980, women's share of the labor force had grown to 42.4 percent, and by 1990 it had risen to 46 percent, approximately where it is now.

Industrialization not only opened up new opportunities to women, it also changed the social and cultural climate in which they worked. As already noted, industrial societies emphasize individualism and achievement, and inevitably this affected how society viewed women. For if men were to be judged by individual worth and not by birth, if ambition and independence in men were to be applauded, why then shouldn't the same standards be applied to women? Why shouldn't women also be encouraged to act assertively and competitively, to pursue achievement as aggressively as men have always done? And if these standards were applied to women, how could it not be noticed that some women were doing very well indeed? Needless to say this was noticed, and as a result the image of women changed. People began to challenge the age-old notion of women as timid and shy creatures, frail and weak, unfit to compete in the hurly-burly of the marketplace. It was time to throw this old chestnut in the scrap heap.

Today young women hoot at the idea that they are temperamentally incapable of competing on equal terms with men. Also they are finding that the resistance to their pursuit of occupational achievement has become fragile and rickety. In many cases the door to advancement stands ajar and the guards blocking women's way often act shamefacedly, disarmed by ambivalence and doubt. Legislation against discrimination has something to do with this, of course; but so has the value industrialization places on gender equality, independence, and achievement.

Still, even with the enthusiastic collaboration of industrialists, the march of women toward economic equality has not been easy. Women encountered numerous obstacles in their path, among them traditions that had long kept women in the home, busy performing the only roles society thought proper for their sex: housewifery and motherhood. In the nineteenth century throngs of writers, lecturers, and clergymen, determined to protect motherhood and the family, thundered against the idea of women working in factories, arguing that factory work coarsened women, endangered their health, and made them unfit to be wives and mothers.[8] Dire necessity might drive a woman into the labor market, but her condition was considered pathetic. Her husband and children must inevitably suffer, it was said—but for this she was more to be pitied than censored.

Comfortably-situated women who pursued careers away from home (the number was small) were considered selfish and devoid of devotion to their families. They were targets of social obloquy, a chilling restraint on their freedom that persisted well into the twentieth century. The treatment handed out to writer Charles R. Morris' mother provides an example of how some middle-class women were treated, even as recently as a generation or two ago, when they went out to work. "My Irish grandmother worked as a cleaning woman much of her married life, and no one regarded it as particularly remarkable. When my mother went to work in the 1950's, on the other hand, it was a subject of much comment . . . the priest regularly sermonized on Sundays about the moral dangers to a family with a working mother. We all kept our heads down."[9] Only an exceptionally strong woman could stand up to this kind of criticism.

And then there were numerous prejudicial practices, often buttressed by law and union regulations, that restricted the employment of women to certain hours of the day, kept them out of jobs thought dangerous to their health, and denied them work when the jobs of men were in jeopardy. Men were considered the family's true breadwinners. The effect of these practices was to keep women in jobs less prestigious and less well paid than those enjoyed by men.

But the sheer number of women in the labor force does not tell the whole story. Equally interesting are the women who previously had been reluctant to work outside the home—married women and mothers of small children. At the turn of the century the typical working woman was young and single; 46 percent of single women worked outside the home, as compared with only 6 percent of all married women. By 1962 this number had increased to a third of all married women, and by 1982 to 51 percent.

That is not all: many of these women had children of preschool age, a marked contrast with the past. Thus in 1948 only 10.8 percent of women with children under six years of age worked outside the home, whereas by 1984 three out of five women with children under three and 52 percent with children under six were in the labor force. Since 1980 most of the increase in female employment has been among women with preschool-age children. For the first time in American history young children at home no longer keep the majority of women out of the labor force.

THE LURE OF THE TECHNO-SERVICE ECONOMY

Dry as dust numbers, no matter how neatly displayed, cannot do justice to the majesty of the radical change in the composition of the workforce and in the growing number of women in almost every occupation brought about by the industrial revolution. But the old revolution is not the whole story. In the last half of the twentieth century a new revolution has taken place, the far-from-finished techno-service revolution, which also introduced startling alterations in women's place in the economy.

What exactly did the techno-service economy do to change the condition of women in the labor force? The question is horribly complex, but an answer may be found in a number of factors that came together at the conclusion of the First World War. They can be grouped into three categories: technological, familial, and economic. In brief, the new system changed the tools with which women work, changed the family network in which women live, and changed the economy in which women are employed. Let us begin with a look at the way in which technology affected how women worked.

Technology made work less burdensome, less exhausting, less linked to sheer brawn. Machines driven by inanimate power made it possible for women to fabricate consumer goods as quickly as men, using equipment that did not require the brute strength only burly men possess—a fact not lost on manufacturers. In addition, machines made obsolete many of the skills men had spent years acquiring (tin-smiths, coopers, saddlers are in little demand today) and which once gave them an immense advantage over women. Many products once made laboriously by hand by craftsmen are now produced in factories on machines run by women.

At least as important as technological change were the changes made in the family. As we have seen, economic change made the family more democratic, more fractious, and less functional. Once caring for her family had easily absorbed a woman's time and energy, and most women who could afford to do so stayed at home, fully occupied with domestic chores and firmly convinced that family concerns took priority over all others, a sentiment society unreservedly approved. But when industrialization stripped the family of many of its functions, time became available for other things, including paid work outside the family.

Also, a job outside the home was possible because families became smaller. As industrialization progressed, the fertility rate steadily declined and women became less tied to childrearing responsibilities. To illustrate, the American birth rate dropped from 55 per thousand in the year 1800 to about 18 shortly before World War II. Following the war, the birth rate rose briefly during the baby boom, only to collapse by the 1970s to its present point, a rate slightly below the replacement level. Granted, some racial, ethnic, and class groups deviate from the mean, but even so families with only one or two children are now commonplace.

Now, we know that a love of children and a desire to nurture them are strong sentiments, powerful enough to bind many women to the home. But what are women to do when there are no longer any children at home? What will occupy their time when the need for their services dwindles, when children are away at school or out on their own in the great big world? These women, often still young and vigorous, can anticipate another thirty or more years of active life, years they do not want to waste bemoaning the miseries of the empty nest. Not surprisingly many women turn to paid work as a way of keeping busy and giving meaning to their lives.

Also important were the changes in the relationship between husbands and wives. On the positive side, the marital relationship became more open and democratic; hence a woman who wanted to work could overcome or override the objections of her husband without bringing crushing obloquy down upon her head. On the negative side, the marital bond grew more fragile; abandonment, separation and divorce became more common. Thus for over a century the divorce rate in the United States rose as industrialization progressed. The techno-service system has done nothing to halt this process. The divorce rate has more than doubled since 1960. Though it appears to have stabilized in recent years, it is still very high. If the present trend continues, as pessimists believe it will, five out of ten marriages made today will end in divorce.[10]

Few women can safely ignore these statistics. Indeed, many older women and their children already know the costs of divorce. Thrown on their own, unable to live on meager and unreliable alimony or child support, they must go to work or live on welfare. Many go to work, if they can find it. Young women, often themselves the children of divorced parents, live with the knowledge that their marriage may not endure and wisely prepare for that possibility by acquiring marketable skills and work experience.

Of course, it is not merely dire necessity that brings women into the labor force. Some go to work gladly, eager to find jobs that promise intellectual and emotional satisfaction and growth. Still others, perhaps the majority, enter the labor market to earn money with which to satisfy their hunger for more consumer products—a new refrigerator, a second car, more and better clothes. Their appetite whetted by consumerism, the demanding child of an affluent industrial society, women join with men in an endless pursuit of the good life, a goal once thought attainable for only a select few.

As everyone knows, the good life (in its hedonistic sense) costs lots of money. Unfortunately, industrial capitalism, despite its record of improving the general standard of living of most people, occasionally starves the very appetites it excites. Periodically, the business cycle throws people out of work, or inflation puts them on a treadmill where they must run ever faster just to stay in place. Whatever the reason, at times the family's income proves inadequate to maintain the desired standard of living, and the wife must put on work clothes and find a job, or keep the one she may have thought of quitting.

Though undoubtedly of great importance, the changes just described do not fully explain the rapid movement of women into the labor force in the past few decades. After all, some of these changes had been at work for several generations; they had made jobs outside the home necessary for some women and possible for others. But the movement of women into paid employment would have been much slower and its effects far smaller had not the techno-service economy flared into preeminence in the last few decades, changing not only the kind of work women could perform but also the ambience in which it would take place.

The techno-service economy did something the factory system never dreamed possible or even desirable; it brought middle-class women into the labor force. As we know, working outside the home had never appealed to middle-class women, certainly not work in factories—noisy, smelly, dirty surroundings, obviously unfit places for ladies. The industrialization of production had meant little to them, except to make certain products cheaper, such as pottery, cloth, thread, and needles. If middle-class women concerned themselves at all with the factory it was to view with alarm the presumed evil effects of factory life on the morals of young working girls or to complain that factories were luring away girls from domestic work, making the problem of finding and keeping servants exasperatingly difficult. And so, unlike lower-class women to whom the factory opened a new world of opportunity, most middle-class women resisted the lure of the industrial system and stayed at home.

But the techno-service system would not be denied. Its technologies eventually entered the home and changed the lives of privileged middle-class women. Labor-saving appliances made managing a house less time consuming, and middle-class women found themselves with more free time than they had ever before known. Some women gave themselves over to having fun, giving parties and attending social events. Some devoted their energies to charity, helping out in hospitals and schools, and setting up private agencies devoted to ameliorating the condition of the poor. And some turned to jobs in the burgeoning service sector, in part just to get out of the house, in part for intellectual challenge, in part for the money with which to buy their freedom from patriarchal control.

Almost as radically as it had changed the production of goods, technology changed the delivery of services. Before the growth of modern technology work in the service sector, mostly performed by women, was associated mainly with dirt and slop, with brooms and mops, with bed pans and soiled sheets, with demeaning toil requiring little intelligence or skill. Technology gave the service worker new tools and interesting skills. Working in offices, hospitals, stores, schools, a middle-class woman could operate equipment of wondrous complexity. Soon the typewriter and telephone (later the computer and the fax machine), the thermometer and the stethoscope, became the familiar tools of middle-class women at work.

However, it was more than technology that made the new system attractive to women; it was the nature of service work. Service work appealed to middle-class women in ways that factory work never had. For one thing, service work seldom makes demands for physical strength that women cannot meet. A hand strong enough to hold a skillet can easily hold a sales pad, punch a computer keyboard, or carry a briefcase. For another thing, service work connotes helping others, an idea congenial to women who think of themselves as helpers—of their families, of their friends, of their communities. Before the turn of the century many women had gained valuable experience dealing with people in their role as volunteer workers in charities that helped the sick and poor. In this way they acquired a proficiency in supervision that was later translated into jobs as visiting nurses, truant officers, child-labor investigators, work to which few men were then attracted.

Service work also attracted women because it often permitted part-time employment and usually allowed easy exit when domestic responsibilities required a woman's presence at home, as well as reentry when the situation at home eased. Moreover, the pay in service work was at least comparable to that earned in factory work, often better, and less subject to layoffs than a job in a mill or factory. But perhaps most important of all, service work was generally safe, clean, respectable—something a middle-class woman could do without jeopardizing her status as a lady.

As in the case of manufacturing, the techno-service economy welcomed women because they were needed. Had employers limited themselves to hiring males, the cost of labor in the rapidly expanding service economy would have skyrocketed. Skilled service workers were scarce, and the competition for intelligent staff was ferocious. Eventually, even tradition-bound companies were forced to toss aside old prejudices. Like it or not, they had to open their doors to women, even in management, even in businesses as stuffy and hidebound as banking. Said Barry M. Allen, First Vice-President of the Bank of Boston, explaining a recent change in hiring practices: "We can't afford to keep out any talented person."[11] Being a woman no longer means automatic exclusion from the manager's desk.

The women who join the workforce today gravitate overwhelmingly toward jobs in the service economy. As a result, about two-thirds of working women are in the service sector; only one in six holds down a job in a goods-producing industry. How different it was a century ago. Then, six out of the ten leading occupations of working women were in the goods-producing sector; now, only one of them, sewers and stitchers, can be called goods producing. Most of the rest are service positions, principally in sales and in the personal care and health, educational, recreational, and financial industries.

Equally significant, most of the jobs created in the next decade will be in the service sector—and these will tend to be women's jobs. Apart from the twenty occupations traditionally held by women—all in the service sector and all expected to grow—the new positions being created in data processing, in legal services, in health and education, and in government are even now being filled mostly by women. The Bureau of Labor estimates that of the ten occupations most likely to add workers in the 1990s, eight are considered women's jobs; consequently, women will account for 65 percent of all new workers. As far as new jobs are concerned, the future belongs to women.[12]

THE USES OF CHAMELEONISM

More than a need for workers motivates employers in the techno-service economy to hire women; commonly-held notions about the character of females are also important. To many men, women appear ideally suited to service work. Women are thought to be exceptionally sensitive to other people's moods, inclined to be sympathetic to their needs, and quite skillful at putting others at ease—character traits that make it relatively easy for a woman to deal with clients in face-to-face encounters.

Women are seen as being more flexible than men, more skillful at mixing with different kinds of people, more able to blend into any crowd. And when it comes to handling irate customers, soothing jangled nerves, and getting along with demanding customers, the sensitive female can generally be counted on to succeed where the more obtuse male would fail. This notion that their temperament (as men see it, that is; women tend not to share the male's perception of the female temperament) is more pliable and accommodating gives women an advantage over men in the service job market. For instance, the rapid movement of women into personnel work, a growing job category for women after 1910, has been attributed to the belief that women possess a natural talent for dealing with people and adjusting grievances.

In effect, what men were saying is that women are chameleons and that this makes service work easier for them than for men. But have men got it right? Are women, in fact, inclined to be chameleons—or if chameleonism is not an ingrained character trait, can they easily assume the skills of a chameleon? There is reason to believe so. The behavior of women, the comments they make about their own sex, and a spate of recent research on the socialization of girls all point to chameleonism among a significant portion of the female population, especially those touched by the traditional female sex role. Despite the strenuous efforts of feminists to eradicate it, this role still influences the thoughts and actions of many women, even the female Elitists in the information economy.

It is significant for the development of chameleonism that the traditional female sex role stresses the weakness of women and their vulnerability to aggression from predatory males. This means that women need all the help they can get. Hence the importance placed on establishing relationships with others—women as friends, men as protectors and husbands. To cement these relationships, females are urged to talk about their troubles, to share confidences, and to seek comfort and reassurance from friends. They are urged to spend time and energy cultivating ties with others and to develop skills that strengthen personal relationships. Above all, they are admonished to anticipate the expectations of others, to control aggressiveness, to conceal anger and leave offensive opinions unexpressed, to say and do what others expect—to fit in as best they can. In a word, they must learn to be chameleons.

Above all, they must do nothing to frighten off men, because, as the traditionalist sees it, the most important relationship of all is with a man in marriage. Eventually, most Americans marry and in time become addicted to the marital state; four out of five remarry after divorce. Intense pressures from parents, married friends, and society are placed on the unwed adult to marry, a pressure which, unfairly, falls more heavily upon females than upon males. Bachelorhood is socially acceptable, but spinsterhood alarms almost everyone. Popular and professional opinion have combined to make many an unmarried woman feel inadequate and incomplete, an unfinished identity awaiting a man to give it form and meaning.

But first a man must be found. Trying to be helpful, parents, friends, the mass media shower the woman with advice and admonitions. She is told to nurture the frail male ego and avoid any behavior that frightens her quarry and makes him skittish. Aggression must be avoided or muted and disguised; an attitude of passivity must be assumed, because the traditional female is expected to play the passive role in courtship—or appear to be doing so—and a posture of compliance should be feigned, within reason. Underlying this advice is the tacit assumption that a woman seeking a husband operates in a buyer's market in which the man is the buyer. No doubt many women find this advice silly and demeaning. They think the traditional sex role an archaic relict of the past, rubbish to be ignored, certainly not applicable to themselves. They will have none of it.

Perhaps they are right. But they need to know that many men have been influenced by the traditional male sex role which contains an ambivalent, schizoid view of women. On the one hand, most men cannot deny that in the domestic and sexual realms women possess highly desirable resources and skills. But on the other hand, listening to tradition, they believe that women are inherently devious, scheming, sexually capricious, powerful creatures, a witch and a wanton who will castrate the male, psychologically and perhaps literally, in order to get her way. Their minds filled with fear and hostility, with wonder and puzzlement about a woman's intentions, traditional males are always alert for any evidence that confirms their prejudices. Even the smallest sign of female competitiveness and aggression is enough to inflame male paranoia. When women behave assertively, when they threaten to win in any contest with men, male anger and fear are aroused, because losing to a woman is intolerable to a traditional male. Faced with the prospect of not doing as well as a woman, some traditional men withdraw and sulk, some flare up in anger. But whatever the response most traditional men feel deeply threatened by female superiority.

Tell this to a woman and she may respond: so what? Sometimes men win, sometimes women do. Winning and losing are part of the game. Why worry about it? Well, because maintaining good relationships with some men becomes difficult when they feel inferior. Most females learn this early. A survey of adolescent girls found that 64 percent believed that boys would like them less if they did better than the boys in a test. Some girls—as skilled chameleons will—hide or deprecate their accomplishments, fearful that others will think them vain; 40 percent of the girls said they worried that other people would think them "stuck-up," and many use chameleon-like methods to fend off this calamity.[13]

The female New Elitist is in a quandary. She works in a highly competitive environment, often with males as superiors or colleagues. She is expected to excel and get ahead in her career. She has been taught to evaluate herself in terms of occupational success, the standard against which men have long been gauged. But what matters winning if it drives away friends who have been made envious by her success? How can she feel content if she believes that competition with males will be thought unfeminine and that victory over men will earn her kudos from society but cost her love and marriage? Even if she is already married or not interested in marriage, or if she works primarily with other women, as many do in the welfare, health, and educational industries, she cannot fail to notice the chill her success introduces in her circle of friends.

And yet if she withdraws from the occupational contest, not only will she pay dearly in money and status, she will suffer a blow to her self-esteem. For in withdrawing she confirms the negative stereotype of women: that women are dependent, moody and flighty, uninterested in work that requires long-term personal commitment, and unable to take seriously the demands that success in a career entails. If her actions confirm this stereotype, is she not in danger of thinking it true of herself? The result may be that she comes to accept as true of herself all the hostile things misogynists have been saying about women. Some women shrug off the accusations made against their sex, refuse to be stymied and sidetracked, and plow ahead in pursuit of their goals: equality and occupational success. But some others fall victim to hostile stereotypes and to the hazards of chameleonism. These women run the risk of becoming self-denigrating and anxious, exactly as the stereotype of women portrays them to be.

Paradoxically, radical feminists have compounded the problems of women by spreading a scurrilous image of the female sex. In order to advance their cause, they paint a picture of women that rivals the most damaging description of women ever offered, even by women-haters. As these feminists see it, oppressive patriarchal society has made women timid and helpless, passive and dependent, gullible and vapid, the crushed and exploited victims of male sexuality and aggression.[14] As expected, this pitiable description of women excites the sympathy of right-thinking people, who then cry out for reform and reparations. But there is this to consider: will not women who buy into this miserable stereotype of women become depressed by it?

The fact that many people hold a stereotypic image of women also helps explain the anger, rancor, and divisiveness that the entrance of women into the labor force, and their exceptional achievements at work, have generated between the sexes. Until relatively recently competition between the sexes had been carefully controlled and muted. Men and women not only performed different tasks, they occupied different physical and psychological space. They kept out of each other's way and rarely competed in any kind of work. Moreover, they usually maintained a certain amount of emotional distance from one another, a degree of formality that modern Americans would find cold and unnatural.

The traditional sexual division of labor prevented or reduced the tensions caused today by competition between the sexes for work, prestige, money, and power. In earlier times, women tended to work at jobs filled mostly by other women and in surroundings populated mostly with women. They avoided jobs in the skilled crafts and professions that tradition had assigned to men, a decision enforced by labor unions and accepted as right and proper by most employers. As long as women stayed by themselves, working mostly in the ranks of unskilled or quasi-skilled labor, the tension between the sexes over competition for jobs, salary increases, and promotion remained low and manageable.

Surprisingly, most women accepted this situation more or less quietly, with a minimum of grumbling and open complaint. For in truth they did not relish the idea of competing with men. In many cases they had entered the work force reluctantly and looked forward to leaving it as soon as possible. Indeed it had never been easy to get women into male-dominated occupations, especially in factories and mills, not even in times of war, not even during World War II, when the pressure on women to work in war-related factories was terrific. According to Walter Karp, "[t]here was nothing spontaneous about the unprecedented influx of women into the wartime shipyards and factories. Far from picking up rivet guns with joy, American women had to be exhorted, cajoled and browbeaten to take traditionally male jobs."[15] Rosie the Riveter, the sweetheart of the homefront, always enthusiastic and smiling, loving every minute at her job, was a figment of wartime propaganda.

This seemingly cheerful acceptance by women of male dominance in the workplace quickly vanished when the new service economy brought large numbers of middle-class women into the labor force. These women began to compete vigorously with men for positions in fields that had long been regarded as the proper domains of men, and they succeeded in replacing males in a variety of occupations long dominated by men. For example a majority of claims adjusters and bill collectors are now women, whereas previously they were almost entirely men. Similarly, women now outnumber men in such fields as real estate and retail merchandising.

Apart from competition with men, the entrance of women into the labor market and their pursuit of occupational success created problems almost no one had imagined. For working women today face a challenge few of their ancestors ever encountered: how to reconcile the conflicting demands of family and career. In trying to juggle the demands of career and family, women often discover that they have taken on more than they can handle. Simply put, they find that there are not enough hours in the day, not enough flexibility in the mind, not enough resiliency in the body for them to do both jobs as they would like. Perhaps Superwomen can simultaneously satisfy employers who require complete commitment to the job, placate husbands who insist on the services of a full-time wife, and win over children who want total attention to their needs, without wrenching physical and emotional costs. But ordinary women, torn by conflicting demands, sometimes end up feeling strung-out. Work outside the home, which was supposed to liberate women, has left some of them feeling exhausted and overwhelmed. To these women the price of success at work appears excessive, not worth the cost in time lost with husband and children, in marital bickering, in nerves strained to the breaking point, in disappointment and frustration.

This frustration is heightened by a gnawing feeling that their work is not appreciated. Even though they are often professionals who think of their work as a calling, not merely as a job, they generally earn less public esteem than they think they deserve. And in truth, some jobs—nursing, teaching, social work—contain an altruistic component. Women in these professions sometimes take risks that prudent citizens sensibly avoid. They teach in dangerous schools, enter violent areas to help clients in need, tend to sick and cranky old folk, and for this they receive scant thanks. There's the rub: sacrifice without appreciation breeds frustration, anger, and bitterness. They feel their sacrifices should be recognized and that their lives should be enriched and fulfilled. Needless to say they are often disappointed.

If some working women complain of being unappreciated, of being just plain tired and emotionally drained, it is not simply because the burdens of the job and family wear them out or that hassles with bosses and fellow workers leave them limp and dispirited, though these take a toil on women as they do on men. It is also because many women find that they must carry the burdens of being a paid employee and homemaker at the same time without much help from their helpmates. Regrettably, many men have been slow to adapt to their new responsibilities as the mate of a working wife.

Some men who are fully at ease in a rapidly changing workplace, who are able to jettison old work-related ideas and practices when necessary, turn out to be traditional spouses who want their meals served on time, their homes kept neat and tidy, their children well trained in good manners and obedience—all this without themselves becoming more than peripherally involved in the tedious business of housekeeping and childrearing. This tends to be true no matter what the family income. A 1995 study of income and housework found that wives do most of the household chores no matter what percentage of the income they bring home or how high the family income.[16] At home the tendency for men is to retreat to their reclining chairs and leave the family chores to their wives.

To make matters worse, some women feel guilty about working, which is easy to understand, for they are often held responsible for the rising rates of divorce, juvenile delinquency, drug addiction, and academic failure that currently afflict America. Echoing complaints of a century ago, modern critics claim that women who insist on working outside the home are damaging themselves, their husbands, and their children—and that for this society is paying a terrible price. Small wonder some working women feel nerve-wracked and frustrated.

It was not supposed to be this way. Winning was supposed to solve most of women's problems. As winners they would shake off feelings of oppression and inferiority, take their rightful places in society, and taste the fruits of victories long denied them. And so it has been for many women. But for many others, the sad fact is that their old problems persist and some new ones have appeared. They had not anticipated the costs of victory. Still, with all its costs, it is at least arguable that winning is preferable to losing. Ask the typical blue-collar worker, losers many of them, whose condition we examine in the next chapter.

10

Blue-Collar Blues

No group feels more badly treated than the working class. No group feels more keenly that its interests are being neglected, that its status is in freefall, that its economic security is in jeopardy. And perhaps no group feels more worried and angry. To sympathetic observers the reason for the workers' discontent seems obvious enough: the techno-service society has treated them shabbily. How can anyone doubt this? Haven't their wages been slashed, their claim to a job ignored, perhaps the job itself eliminated? Is not their condition dire? Haven't they, as one newsmagazine put it, been shafted.[1] And isn't this the cause of their disgruntled mood?

It is not that simple. Economic factors alone do not explain working-class discontent. It is true that many factory workers feel pinched. Some have lost their jobs; others have taken pay cuts; most find pay increases harder to come by. This is painful and no doubt contributes to blue-collar anxiety. But it is not the only cause of their discontent, not even the most important one. In fact, on average, objective conditions have not deteriorated to the extent workers think they have. In many cases they have remained the same; in some cases they have improved.

General opinion notwithstanding, it is not only economic deprivation, a state of the pocketbook, from which some workers suffer; it is also relative social deprivation, a state of the mind. What has in

truth declined for almost all blue-collar workers is their satisfaction
with their social position. When they contrast their position with
what they think it should be, they feel a distinct sense of loss. But it
is less a loss of dollars than a loss of respect.

Many workers are angry because they believe they have been
cheated out of what is rightly theirs: an honored place in society.
They feel unwelcome and ridiculed, like an old suit, out-of-fashion
and shabby, ready for the trash can. The skills and muscles that once
assured them an honored place in society have declined in value, and
as a result so have they. Their values are being replaced by new values
and their needs and those of society no longer mesh harmoniously.
A new social order now calls the tune, and blue-collar workers, like
musicians in a strange orchestra playing an unfamiliar tune, are now
minor performers—off key and getting little applause.

Blue-collar workers feel powerless to protect themselves against
forces they don't understand, and vulnerable to the scorn and slander
of people they despise and fear. They are becoming deracinated.
Their roots are in a world that is rapidly losing influence and, as a
result, so are they. The old manufacturing economy in which they
played an important role no longer rules the economic roost. Its place
has been taken by a new system, the information society produced by
the Second Great Transformation—a system to which they are ill-
adapted and in which they feel poorly rewarded.

Their place in this world is not the one they expected and feel they
rightly deserve. As they see it, their contributions to society are un-
dervalued and taken for granted. Unfortunately society no longer sees
it their way, and they are having difficulty accepting this sad fact. In
truth, they have suffered the cruelest fate that can befall a social class:
they have lost a social revolution. Through no fault of their own they
have been grievously hurt by the techno-service system's triumph
over manufacturing. They have become losers, and losing is hard to
take. What is even sadder, they still do not fully understand what is
going on.

But it is not only that their work no longer wins the kudos it once
did; it is also that the new society celebrates a culture they find re-
pellent and empowers an elite class they fear and hate. The new culture is permeated by the Chameleon Complex, which serves the
interests of the New Elite, and toward both the culture and its elite
bearers the blue-collar class feels only visceral loathing.

Of course, blue-collar workers are themselves not untouched by the Chameleon Complex; every group has its chameleons. But chameleonism is less prevalent among factory workers. A skill at dissimulation, which New Elitists number among the useful tools of their trades, while not unknown among blue-collar workers, is not a valued commodity in the factory. As a rule, factory work seldom requires disguise and dissimulation; no one rewards the blue-collar worker for trimming with the situational winds. Quick, efficient, high-quality production is what matters.

Mostly, factory workers produce objects for unknown customers, whose personality needs they need never consider. No one asks the production worker to greet the customer with a smile and an offer to be of service. Nor is the workplace as competitive for blue-collar workers as it is for knowledge creators and information processors. Competition exists, of course, on the factory floor, but it tends to be controlled by company and union rules. Also, the production worker has less opportunity to threaten others or be threatened by them, and thus less reason to adopt the chameleon's disguise.

On those occasions when they try to play the chameleon's game, dealing in intangible images rather than material objects, the factory worker's relative lack of the verbal and interpersonal skills intrinsic to the Chameleon Complex is a distinct liability. The Chameleon Complex may be an asset to middle-class men and women; its absence can be a handicap for blue-collar workers trying to get ahead in situations where impression management counts a lot. Perhaps for all these reasons, chameleonism strikes blue-collar workers as downright dishonest. And they feel awkward and out of place in a society that tacitly accepts chameleonism as the norm.

THE END OF AN ERA

Even though, as we have shown in Chapter 2, the economy remains strong, it would be foolish to deny that some workers have experienced severe economic loss and that this has contributed to their anxiety. Massive economic change—the Second Great Transformation—is costing some workers their jobs. This has caused pain and it deserves discussion, even though, as I believe, it is only one of several factors contributing to the current mood of discontent among blue-collar workers.

Workers are learning that lean and mean corporations are hard to live with, that job security is something their parents may have known but which is no longer certain for them. They are learning that improved productivity and economic growth do not necessarily create jobs for everyone, and that a continually rising standard of living can no longer be taken for granted. In brief, they are learning an old, if obvious, lesson—that slim wallets depress the spirit and joblessness can lead to despair. Unfortunately, Americans are ill-prepared for the school of economic hard knocks. They have grown accustomed to more work benefits, greater job security, and larger paychecks than workers have ever known before.

The current plight of workers mauled by economic change is particularly excruciating because for a brief period, from the end of World War II to the early 1970s, blue-collar workers enjoyed an astounding improvement in social position and living standard. During that period the economy became significantly more productive, enriching the lives of people in almost every station in life. Never before had the material condition of so many Americans changed so much for the better in so short a time with such far-reaching consequences.

The extraordinary growth of the American economy after 1945 created a wealth of good-paying jobs that was unprecedented anywhere in the world. Skilled workers, and even those with few if any skills, enjoyed incomes never dreamed of by previous generations. Real earnings of the typical worker were twice as high around 1972 than they had been in the late 1940s.[2] Automatically, almost magically, the children of the working class, many of them factory workers like their parents, stepped on the escalator that is the American Dream, moved into well-paying jobs, bought houses in the suburbs, and took on the title and accoutrements of the middle class. Ambitious war veterans from every social stratum equipped themselves with college degrees bought with money provided by the GI Bill, and buoyed by a burgeoning economy became managers, entrepreneurs, and professionals, joining the ranks of the upper-middle class.

But this period of exuberant economic growth and fabulous social mobility did not last. In mid-1973, the bright days of seemingly endless and effortless growth came to an end. The economy, which had been growing at a brisk average rate of 3.9 percent during the period 1950 to 1970, slowed to a modest growth rate of 1 or 2 percent.

Jobs became scarcer and real wages increased slowly; the upward movement of average family income slowed to a crawl.[3]

Among the first to feel the pinch of the slowdown were factory workers doing routine, repetitive work. Many of them began to live in fear of the ax. Across the nation, workers who once felt secure started to churn with anxiety about their future in companies for which they had worked for many years and to which they had given, as the saying goes, the best years of their lives. Looking about them or following the news in the media, they discovered that workers were losing their jobs. Many companies began reacting to grim economic news: they were losing money. Profit margins had slipped disastrously. Pretax profits, which had averaged 16.9 percent in the 1950s, fell to 10.7 percent in the 1970s and to 8.7 percent in the 1980s. Companies had to respond to this progressive decline or go under. Some in fact became bankrupt, others were taken over by competitors, but many survived.

Stung by foreign competition, desperate to survive in a fiercely competitive global market, eager to fend off angry stockholders and keep their own jobs, corporate managers undertook a number of draconian measures to return their companies to profitability. For one thing, some of them began moving production abroad to locations where routine work could be quickly learned and efficiently performed, where workers could make things comparable in quality to that obtained from more highly-paid Americans.

Consider these sobering statistics. It costs about $16 an hour to employ a production worker in the United States, as compared with $2.40 in Mexico, $1.50 in Poland, and 50 cents or less in China, India, Malaysia, and Indonesia. Auto manufacturing highlights the extent of international wage differentials. Mexican workers producing 1993 Ford Escorts earned $2.38 an hour; Americans working on the same car earned $17.50 an hour. With wage differentials this large it does not take a rocket scientist to figure out how the *Fortune* 500 firms across America were able to cut their American payroll from 16.2 million in 1990 to 11.8 million in 1993 and still keep production high. Many of them had transferred some of their production to low-cost countries.

Employers in poor countries often force their workers to accept wages Americans would not tolerate. Some workers in Shenzhen, China, earn as little as one yuan (12 American cents) an hour, and work 12 to 13 hour days, seven days a week. In India millions of children, some as young as seven years of age, weave carpets for a pittance. Factory conditions are often Dickensian—dark and dismal and dangerous. Hundreds of workers die needlessly in factory fires, trapped in buildings that lack the simplest precautions against accidental conflagration or provisions for escape once a fire breaks out. Industrial accidents are common; the risk of being accidentally killed in a factory is six times higher in South Korea and fifteen times higher in Pakistan than in the United States. Competition for manufacturing jobs with workers willing to work under such conditions seems hopelessly unfair to many Americans.[4]

Transferring some of their production to low-wage countries was only one of the strategies companies employed to stay afloat in turbulent economic waters. There were others. Where possible manufacturers began employing robots and computers, increasing productivity but also putting people out of work. Like the Luddites (1811–16), who smashed machines in the textile mills of industrializing England in a futile effort to save their jobs, few workers have difficulty comprehending the connection between technology and unemployment. In 1930, John Maynard Keynes saw it too. "We are being afflicted with a new disease . . . technological unemployment," he explained to policy makers worried by a sinking economy that, as time would show, was slowly slipping into the worst depression of modern times.[5] And even more recently, economist Paul Krugman reminded us that machine-driven efficiency inevitably hurts some workers. The gain in long term riches must be paid for in the short run by production workers whose jobs and skills are being swallowed up by technological progress. This is regrettable but unavoidable, he concluded. There is no gain without pain.

In addition to transferring production abroad and introducing advanced technologies, managers began to reduce their workforces. In some industries, appreciable numbers of production workers were laid off or forced into retirement. In one year alone, 1993, the top 100 American electronic companies eliminated 480,000 jobs. For example, Compaq Computer Corporation, the world's biggest maker of computers, laid off 20 percent of its staff. In a different field, Caterpillar, the manufacturer of construction and mining machinery, took an even harsher step: it slashed its work force 31 percent. U.S. West, a Baby Bell telephone company headquartered in Englewood, Colorado, began phasing out 9,000 jobs, about one-seventh of its work force.

American Telephone and Telegraph, mother of phone companies, announced in 1996 that it would lay off no less than 40,000 of its employees. Albert J. Dunlap ("Chainsaw Al" to his critics), chairman of the Sunbeam Corporation, announced in 1997 that he would slash Sunbeam's overall workforce in half, having previously lopped off one-third of the workforce at the Scott Paper Company in just 28 months.[6]

Rather than lay off employees, some corporations seek to reduce expenses by simply not filling vacant slots, forcing the remaining employees to carry the workload of their former co-workers. At the General Motors Fisher Body plant in Flint, Michigan, employees gripe that they are being asked to do what used to be several different jobs. "If somebody retires, all they do is take the work and give it to other people," said one worker. That complaint is echoed by others in many industries across the country. Said one employee of Gamma, a large photo lab in Chicago, which had dismissed 16 percent of the staff the year before: "Everyone has to do everyone's job in addition to their own."[7] When the workload becomes too burdensome and the complaints of workers too noisy to be ignored, some companies fill full-time positions with part-time or temporary hired hands, who receive no expensive benefits, health insurance, unemployment payments, and paid vacations, and can be laid off at a moment's notice.

Another tactic is to pile on the overtime. Some companies use overtime to wring the most out of their facilities without having to hire new people or expand the plant. The factory workweek in 1994, a robust year when the economy grew at a 4 percent annual rate, averaged a near record 42 hours, including 4.6 hours of overtime. The big-three auto makers pushed this figure to ten hours a week overtime. "We are the workingest people in the world," says Audrey Freedman, a labor economist.[8] But workers complain of exhaustion. One worker even welcomed a brief strike just to get a few days off. Still, notwithstanding bone-weariness and the loss of precious time with family and friends, overtime pay is welcome to most workers and princely to some. Many autoworkers are earning $65,000 to $70,000 a year, and electricians on plant-maintenance crews working seven-day weeks can push their income to as much as $100,000 annually.[9] Paying overtime is expensive to the company, of course, but it is cheaper than building new plants and hiring new workers.

Some companies sought to increase production without cutting the work force or substantially increasing overtime. The Birmingham

Steel Corporation took this route. As recently as 1987, it had produced 167,000 tons of steel with 184 workers, an average of 912 tons
per worker. Six years later, after tightening production procedures
and strictly controlling new hiring, it produced 276,000 tons with
207 workers, an average of 1,335 per person, which works out to an
8 percent increase in productivity per year, a remarkable figure by
any standard. Many other industries have also become more productive, bringing down costs and boosting production. In the entire
country, over all industrial production was 40 percent higher in 1994
and four times higher than in 1950. In effect, more was being made
with fewer people.

MANUFACTURING DECLINE

Viewed historically, the effects of increased productivity on blue-
collar employment were dramatic. From 1919 to 1929 manufacturing
output increased by 60 percent, but the manufacturing workforce actually declined by 0.6 percent. During the period from 1957 to 1964,
while output doubled, the number of production workers shrank by
3 percent; and from 1979 to 1992 the manufacturing workforce declined by 15 percent even though the output increased by 35 percent.
The hemorrhaging of blue-collar jobs continues: there were 21 million factory jobs in 1973, accounting for 23 percent of the work force;
by 1994 there were 18 million such jobs, accounting for 16 percent
of the total, close to the present figure. About one million fewer
people worked in manufacturing in 1994 than had been the case four
years earlier.[10]

In the long run higher productivity means higher wages, economists hasten to assure us, although as Keynes once wryly remarked,
when someone predicted the economy would improve eventually, in
the long run we are all dead. Even so, despite increased productivity,
income increases have come slowly, certainly not as rapidly as in earlier years. Nor can it be denied that some groups have lost ground.
Workers in bars and restaurants, for example, saw their base wages
fall, though tips helped soften this drop. The biggest losers of all
were men who had never completed high school; their earnings fell
14 percent.

To the young unskilled worker economic distress came as a shock.
Not so very long ago a husky man with large biceps, a strong back,

and a willingness to work could always find a good job. Education and skill counted for much less then than they do now. Unskilled manual workers were in demand, and work was easy to find. For decades the nation's factories had offered prosperity to people without diplomas or special skills, migrants from the hills of Appalachia and the cotton fields of the Mississippi delta, or immigrants from the villages of Europe. "I remember," said Lawrence Hunter, a black machine operator, referring to the employment situation in Milwaukee in the 1950s when he was a young man, "when you could quit one job one day and go out the next day and get a better job making more money. You could go to a foundry and get a job any day."[11]

Now things have changed. "A kid used to be able to drop out of school and get a job with his old man at General Motors," said Arnold Packer, executive director of a Labor Department commission studying ways to improve the education and preparation of workers. "Now the old man is lucky if he can keep his job, and his kid has to start somewhere else at the minimum wage."[12] Young blue-collar workers are said to lack the educational background and stamina to get and hold a demanding skilled job. "They get out there on their own," said Joseph W. Schroeder, a manager at one of the Michigan State Employment offices, "they want a job, their own place and a telephone. And they're unskilled. They haven't been taught to work. In dealing with young people the problem that employers tell me about is that they can't read or write very well. They can't fill out a job application." It is not only employers who speak this way. Said Gordon Malmgren, an agent for a carpenter's union, "They're a lot dumber and burned out, half of them." He found that often people who want to be carpenters "don't have the arithmetic they should. It was beat into me."[13] Now that low-skilled work with high wages has become scarce, young workers without job skills and little education often end up in dead-end jobs.

It was not always this way. Not all that long ago college graduates did not make much more money than high school graduates or even some school dropouts. Few doctors were rich, most lawyers struggled to make a living, many college graduates ended up doing routine clerical work for modest pay. The average annual incomes of college graduates and that of their peers who had only finished high school were not far apart. When the costs of going to college and delaying entering the workforce for years were factored in, the factory worker could justifiably feel that little was lost by not continuing on the academic treadmill. Now the gap between the life-time earnings of a college graduate and those of a worker without a college degree has widened significantly. It is estimated that college graduates will earn over their lifetimes 1.4 million dollars, as compared with $609,000 for workers with only a high school diploma.

Clearly some workers are hurting badly. Public assistance helps, but the bitter bread bought with welfare checks and the handouts from friends and relatives can tear families apart. Proud Americans find charity hard to swallow. But a preoccupation with dramatic cases of personal and family disintegration following job loss, and an obsession with the statistics of job loss, endlessly echoed by groups with political axes to grind, lead to a misleading conclusion: that the economy is in trouble and that this is the main reason for blue-collar disgruntlement.

The facts say otherwise. The economy is amazingly resilient and so are many of its workers. Some troubled industries modernized—for example, the steelworks of the Midwest—and are once again profitable. The "rust belt," once given up for lost, has recovered and is doing well. Most cities battered by an unexpected plant shutdown eventually pull themselves together and move on. A Federal Reserve study reported that many of these cities swapped manufacturing for service jobs and prospered.[14] The economy is still creating millions of jobs annually, some of them of the hamburger-flipping variety, it is true; but many are high-skilled positions with good pay and decent fringe benefits. Despite relentless corporate ups and downs, which understandably has given some workers a case of economic nausea, the percentage of new jobs that pay above-average salaries has doubled since 1992.

Many people are now getting jobs that are far better that the ones they lost. After studying the effects of corporate restructuring, Mark Zandi, chief economist at Regional Financial Associates, an economic consulting firm in West Chester, Pa., concluded that "we're seeing a lot of job growth in sectors and occupations that are high paying."[15] New jobs are constantly coming on the labor market because the economy continues to grow. In 1997 it grew at a brisk annual rate of about 4 percent and unemployment fell to 5.3 percent, the lowest in four years and close to an economist's definition of full employment. And despite complaints of stagnant or reduced wages, blue-collar workers are, on average, comparatively well paid. American workers in manufacturing, many of whom are doing low-skilled work, are on the average among the highest paid in the world.

THE WAR AGAINST THE WORKING CLASS

Why then have so many people responded so strongly to stories of economic misery? In part because the media rapidly spread the bad news to national audiences, who wonder if it will be their turn next. But more important, many blue-collar workers feel they have become the targets of an organized campaign to harass and vilify them. They have come to feel surrounded by enemies, by malefactors who make trouble and who delight in maligning the worker. And not only do they believe things are not going as well for them as they ought, they think things are going all too well for people not a whit more worthy. But who exactly do they blame? Who are the people getting more than their fair share?

We can rule out the inheritors of great fortunes, the possessors of old family names and estates. They are a tiny, remote, exclusive group, a mere blip on the screen of public consciousness, not serious targets of hostility. Equally excluded are the princes of the cities, the performers and entertainers, the lucky winners in life's lottery, the select few whom talent and fate have vaulted into the multi-million-dollar dream- land of the public's fantasies. These people live in sybaritic luxury, jet to far off places to test the food, waters, and sexual attractions of exotic lands in secluded hideaways. Probably few working-class Americans lose much sleep brooding about these favorites of fortune.

Who then do they blame for their unhappy condition? Who are the people who make them feel unappreciated and insecure? The villain is the New Elite, the upwardly-mobile, bright, hardworking, eager for power and wealth, information processors who dominate the techno-service society.

Elitists rub blue-collar workers the wrong way. For one thing, the Elite's wealth and power are too new, too different, too offensive to working-class sensibilities to have won the acceptance given to the inheritors of old money and to the possessors of valued talent and quirky good fortune. For another thing, the masters of the infor- mation society make no bones about their own moral and intellectual superiority. With grating hauteur, they have announced to the world that their special mission is to save America and make it atone for its sins. Such pretensions to superiority stick in the worker's craw. Worse yet, as a demonstration of its moral superiority the Elite is pushing affirmative action policies that undermine the workers' sense of security and confidence in themselves. It is this loss of security and self-confidence, this feeling of having lost status respect, at least as much as anything else, that accounts for blue-collar disaffection.

The hostility many workers feel for the New Elite surfaced during the debates about the wisdom of enlarging the free trade pact with Canada to include Mexico. Elitists generally supported the North American Free Trade Agreement. Said one young lawyer, interviewed as she was catching a train bound for a Chicago suburb, "We've got to keep up with the world. It's just smart economic policy." Other lawyers, stockbrokers, and accountants catching the same train also enthusiastically supported the treaty. It was, as one man put it, a "no brainer." As he saw it, the United States has everything to gain and nothing to lose by opening its gates to trade with Mexico.

But to many workers the issue looked entirely different. To Sharon Jones, a 36-year-old union worker who cleans train cars for $8 an hour, the treaty presented a threat to her livelihood. "It's going to take our jobs away," she said. And then she added, in angry tones that revealed the blue-collar suspicion of the credentialed class, "I know the rich people say it won't. But what do they care about working people? The only ones looking to protect people like us is the A.F.L.-C.I.O. And if the union says it's bad, I trust them. Got no reason to trust those other folks." And to another worker, a Chicago truck driver named Dennis McGue, the treaty looked like the work of "fancy-pants elites" who cared nothing for the workers. "I guess when you live up on a hill," he said, "you just don't see the people in the valley."[16]

The "people on the hill" generally know little about the "people in the valley" and care little that the blue-collar class has had to endure a steady deterioration in status. Nor are they impressed when factory workers point to the importance of their work. Quite the reverse. For one thing, many arts and skills are in decline. Ancient crafts have been broken into simple operations, routinized and robbed of intrinsic merit. Old skills, painfully acquired through long years of apprenticeship, have fallen into disuse, replaced by robots and computers. And for another thing, even granted that workers still make things that move on roads and fly through the air, that clothe and house the nation, that arm the military and win wars, these are the products of an old regime, the manufacturing system, now in relative decline. A new system, the information economy, is in ascendance, and its masters take for granted the goods the old system still builds. As the New Elite sees it, building bridges and roads, making cars and airplanes, count for less in the national scheme of things than building pyramids of words. Possessing and processing information are what really matter; manual work can be delegated to lesser breeds.

This attitude baffles and infuriates most blue-collar workers. It is not what they had expected. In the past, society understood their importance and visibly showed its respect. Organized in powerful labor unions, as many of them were, blue-collar workers were people to whom politicians and employers paid heed. They lobbied for legislation to protect their interests; they demanded wage increases that appreciably lifted their pay. And if their demands were not met they tied a company up in strikes that in time would bring it to its knees. Taken all in all, with its voice in the councils of government, its contributions to political parties and the clout that resulted from judiciously placed money, organized labor had won a place at the table of power. It negotiated as equals with employers and politicians over its share of the nation's economic pie. And as labor's influence grew, the worker enjoyed the esteem that power always brings.

Needless to say, much has changed since the glory days of working-class influence. Blue-collar clout has declined as the unions, particularly in manufacturing industries, have lost members. In the 1950s about a quarter of all workers in the private sector belonged to labor unions. Today, only 11 percent are union members, about the same as in the 1930s. And in a marked change with the past, while blue-collar membership declined service sector membership grew: today service workers are the most rapidly growing segment of unionized labor.[17]

As though economic disappointment and declining influence were not trouble enough, workers must also contend with attacks upon their values and personal worth. At times the media portray them, especially the white males, as louts, beer-sodden inebriates, mindless television addicts, coarse boors oblivious to the needs of women, lesbians, and gays, to the sensibilities of the crippled, the old, the fat, the ugly, and other fashionable minorities. Their lives are ridiculed as shallow and crude, wasted years spent in the pursuit of tawdry pleasure, without commitment to ideas, to the joys of self-discovery, and to the advancement of high culture. They feel under attack from all sides. Call this paranoia if you like. Say it will go away when times get better, when factory jobs once again become well paid and secure, when the golden past is somehow recaptured. But remember that working class anxiety persists in these relatively good times, that it hangs on even as the gross national product grows briskly, employment goes up and inflation down.

This is not to say that a bigger pay check and an ampler bank balance would not be welcome. Obviously, this would ease the pain. But it will not erase it. The working class is hurting because it feels rejected, and the rejection is real. Working-class values, though enjoying something of a revival of emphasis in the speeches of politicians desperate to win the worker's vote, no longer enjoy the general favor they once did. Indeed, the workers' culture appears downright ludicrous to the New Elite.

Elitists dismiss working-class culture as low-brow trash, a detritus of sentimental country music and abrasive rock, of mindless violence on television and in motion pictures, and of children's games played by grownups for fantastic salaries in baseball parks, on football fields, and on basketball courts around the country. A comment by novelist Joyce Carol Oates, complaining about what she sees as the worker's ungenerous attitude toward immigrants and blacks, succinctly sums up the elite's opinion of workers: "[w]hen these people (unionized workers) get power, all they want is a house in the suburbs, some of them, and their cars and dishwashers."[18] More attention should be given, she implies, to social justice, to good music, and, not incidentally, to good books.

The New Elite also accuses the blue-collar worker of being an environmental despoiler. It charges the logger, truck driver, bulldozer operator, and pesticide sprayer with riding roughshod over the fragile ecosystem, endangering the survival of trees, insects, rodents, fishes, birds, flowers, cacti, rare plants, and snakes. The wetlands, the deserts, the atmosphere, the ozone layer—all suffer from blue-collar carelessness and indifference. In the face of this barrage of criticism, some workers find it hard to keep their heads up. Others feel unfairly treated and eventually turn against their detractors.

Perhaps most damaging is the charge that factory workers are dumb. Social researchers, psychometricians, and other elite members of the information society bluntly question the blue-collar worker's ability to cope with the demands of the information age. They assert that the average blue-collar worker lacks the intelligence to cope with the technical requirements of the information system. Blue-collar IQ scores, researchers report, tend to fall on the wrong side of the bell curve, below the median. In the judgment of Richard Herrnstein and Charles Murray, authors of *The Bell Curve*, blue-collar workers tend to be deficient in "cognitive ability," the capacity to handle abstractions and process information.[19] Many of them cannot puzzle out the instructions in work manuals or understand complex job processes, and for these reasons are doomed to stay in the lower reaches of the workforce. Rattled by this low assessment of their intelligence, some workers wonder whether the elite may not be right. Certainly, the jabberwocky jargon of computer technology leaves most of them at sea, adrift and bewildered. Worse than that, they feel diminished.

But it is not the assessment of their IQ that most troubles blue-collar workers. What troubles them even more is the feeling that they no longer fit into the economy in the comfortable, reassuring way they once did, that they no longer mesh neatly with the rest of society—and that no one cares. In this conclusion they are entirely correct. They are, in fact, out-of-synch with the new system. They had been educated to work in harmony with other parts of a complex machine called the manufacturing system. But since this system has been downgraded by the techno-service economy, which needs a different kind of workforce, they sense, quite accurately, that they have been relegated to second place, along with the system they were trained to fit.

In a manufacturing system the factory is the major trainer of workers. The factory is a forceful school: its spirit enters the mind and marrow of the worker. It is in the factory that workers acquire many of the traits that define their character: respect for authority and tradition, a need for order and predictability, an admiration for technical competence. The rhythm of its machines, the constant insistence on efficiency and reliability, these attributes of the factory subtly shape workers in ways that make them suitable for life in an industrial society. Day in and day out, by example and direct instruction, the modern factory teaches him how to function in a formally organized, deeply hierarchical system, characterized by a complex division of labor, an emphasis on specialization and technical skill, a devotion to competence and efficiency.

In the factory workers contribute to the making of useful objects, some of them marvelously precise and beautiful. In the factory they observe highly skilled technicians performing exquisitely complicated tasks with ease and regularity. In the factory they discover that competence pays and shoddy work earns meager rewards, perhaps even dismissal. The workplace teaches that excellence in work counts for something, that without order nothing gets done, that diligence and self-discipline pay off—all notions of what matters in a manufacturing society.

Surrounded by machines of extraordinary complexity, constantly admonished to stay in step with others in the production line, the factory worker tends to develop an admiration for a well-functioning organization. Working in the tightly organized structure of the modern factory, the worker learns to acquiesce to institutional power—provided it is buttressed by moral authority, managerial competence, and technical skill. When these are present the constrictions of the modern workplace meet little resistance from most workers. Factory workers will accept constant supervision and the bossy dictates of the clock, will submit to restrictions on their ability to move about and allocate their time, will endure dull, repetitive work with minimum fuss and complaint—as long as the organization for which they toil is considered competent and fair. When that is the case they often develop a singular loyalty to their employers. The company's logo and products take on symbolic, almost sacred connotations. Workers will celebrate the company's victories and fight to preserve its place in their industry. The effect of all this is not to make them docile—no one has ever called American workers docile—but to make them supportive of organizational order and tradition.

Tradition appeals to blue-collar workers. They tend to distrust change and would like to keep things as they are—familiar, comfortable, and predictable. Socially conservative, they consider affronts to the system, insults to its symbols and mockery of its values, as nothing less than invitations to anarchy. Respect for religious and national symbols—the crucifix, the flag, the national anthem, oaths of allegiance, patriotic parades—forms a crucial part of their culture. Consequently, flag-burning or the sacrilegious depiction of sacred objects (for instance, a crucifix immersed in a jar of the artist's urine, Andres Serrano's contribution to art, which prompted a move by Senator Jesse Helms to bar federal financing for "obscene and indecent" art) are more than esthetically offensive; they are felt to deeply subvert the traditions to which workers are emotionally bound. When the foundation wonks and trendies who edit and write for elite magazines make fun of the working class, when reckless, self-besotted intellectuals attack the symbols and pieties of blue-collar workers, they bewilder and anger them to a degree the Elite does not yet understand.

Perhaps workers would feel better if they could strike back at their detractors, the mockers of their character and values. But how to do this? It is not easy; there are problems. For one thing, Elitists are difficult to get at. They often live in protected city enclaves or in gated suburbs; they avoid public transportation and parks; they send their children to private or special schools. Consequently, the paths of the worker and the Elite seldom cross. Short of taking out full-page advertisements in the *New York Times*, how can workers get their message across? (Weirdly, the copy would probably be written by Elitists in the pay of labor unions. Hired guns, some Elitists are ready to serve any master.) Even with aid of experts, the worker would find the Elite an elusive target, hard to locate, harder yet to hit.

For another thing, the Elite counters the complaints of workers with disarming arguments. When workers complain about workforce reductions and plant shutdowns, they are told this drastic action had to be taken, even though it meant throwing people out of work and shattering their lives. The plant had to be closed because it was losing money. People had to be laid off because meticulously conducted studies showed the work force was bloated and the work shoddy. That these actions caused some people pain was regrettable, but it was for the greater good of the company and the country. Workers often find these arguments hard to refute. Sheepishly, they admit the workforce had become too large and the work may have been sloppy. Why else were Americans buying Japanese cars in preference to American ones?

Blue-collar workers cannot hope to beat the Elite at its own game. Elite arguments were fashioned by people who are extremely skilled in the use of language, expert at using words to confuse as well as to enlighten, weaving a web of verbiage to trap the unwary. Words make workers uncomfortable. They are accustomed to making tangible objects and tend to judge the value of things by their obvious utility. They are suspicious of the tools Elitists use to ply their trades: words and images, mysterious devices of dubious value. But without words and the skill to use them, workers lack the right weapons to deal with the Elite. And so, when told that their anger is not justified and must not be expressed, that it must be swallowed, bottled up, reasoned away, and treated with scorn for the selfish, ugly thing it is, they are dumbstruck, literally at a loss for words.

Though baffled and beaten into silence by abstruse argument and softened by appeals to their better nature, many workers nevertheless remain angry. Occasionally, their anger erupts in bursts of sporadic violence or electoral revolt. The abrupt dismissal of many Democratic party politicians in the 1994 midterm elections was said to have been due to the revolt of blue-collar voters furious at the way elite politicians had been treating them. At other times blue-collar anger has taken the form of nativist outbursts at immigrants, sporadic bombings of government buildings, and attempts to set up sovereign enclaves in isolated areas—for example, an Aryan nation in the Northwest or a separate republic in Texas.

But usually the rage is hidden, buried beneath a mountain of denial, repressed from consciousness. Nonetheless, the anger is still there. It can be denied, but it can't be eliminated by denial. Boiling beneath the surface and unable to find an acceptable outlet, repressed rage takes a terrible revenge on people who will not admit its existence. For rage will be heard from, whether its possessor likes it or not. Repressed anger surfaces in feelings of irrational fear and restlessness and in a sense of drift and alienation. Its effects can be seen in the pervasive anxiety that afflicts blue-collar losers.

What have blue-collar workers done to merit this affliction? Why have they become the target of so much New Elite hostility? The answer can be found in the Elite's estimation of blue-collar character, culture, and politics. As already noted, Elitists consider working-class culture both vulgar and reactionary, and they consider the bearers of that culture the relics of a past best ignored and forgotten. But this is, at best, only a partial answer. What offends the Elite even more is the blue-collar worker's hostility to social justice—at least as Elitists define the term. Specifically, Elitists charge the blue-collar workers with resisting affirmative action, a critical part of the Elite's program to create an egalitarian society.

But the hostility the Elite feels for the working class is minor compared to its hatred of the business class. As the Elite sees it, corporate power is the principal obstacle to the New Elite taking power and turning the country in the direction it seeks—towards a just and perfect society in which everyone can enjoy fair access to the nation's resources. Elitists dream of an open society in which everyone, of whatever colour, sex, or sexual orientation, can pursue the grail of self-realization—and Elitists will not tolerate anyone who tampers with their dream. We turn now to an examination of the Elite's treatment of the business class—the putative killers of the dream.

11

The Business Class
Under Attack

Elitists deny that they hanker for unattainable perfection. What they want seems perfectly reasonable to them: nothing more than what children daily pledge allegiance to in schoolrooms across the country—one nation, indivisible, with liberty and justice for all. Surely, it is not asking too much to expect of a country which professes to believe that all men are created equal and endowed by their creator with certain inalienable rights, among them life, liberty, and the pursuit of happiness, that it practice what it preaches. The pursuit of happiness has been going on for more than two centuries, the disenchanted Elitist points out, and yet liberty is far from secure, injustice is rampant and growing, and equality remains as remote as ever.

Why after generations of struggle are we still so far from making good on our promise of equality and justice for all? Whatever happened to the more perfect union the founders promised us? What is the problem? Stupid question, thinks many an Elitist. Surely by now the answer must be obvious: the problem is the system and the people who control it—the people who want to keep things as they are, who profit from a society that is coercive, unequal, and unfair, the business class and its allies. These bad people stand between the New Elite and its dream of a perfect society.

The New Elitists grew up in the information age. As children they daily sat before a television set and watched the good guys contend with the bad guys in battles in which right and wrong were comfortingly clear. Now, as adults, social and moral complexity bores them. They tend to grow impatient with abstruse explanations, with broad generalizations about vast historical forces that throw societies into turmoil, disrupt lives, and prevent or retard desired change. Such explanations irritate them, and they brush them aside impatiently as irrelevant complications. Simple conspiracy theories are much more to their liking.

To many Elitists, rebels in their youth and often hostile toward any authority—familial, educational, military, or governmental—it seems clear that a conspiracy against the public good exists at the highest levels of society. The conspirators are the rich and powerful, the corporate and financial managers, the business establishment which controls the economy and selfishly resists all measures to advance equality and social justice.[1]

As the New Elite sees it, the business class is a cabal of wealthy industrialists and merchants, chief executives and managers, investment bankers and financiers who fight every move to raise taxes, redistribute income, protect the environment, care for the disadvantaged, and extend political rights to minorities. Said to be privately in touch with each other, the members of the business establishment coordinate their activities, manipulate government at all levels to support legislation friendly to their interests, and try to sink anything threatening to business profits and power. Radical Elitists have concluded that this conspiracy cannot be reasoned with; it must be driven from power.

The New Elite is engaged in a furious struggle to seize the reins of power from the faltering hands of some elements of the business establishment that has been grievously weakened by self-doubt, confused about its role in society, and fearful that its days of dominance are about to end. In contrast, the New Elitists brim with confidence about their ability to guide America into the future. They want to control the country's polity and economy and—most important, for they are idealists—they are determined to promote social justice and shape the content of the nation's culture. They have no doubt about the need to unmask the conspiracy that keeps the business class in power and bring it down. They are making a revolution and they feel certain of eventual victory. Equipped with information-age skills, bustling with energy and armed with an inspiring ideology, they present the greatest challenge the business class has faced in this century.

Most New Elitists would probably be startled to hear themselves called revolutionaries. They certainly do not look like revolutionaries. True, they occasionally dress unconventionally, but they are not Maoists clothed in obligatory bluc-quilted jackets. Blue jeans are common among computer programmers; whereas dark coats and subdued ties enjoy favor among stockbrokers and lawyers. Others dress pretty much as they please. Nor do they carry conventional weapons: no Uzis, Molotoff cocktails, car bombs. Their weapons are computers, fax machines, cellular telephones, and other products of electronic wizardry. Working in offices, silently seated before computers or bent over spreadsheets, manuscripts, and other documents, or when on the move, sporting laptop computers and cellular telephones, they look more like priests of some religious sect than practitioners of revolution. But notwithstanding appearances, they are drastically changing the order of things. They have fashioned a vision of a new world, free of imperfection and dedicated to egalitarianism and self-fulfillment, a vision embodied in a powerful ideology which vindicates their own motives and vilifies those of the business class.

One might suppose that the boom produced by the Second Great Transformation would have made the business class immune to Elitist criticism. Some entrepreneurs were clever enough to see where change was heading, and plunged into the newly emerging information economy, building computers, writing software, establishing data processing services—and as a result have become fabulously wealthy. Of course, not every business prospered; some businessmen were not nimble enough to change as the economy changed and suffered losses; some went down and disappeared. Their fate was dramatized in early 1997 when the Dow-Jones Company dropped such manufacturing troglodytes as Bethlehem Steel and Westinghouse from its industrial index and replaced them with the information-oriented companies Hewlett-Packard (computers) and The Travelers Group (insurance and information services). But by conventional criteria many business practioners have become winners—rich in worldly goods and heavy hitters in circles that wield power. And winners can usually shrug off criticism.

But material success has not protected the business class from self-doubt. It is no longer secure in its own superiority, no longer certain that its values and practices represent the best society can provide, no longer sure that its vision of the future will prevail. For that matter it can no longer be said to have a vision that attracts almost universal support, as was the case several generations ago when the manufacturing system dominated the economy. Its wealth and power aside, the business class, paradoxically, is a winner that fears it is becoming a loser—and it might well be right.

The problem for the business class is that it is the target of unceasing criticism and vilification that has undermined its self-confidence. Its critics are New Elitists, who accuse the business class of using its power to corrupt government officials, despoil the environment, and cruelly exploit the poor. Protestations of innocence meet with stony indifference or angry rejection. Examples of corporate benevolence are dismissed as trivial expiation for past transgressions and as evidence of overwhelming guilt for sins against society. The businessman's argument that under his influence society has prospered as never before, that the general level of prosperity is higher than at any other point in history, evokes contemptuous disbelief. In the eyes of the New Elite, the business class is society's enemy number one.

The depth of the anger New Elitists feel toward the corporate class cannot be understood as simply an outgrowth of a clash of interests. It is that, of course. But it is also a product of an animus deeply rooted in western culture which is finding its most recent voice in the New Elite's aversion to the businessman and the bourgeois way of life. This chapter examines the historical roots of this hostility and shows how business hatred became a tool in the hands of the Elite, which plans to unseat the corporate class and take its place.

BUSINESS HATRED

At first glance the Elitists' attack on the business class seems parricidal. They are, after all, usually the children of affluent parents, some of whom were in business or in professions allied to business, who showered every advantage on their offspring. It was probably dad's money that paid for their expensive education, and dad's connections that helped them get their first job. Also, Elitists sometimes work in business environs as professionals servicing profit-seeking enterprises. And, furthermore, they are among the most handsomely paid people in the country. It would seem they are attacking the very class to which they belong and biting the hand that feeds them.

But in fact the New Elite is critically different from the business class—economically, culturally, and psychologically. It is important to note that the New Elite and the business class are not homogeneous groups. Individual variations exist in both groups. To some extent membership in the two groups overlap. Some Elitists are in business; some business people are members of the New Elite. Nonetheless, the central tendencies of the two groups are different. Economically, the business class is closely linked to commerce and industry, to the production of durable products for sale at home and abroad. Culturally, it espouses an ideology of efficiency. Its greatest boast is that it has created a system that works, that the things it makes work, and that it has shown that working is man's sweetest use of time. Psychologically, the business class exalts, and to some extent still exhibits, a character structure derived from the very system the Elite criticizes—the old bourgeois manufacturing economy.

Though once rebellious, in the seventeenth and eighteenth centuries when it was eager to throw off the shackles of feudal privilege, the business class has grown culturally conservative. It now clings to tradition (by which it means the rules and ways of its class) and angrily defends any challenge to established values. It feels threatened by new ways of dressing, speaking, having fun, making music, and cavorting to modern rhythms. To its eyes and ears the new lifestyles of young Elitists are vulgar, absurdly juvenile, and self-indulgent. It is nostalgic for the culture of a mythical past, when the streets were safe and the working class and minorities knew their place, when the business class was cock of the walk.

Psychologically, the typical businessman is a bundle of needs and traits that can be summed up in his model of the ideal man—Darwinian Man—whose character he admires. This model is a complex figure, mixing in one person strangely contrasting elements: the ambitious, free-booting, lusty, risk-taking inclinations of the nineteenth-century entrepreneur; the careful, steady business acumen of the crafty eighteenth-century merchant; the devotion to hard work, frugality, temperance, self-discipline of the seventeenth-century Puritan. Taken singly these characteristics are not new, of course; they have threaded their way through history before and could have been found in other times and places. But never before have they been encapsulated in one character type—the bourgeois Darwinian Man—and presented as a model for all to emulate.

In contrast, the new Elitists make a point of not being bourgeois. Unlike the business class they seldom make material things; rather they move in the world of the incorporeal information economy. Though they may offer their services to businessmen, may in fact work in corporations, they are not full-time business people. In their contact with the business world they usually function as problem-solvers, financial experts, public relations flacks, idea generators, facilitators of corporate melding and restructuring, legal counselors, advertising writers and sales campaign promoters, and other service specialists. Most of the time they talk only to one another. Logging on to computer networks, meeting in special groups to organize campaigns to make or sell products or services, they chatter away at each other, making deals, creating and processing data, solving problems.

As denizens of the knowledge community, they have a vested interest in credentials that certify expertise in marshaling, interpreting, distributing, and conserving information. They take pride in their formal training. The casual attitude the business class tends to take toward certificates, degrees, and other honorific marks of academic attainment baffles them. (A businessman may boast of being self-made, a rough jewel untarnished by advanced schooling; the New Elitist seldom does so.) Elitists may not hang their diplomas on the wall, but they are keenly aware of the nature and provenance of their degrees and in subtle ways take care that others know about their academic training. A good degree from a good school is like money in the bank.

Academic credentials ease the Elitist's access to the government, which has grown accustomed to rank and use people according to their years in school and diplomas earned. This is important because many Elitists have become dependent on government for their livelihood. It is in part for this reason that they see government differently than does the average businessman. To the businessman the government is either a meddling enemy or a compliant cash cow to be milked, a rich source of subsidies and protection for privileged or inefficient corporations, certainly not something to love. Most businessmen would rather be caught cheating on their wives than be heard saying a good word about government.

In contrast, the Elite generally beams approvingly upon government, seeing it as not only a lucrative and reliable source of employment but also as an instrument for promoting greater equality and social justice. Consequently, unlike the businessman, the Elite is not alarmed by the growth of government, nor is it opposed to the welfare state. Some abuses need to be remedied, some fine tuning may be necessary, it concedes, but in principle the New Elite finds nothing objectionable about the government assuming a major share of the responsibility for aiding the poor and disadvantaged, using its power to redistribute income, to erase racial and sexual barriers to economic opportunity, and to level invidious distinctions between groups. The goal of the New Elite is not to reduce the government's role in everyday life but to find ways to expand it. If it takes a bigger government to promote social justice, the Elitist reasons, so be it.

Many New Elitists work for government bureaucracies, processing information and performing services considered invaluable. How could those mountains of paper and intimidating rows of cabinets filled with computer tapes and disks be moved, leveled, tunneled, traversed, and scanned without the aid of workers trained in data management? Most bureaucracies, inundated by tons of data, would founder into bewildered impotence without the diligent assistance of data processors—or so it is said. Other Elitists work in private service agencies, doing yeoman work dispensing warnings about endangered species and global warming, giving advice on what foods to eat or avoid, offering guidance on how to sexually satisfy one's spouse or significant other without getting AIDS, providing instructions about how to avoid getting fat, mugged, or raped, and many other kinds of ostensibly useful information. Still other Elitists depend on government largess to carry on creative work in the arts and sciences. Who else would build the vast laboratories in which scientists delve into nature's secrets? Who would nurture local arts and crafts, and support the orchestras and theaters in which fledgling artists test their wings, if not the government?

Although Elitists are problem solvers and hence not indifferent to the need for efficiency, they believe the businessman's obsession with efficient production seriously obstructs self-realization, the prism through which they view the world. Too much time spent worrying about efficiency leaves too little time to contemplate and improve the self; too much time spent making things leaves too little time to enjoy them. To the hedonistic Elitist the businessman's obsession with efficiency appears as ludicrous as his business practices appear villainous.

THE ROOTS OF BUSINESS HATRED

The New Elite's hostility usually shocks businessmen, who routinely express disbelief that their character should be so maligned.

But they ought not to be surprised. Indeed, only an abysmal ignorance of history can explain the businessmen's startled dismay at the
indictments hurled against them. Truth to tell, the business class has
rarely enjoyed good repute. Almost everywhere it has been the target
of unremitting disparagement, as befits the *nouveau riche* whose
money lacks the patina of respectability that only time can give. Let
us briefly examine this hatred of the businessman. It lies deeply rooted
in Western memory, a reservoir of ancient attitudes which will help
explain the fury many Elitists feel for the business class.

A contempt for people who grow rich in trade runs deep in western
tradition. It was, for example, pronounced among the ancient Greeks
and Romans. Not that they had anything against money. In fact, the
ancient Greeks considered wealth (along with health and heroic glory)
one of the prerequisites for an enjoyable and useful life.[2] It is rather
that they despised practical (physical) work of all kinds. Aristotle believed working for wages in the "industrial arts," by which he meant
any utilitarian labor other than farming, degraded the mind. The
Greeks, who bequeathed a legacy of rational speculation to Western
Civilization, gave economic practicality no place in their philosophy.
Exploring labor costs and capital appreciation, amortizing and depre-
ciating assets, plowing back profits in business production—these
grubby aspects of economic enterprise simply did not interest them.

Among the Greeks "the strong drive to acquire wealth was not
translated into a drive to create capital; stated differently, the prevailing mentality was acquisitive but not productive."[3] Trade and industry did, of course, exist in ancient Greece, but it was primitive,
little admired and of secondary importance. A free-born Athenian
would not touch business if he could help it. Business was given over
to slaves, freedmen, and foreigners, who were treated as outsiders no
matter how long they or their family had lived in Athens. Marrying
rich was fine, inheriting wealth was better, but money grubbing in
commerce and industry was beneath the dignity of free-born men.

In money matters the Romans differed little from the Greeks. Like
the Greek, the Roman's love of money was proverbial, as the hapless
peoples who fell victim to Rome's armies quickly learned. And the
Roman's contempt for business was fully as great as the Hellene's.
To the Roman there were only two honorable ways to get rich: fighting and farming. In the Republic both activities were performed by
the same person, the free land-owning farmer, who would, when
called by the state, lay aside the plow, take up the sword, and go off

to war. If lucky, the soldier would return laden with plunder with which he could buy more land and slaves. It was not wealth as such that offended the sensibilities of the Romans; it was the way the commercial class acquired it—in workshops and counting houses, whose very ambience, according to Cicero, would poison the minds of free men foolish enough to enter it.[4]

After the collapse of the Roman Empire, the status of the businessman grew worse. In the Dark Ages industry outside the manor all but disappeared, and commerce dwindled to a pitiable fragment of its former self. Trade between towns was crippled by bad roads, constant warfare among princes, and raids by barons and bandits, who found merchant caravans too easy pickings to resist. It took time for the barons to learn that it was foolish to kill the golden goose. Only slowly did it dawn on them that it was more profitable in the long run to protect the merchant, periodically plucking his gold, taxing him heavily in the towns, and imposing tolls at intervals along the road and at bridges when he ventured outside the town walls, than to push him into hopeless, immobile poverty. Even so, life for most merchants was harsh and uncertain. Business profits were meager and unreliable, and prospects for improvement gloomy.[5]

On trips in search of trade and profit the Western merchant's life was always at risk and all too likely to end painfully at the hands of some brutish ruffian highwayman. It took courage, even when accompanied by other merchants and occasionally by armed guards, to set out by land on business trips to towns only a few days or weeks journey away. Travel by water was faster and easier and somewhat safer. No barons or highwaymen barred the way, but the seas were infested with pirates or in the control of Muslim powers who felt no compunction about robbing and killing infidel travelers. A merchant could quickly lose everything in a storm, a pirate raid, a chance encounter with an uncooperative, money-hungry chieftain or rapacious prince.

Although the barons and their knights did not cavil at taking the merchant's money, they found associating with townspeople distinctly irritating and confusing. The warrior did not know what to make of this new breed of men. That they were inferior to the fighting man there could be no doubt. The knight, proud of his courage and martial skill, despised the unwarlike townsman and made no effort to disguise his distaste for a life devoted to money grubbing. Convinced of the merchant's base nature, he treated the tradesman with contumely and kept him at a distance, making sure he knew his place and that he behaved with proper deference toward the nobility. But then there was the annoying fact of the townsman's wealth and growing economic power. This seemed to the warrior "so much the more hateful in that it was obtained by means which were at once mysterious and directly opposed to his own interests."[6] Loathing bourgeois culture and fearing business power, the warrior easily came to hate the business class. Vestiges of this ancient animosity can still be found among landowning aristocrats to this day.

The attitude of the medieval Church toward commerce made matters worse; for Christianity, conservatively interpreted, made conducting business difficult, even morally reprehensible, when interest on loans and large profits entered into commercial exchange. The Church could never quite reconcile itself to the crass world of commerce. It had developed in an agricultural society at a time when it was customary to put most people into one of three strata: a landowning aristocracy whose function it was to fight, a peasantry which was expected to work, and a clergy which prayed for the salvation of men's souls. The commercial class, what there was of it, had no explicable place in the Church's theology; its function was little understood, barely tolerated, and always peripheral to the social system. The merchant's goals—getting rich and living well—were considered gross, worldly, and shortsighted. His preoccupation with the mundane world slighted what should have been his real concern, the salvation of his soul. To the Church, whose doctrinal tenets emphasized a commitment to other-worldly concerns, this base preoccupation with material pursuits jeopardized the merchant's chance of saving his soul.

The Church's ascetic ideals suited a subsistence rural economy in which efficiency of production merited no praise whatsoever and received no more attention than was needed for survival. Work on the Sabbath and on religious holidays (of which there were many) was forbidden. Gluttony and pride were cardinal sins, and bourgeois excesses in dress and feasting quickly brought into play sumptuary laws, mandated by the clergy and enforced by the nobility, that sought, usually unsuccessfully, to curb the townsman's penchant to eat, drink, and be as merry as his situation permitted. The merchant (pre-Calvinist variety) saw no reason to stint on food, drink, and apparel, and apportioned his time and life with his own interests in mind. His safety from foreign and domestic predators he turned over to the warrior, his soul's protection he assigned to the keeping of the priest, his work he took into his own hands. His major concern, the main absorber of his time and energy, was making money.

Religious hostility to the businessman, as Henri Pirenne wrote, "prevented the merchants from growing rich with a free conscience and from reconciling the practice of business with the prescriptions of religion."[7] If making money was to spend life badly, lending money at interest a sin, and making a profit a sign of avarice, then the merchant's chance of standing in well with the public was indeed slim and his chance of entering the gates of heaven slimmer yet. People might be hoodwinked, but God's wrath and eventual punishment could not easily be evaded. A class marked out for punishment for avarice and cupidity could hardly hold itself out as an exemplar of civic virtue. Businessmen are finding it difficult to do so even today.

City-dwelling merchants, though unskilled in martial arms and indifferent to the rules of chivalry, nevertheless rarely hesitated to chisel away at the aristocratic way of doing things whenever it got in the way of doing business and making money. Not surprisingly, the aristocracy imputed to this group every conceivable vice. As the aristocracy saw it, "the merchants are rootless, greedy, the source of all evil; they promote luxury and weakness; they distort nature by traveling to far-off lands, violating the natural barriers of the seas and bringing back what nature will not permit us to grow at home."[8] These complaints are still being echoed today in accusations that businessmen use science and technology to violate the natural order of things by genetically altering the fundamental nature of fruits and vegetables, thus enabling them to mature and survive out of season.

How did the peasants, who made up at least 90 percent of the population, feel about the businessman? We don't really know. As far as we know, no one made a note of it. Probably the literate segment of society, the lay clergy and educated members of the church hierarchy, the only people capable of compiling a record of peasant opinion, gave little attention to what the illiterate peasant thought of his betters. This is too bad, because it would be interesting to know if medieval peasants felt toward the merchant class the same way the present-day blue-collar workers feel toward the New Elite. For example, did peasants think merchants too rich, too powerful, too self-absorbed, too little interested in the welfare of the class beneath them? Most likely they did, but we do not know for certain. Lacking an interest in the peasant's political views, the clergy seems not to have bothered to write them down.

If the educated clergy thought about the peasant at all, it was to speculate about his state of grace and the eventual destination of his immortal soul. Neither was cause for congratulation. As the clergy saw it, the average peasant was an inveterate sinner. He fornicated lustily, argued violently (an eating knife was always kept in his belt), and ate glutonously when food was plentiful, which fortunately for his soul's salvation was not often. Hunger stalked the lives of most peasants much of the time. Bad harvests, harsh winters, constant warfare, and intermittent civil disorder made food scarce. Food was always on his mind. His dreams and fantasies were filled with imagery about food. The fabled land of Cockaigne, in which he half believed, featured houses made of food, free for the taking. (The original author of Hansel and Gretel and the gingerbread house would have known of this mysterious land.) For the peasant an idyllic life, such as could be had in Cockaigne, meant free lunches, not free love. Everything considered, the peasant's chances of entering heaven seemed poor, at least not without a lengthy stay-over in purgatory.

Chances are the peasant shared with the aristocracy and the clergy a sharply unfriendly view of the merchant class. Peasant behavior in the Peasant Revolt of 1381 during Richard II's reign would seem to bear this out. Among the targets of peasant fury were the merchants who had raised prices unconscionably during periods of scarcity. Wat Tyler took particular pleasure in setting their homes and warehouses aflame, and more than a few lost their lives.[9]

To sum up: the businessman was almost universally disliked right up to the industrial revolution. He presented a threat to an established order based upon agriculture, inherited wealth, land tenure, a special connection with divine power, and the ability to make war. The feudal system had the support of the Church, which gave it moral sanction and sought to protect it from social change. The business class lacked this advantage. Nothing stood between it and the enmity of the other classes—nothing but its money.

BUSINESS HATRED IN MODERN TIMES

With the advent of industrialization the social status of the businessman improved remarkably. From being a near-pariah, he gradually became a person of stature—respectable, rich, powerful. Using the marvelous machines invented by ingenious mechanics, and his own invention, the efficient factory system, he produced a cornucopia of cheap durable goods. He expanded the network of banks and pumped money into the life-stream of the economy, stimulating trade and encouraging economic development at home and abroad. In time the sinews of industrial capitalism made him strong: seizing the levers of economic and political power he became a person to be reckoned with.

No longer need he defer to arrogant aristocrats, no longer need he beg the government for permission to do business, no longer need he listen in silence to the scolding of the clergy—he could manipulate and dominate them all. The aristocrats he easily bought off, lending them money, marrying his daughters to indigent barons and earls, purchasing estates and manors and eventually becoming a knight himself. The government he slowly took over, infiltrating the political parties, putting his own men in office, and forcing into law those policies that advanced his interests. The clergy he won over with munificent gifts to religious orders and monasteries, with an espousal of religious values, and with the careful public observance of conventional rules of behavior. He became a person to be feared, envied, and even admired.

But in overthrowing the ancient regime he unintentionally made a terrible and implacable enemy, the cultural elite of the time—the critics, novelists, poets, composers, sculptors, and painters of the nineteenth century. They became his nemesis, the bane of his life, the disturber of his peace of mind. Sad to say, he never understood what he had done to offend them. Why did they hate him so? For his part he rather admired literary-artistic people, in a somewhat condescending way to be sure, but nonetheless with genuine, if uninformed, awe for their skill and artistry. He bought their pictures, subscribed to their novels, and praised their poems (he was much too busy to read them, of course, but his wife did), watched their operas, and listened to their music. What more did they want? What more could he do? He never understood their hostility, because he could not understand that he had produced a civilization the literary-artistic elites found utterly abominable. And for this they would never forgive him.

Like a misunderstanding between kinsmen in an ancient Greek tragedy, the fatal consequence of immutable destiny, of a flaw in character, and of a misjudgment of intentions that is both devastating and inevitable, the conflict between the businessman and the literary-artistic elite was bound to happen; they saw the world too differently to live together amicably. What one thought inspiring and beautiful, the other found mindless and ugly. What appealed most to the businessman about the world he was creating were precisely the things the intellectual and the artist found most detestable.

The businessman took from the French Enlightenment the notion that reason is the best guide for all human endeavor. Rationality, the unemotional calibration of means to ends, gave to sentiment no legitimate role in economic affairs. Sentimental ties to kinfolk and friends, obligations to workers other than the money paid for services rendered, emotional appeals for help, all these were to be resisted as impediments to efficient production. The Goddess Reason, which the French revolutionaries of 1789 had enshrined in their political philosophy, was transmogrified in the theology of conservative business from an incendiary supporter of revolution into a bulwark of capitalist enterprise, a goddess of machines, production, and profit. The new industrial world required a modern pantheon of serviceable deities, and Reason eminently belonged in that select group.

The businessman was proud of his ability to use reason, science, and technology to extract from nature its hidden treasures and to harness its power for man's benefit. His class was the first to treat science as something more than an intellectual game to tickle the imagination, or technology as something more than a source of toys to amuse children; he insisted that they have practical uses. How could he not be practical about science and technology when practicality is what business is all about? And so the businessman, with undisguised hubris, boasted of his ability to employ science and technology to wring from nature those bounteous gifts of mineral wealth and energy it had so long withheld or had granted only grudgingly. To the businessman, beauteous nature, like a pretty barmaid or a secretary, could not get by on good looks alone; she must prove herself worthy by being useful.

Utility was at the core of the businessman's worldview. Business-men tended to assess their own value and that of others, and the value of most products of human endeavor, according to how well each measured up against a standard of usefulness. True disciples of John Locke and Jeremy Bentham, philosophers of utility, they took for granted that a product was useful to the degree that it contributed to human material well-being and happiness. Since machines were de-monstrably useful, efficiently increasing the production of numerous goods for the general public, they used them whenever possible and profitable. Everyone gained in the process, even the working poor. It was the machine, as Joseph Schumpeter pointed out, that made it possible for every shopgirl to purchase silk stockings, a luxury which once only the rich could afford.[10]

THE MORAL BASIS OF BUSINESS-CLASS POWER

The New Elite's attack on the business class should not be dis-missed as the ranting of disaffected eggheads, crazy esthetes, and am-bitious careerists. Far from being trivial, it is serious. It can be mortal because it challenges the moral right of the business class to hold power. In order to wield power effectively, every ruling class must convince the populace of its moral right to govern. Granted, a ruling class may win power by force of arms and even keep it for a time, but it will not hold it for very long unless the people believe this power is morally justified, sanctioned by motives that transcend per-sonal advantage. Without strong moral legitimacy, power is always shaky and prone to fracture under the stress of hardship and privation. When times grow intolerable, popular grumbling about inequalities in wealth and privilege mount, violent dissent and rebellion break out, and eventually the regime collapses.

A number of things can lend legitimacy to power—for example, lineage, arcane knowledge, and religion. None of them works all the time, of course, though some work better than others. Religion has by far the best track record, but there are many examples of painful failure. King Charles I of England appeared secure for a while, for he played it safe, appealing to both lineage and religion—his family connections and the divine right of kings. But a counter-religion, Puritanism, proved too strong and Charles lost his head. On the other hand, religion coupled with special knowledge—the nature of the gods and the timing of the Nile floods—helped keep the priesthood in pharonic Egypt in power for millennia.

In the beginning the business class also found its legitimacy in a religion, ascetic Protestantism. On first inspection, an ascetic religion would seem an unlikely supporter of business, which makes worldly gain one of its main goals. Ascetics are not supposed to be interested in worldly goods. Nevertheless, as Max Weber implied, ascetic Protestantism gave to capitalism a supportive moral thrust that carried it to new heights. Ascetic Protestantism elevated work from a curse to a religious calling. It contributed to the development of a new character type, bourgeois Darwinian Man, self-disciplined, sober, prudent, hard working, ambitious and driven to succeed. This constellation of moral traits, aggressive tendencies, and repressed needs gave the Protestant businessman a distinctly better chance of being successful in the newly competitive world of commerce than his more relaxed, self-indulgent, less driven competitor. Buttressed by religious conviction, the businessman became an instrument of God, an enricher of the world, a terrible sword to cut down the ancient barriers to worldly success.

Success in business was seen as a sign of good character and of God's favor. Naturally, it was understood that business success did not in itself guarantee God's good will. God is not so easily won over. But surely, it was argued, success in business could be taken as a sign that God smiled on one's efforts to get rich, and from this it seemed logical to infer that God had decided favorably about one's ultimate destiny, a secure place in heaven. Admittedly, this line of reasoning was self-serving, though entirely human, and perhaps even mistaken. Can one ever be sure how God's mind works? Still, the effect of ascetic Protestantism on the businessman was to combine, in a mysterious alchemy, two unlikely ingredients—a wish to grow rich and a gnawing hunger to know how one stood with the deity.

Eventually, as a result of a long process of secularization and industrialization extending over generations, during which the Protestant Ethic evolved into the Spirit of Capitalism, the connection between business and religion became attenuated. By the late nineteenth century the connection had pretty much disappeared, and most businessmen quietly abandoned any serious effort to justify their work in religious terms. They did not stop, however, trying to give capitalism a moral basis. No ruling class, not even the complacent business class, is so stupid as to ignore the importance of a moral explanation for its power. A justification was found; it was, however, secular rather than religious.

Probably no contemporary businessman would dream of trying to justify the system that made him rich and powerful as God's will, as John D. Rockefeller did, albeit with little success. (Money was posthumously successful. The Rockefeller Foundation and other philanthropies have clothed the family dynasty with more public approval than the founder ever knew in his lifetime. Forgotten are his machinations in building Standard Oil.) Henry Ford, perhaps learning from Rockefeller's experience, never tried it at all. And few, if any, modern businessmen even give it a thought. God and organized religion are no longer seen as necessarily on capitalism's side.

If religion no longer gives the business class moral underpinning, what is it to do? It must do something. The need to justify its power has not lessened. If anything, it has grown greater as the attacks on businessmen have increased. What it has done, in fact, is to offer a secular justification for the business system that it believes is attuned to the sensibilities of the industrial age.

The business class now argues that it deserves popular support because of its contributions to the public welfare—an efficient economy, a freer polity, and a more just society. The businessman argues that his system is a marvel of efficiency, that no other system can match its ability to produce goods and services and generate as much wealth with as much consistency. This would seem to be a hard argument to refute. Even Karl Marx agreed with it. Strange to say, the founder of a movement dedicated to capitalism's overthrow was an admirer of capitalism. He thought it a dynamo of production. But he believed it had seen its best days and was doomed to die. The free market was too irrational and chaotic, too bedeviled by inner contradictions to survive. Communism would inevitably take charge simply because central planners in government bureaucracies, guided by experts surrounded by mountains of impeccable information, would be more efficient than individual capitalists at organizing production and distributing the fruits of an industrial economy. In a way, fate has been kind to Marx; he escaped having to explain the economic collapse of the Soviet Union or the evolution of Chinese communism into oriental despotism with a capitalist face.

The trouble with trying to justify capitalism in terms of its technical virtuosity, as Irving Kristol pointed out, is not that efficiency is unimportant—rather, that it is morally uninspiring.[11] Corporate managers may feel their pulses quicken and their hearts race at capitalism's promise to increase productivity and enlarge the Gross Domestic Product. But to the idealistic young this is watery stuff, very thin gruel to satisfy a gnawing hunger for spiritual uplift and personal growth. Bread is fine, one cannot live without it, but even the finest bread smeared with the most delectable imported cheese becomes tasteless when life lacks meaning. And for life in a business-dominated system, as in any society, to have meaning, it must help people understand why they are living—or so the moralists say.

Even though material improvement may not make life more meaningful, and even though not everyone's condition has improved to the same degree, it seems fair to say that on the whole the material lot of the average citizen in the United States has in fact markedly improved under the aegis of the business class. As to freedom, the businessman tends to think of freedom primarily in economic terms, as the right to make choices in the marketplace, to buy or sell whatever one chooses to anyone, without government permission or interference—hence the emphasis on breaking the power of government to establish monopolies, to set high tariffs on commodities, and to control prices. (There is less objection to the government putting tariffs on certain imported goods or encouraging low wages, and keeping labor docile.) Breaking the power of government required enlarging the electorate, and this the business class promoted in the belief that the new voters would support the economic objectives of business.

The claim of the business class to have created a more just society is based on the belief—rather naive, as we see now—that prosperity will naturally lead to greater civic virtue and hence to a just society. This faith in the power of money to smooth out the rough edges of the system stems from the assumption that privation brings out the worst in people, and that material abundance would solve all social problems by removing their economic cause. This is an idea to which the business class still fondly clings. Routinely it offers increased economic growth as a standard prescription for eliminating social injustice, arguing that greater economic growth will as a matter of course generate the money needed to treat the ills of society, particularly the deplorable condition of the poor, the sick, and the unlucky.

None of these arguments convinces the New Elite. To the New Elite, businessmen are hypocrites who hide their selfish actions behind claims to benevolent consequences. This claim, Elitists say, is false and self-serving, based on willful ignorance and an uncanny ability to ignore unpleasant facts. For how can businessmen say the material condition of society has improved when the poor are still with us, when homeless indigents roam the streets by day and sleep in cardboard boxes on wintry nights, when the rich grow fat and the poor struggle to put meat on the table?

How can the businessman say he has created a more just society when civil rights are being violated and oppression degrades innocent victims, though many of them, it turns out, are self-designated victims, protected by law and favored with governmental largess. Since the number of these victims is ballooning rapidly, something must be amiss. The business society has failed to deliver the even-handed justice promised to all, rich and poor, high and low alike. What kind of freedom has the businessman increased? The freedom to make money, of course. But real freedom, as the New Elite defines it, still languishes in neglect.

Freedom to the New Elite means more than not having to cope with governmental obstruction in the marketplace. It means the right to live pretty much as one pleases so long as no other person is harmed; it means, among other things, the right to be openly gay or lesbian, to have an abortion, to smoke pot, to view pornography, to teach multiculturalism in the schoolroom, to challenge all orthodoxies, its own excepted. And to radical egalitarian New Elitists true justice means not only impartial and equal treatment—before the law, in the workplace, and in the pursuit of success; it means, most importantly, the right to a condition of life equal to that of anyone, equal in status and power and possessions, without regard to individual merit or contribution.

FRUIT JARS AND THEME PARKS

When the business class speaks of the benign effect of business on the moral condition of society, it sometimes nostalgically evokes the memory of a business world that has all but vanished. Well into the early years of the twentieth century most American businesses were small, family-owned, and family-managed. The owner of a business usually lived in the community in which he made his money. In many cases this was a town or small city where he would be recognized on sight and greeted politely, though not with servility. As a man of substance, he was expected to live in a way that helped people understand how a meaningful and moral life should be led. He took part in local affairs, attended and supported a local church, sent his children to local schools, and gave generously to local charities. He was expected to be a visible force for the common good.

To accomplish this goal, his money, though certainly useful, would not alone suffice. He had to show that he was not merely rich in dollars; he had also to prove that he was rich in character, that he was above all a person of high moral stature, generous and responsive to the needs of the community, an uplifting model for his less prosperous fellow citizens. As difficult as it is for Americans today to believe, it was this moral component, exemplified in his family life and public benevolence, as much as in his money, that made the businessman an object of admiration, a person to copy, a cultural hero in the nineteenth and early twentieth centuries.

Examples of this kind of hero were the five Ball brothers of Muncie, Indiana.[12] After trying their hands at various work—one was a farm hand and timber cutter, one a physician, the others small manufacturers of fishing kits—the brothers turned to the glass business. In 1887, on a $7,000 investment, they built a factory to make fruit jars; by 1935 the Ball company was the largest manufacturer of fruit jars in the world. For generations, preserving food and the Ball jar were inseparable, and even today anyone who preserves fruits or vegetables will know what a Ball jar looks like.

Success did not come easy. The brothers were frugal, hardworking hustlers who took part in every aspect of the company's operation. On the factory floor they practiced a form of hands-on management that no doubt contributed to the success of the company. Said one person of a Ball brother who had been in charge of production in the plant: "He always worked on a level with his employees. He never asked a man to do something he would not do himself." By the mid-1930s the Ball family, considerably enlarged through marriage and progeny, had investments in other enterprises besides manufacturing jars. They owned the city's largest department store, held controlling shares in the local bank, acquired an interest in a milk company and a nearby brewery, built a major real estate development in the northwest section of the city, and owned entirely the city's interconnecting trunk railways. Critics of the Balls complained that their business success stemmed in no small part from the low wages paid to their workers, forty-two cents an hour in 1935, paltry pay even in that grim depression year. The Balls justified their wage policy by arguing that only by keeping labor costs low could the company remain profitable. Higher wages, they said, would drive the company out of business and everyone would suffer, owners and workers alike, a rationale for keeping wages down still in vogue today.

On the other hand, low wages aside, the family had a reputation for looking out for its workers. The Balls knew many of their workers by name; they took an interest in the older workers especially, and during the depression carried some unnecessary workers on the payroll. It was characteristic of the company that when a woman was told she would be laid off during a slack period and began to cry, explaining that her husband was out of work and that her family was living on water and five loaves of bread a week, the management responded to her plight. She was told, "Send your old man around and I'll give him a job." And he was hired.

The family was involved in almost every aspect of community life. Staunch conservatives, they were active in the local Republican Party, the Masonic Temple, and the Chamber of Commerce. Education was of particular interest to them. A member of the family served on the school board; and the local State Teacher's College, which would eventually carry the family's name, received sums large enough to endow programs and erect buildings. They contributed generously to the Community Fund, the Y.M.C.A. and Y.W.C.A., and to numerous local charities. The Ball Memorial Hospital was an outright gift by the family to the city.

The Balls considered religion a civilizing influence on the community, and several local churches benefited from family generosity, which was sufficient to enable several churches to carry out their building programs. No scandal marred the family name, and its reputation for integrity steadied the local bank and reassured the community during the grim depression years when many banks across the country were closing, leaving depositors shaken and destitute. To sum up, the Balls were an omnipresent force in the community, and even their critics admitted that their influence was on the whole a good one.

It would be claiming too much to say that the Balls and people like them in communities around the country were enough to give moral legitimacy to the business system in the United States. This was too difficult a task for a relatively small group of entrepreneurs to accomplish on their own. But at times they strengthened the moral backbone of the community in which they lived and helped soften the rising anger against the business system that hard times were beginning to create. In any event, the issue of their role in legitimating capitalism became moot, or at least less relevant, as their importance declined. As major players in the economic game, small family-owned companies have become a dwindling force. Whatever part they may have once played in representing the business class to the public, that role is now a thing of the past. They can no longer be depended upon to lend a benevolent aura to the businessman's image. A new figure now fashions the public's perception of the business class—the corporate manager.

The power of the New Elite to shape the public's image of the business class can be seen by contrasting the way the media once treated the entrepreneur with how the contemporary corporate manager fares today at the hands of the elite media. Whereas, in the past, the successful businessman was someone to be treated gingerly and with respect (the mudrakers's treatment of magnates such as Rockefeller aside), the corporate manager today is often regarded with suspicion and resentment. The media revel in laying open his follies, misjudgments, and excessive remuneration for a job all too often badly done. He is blamed for corporate downsizing and business failure, called greedy and incompetent. In the eyes of the media the corporate manager, far from being a benevolent figure, has become a symbol of heartlessness, a cold manipulator of people, a tyrant obsessed with profit and indifferent to the pain his policies engender.

This change in viewpoint is in part the work of the New Elite, whose members produce the material that fill the media. But it also reflects a change in the economy. When the publicly-owned corporation replaced the family-operated business as the keystone of America's economic edifice, the corporate manager became the representative of business to the public. Unfortunately, corporate managers tend not to be inspiring figures. Often they are financial experts or engineers, colorless, reserved, and dedicated to the bottom line. They work for companies they neither own nor necessarily love; their only loyalty is to their careers, their families, and perhaps a few associates. When they can better themselves, they think nothing of pulling up stakes and abandoning the company to take care of itself. Their ties to the community are tenuous and contact with employees minimal, since they cannot possibly know more than a tiny fraction of the hundreds or thousands of people who make up the company's work force. Nor are they widely known outside the company's ambit. How many Americans know the name of the president of General Motors, the world's largest corporation; or the identity of the man who manages Boeing, the world's largest aircraft manufacturer? In large measure, they are invisible to the general public.

Occasionally a corporate manager gains the public's attention, and becomes a celebrity, someone who represents forces greater than his company. This happened to Michael Eisner, chief executive officer of the Walt Disney Company, when his company proposed building a Civil War theme park near the Bull Run (Manasas) battlefield, not far from Washington, District of Columbia. The reaction of the media and the public to Eisner's proposal highlights the enormous change in the way the contemporary businessman is seen as compared with the treatment he would have received in the past.

Perhaps to Eisner's surprise his proposal met with something less than unanimous support. True, the Virginia legislature liked it; the park was seen as a potential boost to tourism and a source of revenue to the state. But to a group of Civil War buffs, historians and other academics, writers, and environmentalists the idea was anathema. They expressed disbelief, outrage, and horror at the idea that the most tragic war in American history could be fit material for an amusement park, where distortion and trivialization were inevitable. A combat team was quickly assembled and dispatched to the media. Op-ed articles were written, appearances made on television, presentations given to Congress—all condemning the proposed park as an environmental disaster in the making and an affront to the memory of the men who had died in the war.

In vain Eisner protested that the park would be a contribution to the cultural life of the nation, not a detriment, a faithful rendition of history, not a distortion. By mixing fun with education, the park would make the past vivid to people for whom the Civil War was an all-but-forgotten episode in American history. He assured the public that proper solicitude would be given to the feelings of all the parties in the war, and that every effort would be made to make the exhibitions factually accurate. This alone shows how naive Eisner and his associates were. Historians have been arguing for more than 130 years about the facts of the Civil War. Even now what caused it and why it was won—or lost—are questions that still engender lively, often bitter, debate. Whatever made a group of businessmen think they knew or could learn the "facts" of the war?

But all these protestations of good faith were to no avail. The clamor against the theme park grew louder and more angry with every day. Finally, recognizing that the company could not afford to alienate the public, which tends to be suspicious of corporate motives and not at all inclined to regard corporation managers as disinterested educators, the proposal was dropped. But had he angered the public? We do not know. No national survey was ever taken to find out what the public, that great anonymous mass of ticket buyers who crowd into theme parks like Disneyland every day, making corporations rich and shareholders happy, really thought about a Civil War theme park. Perhaps people think education should be fun, even instruction about a national calamity like the Civil War, and would pay good money to hear a robot Abraham Lincoln recite the Gettysburg Address or visit a true-to-life slave quarter (Eisner believed this would be particularly educational), and the like.

Probably without his ever recognizing it, Eisner had tangled with a particularly articulate portion of the New Elite, which took it for granted that the motives of corporate management were base, that its sensibilities were coarse, and that its pursuit of profit would inevitably debase the memory of the Civil War. For how could a merchant of fantasy, a maker of cartoons, and a manufacturer of Mickey Mouse beer mugs and Goofy T-shirts understand the meaning of a catastrophe that had taken the lives of more than 600,000 Americans? It was assumed that he could not. That Eisner fought as long as he did demonstrates again the obtuseness of the business class in its dealings with the New Elite, the failure to understand the folly of jousting with intellectuals on their own turf—the field of words and ideas.

That Eisner, running headlong into the buzzsaw of an adversarial culture operated by the New Elite, had been pitilessly shredded was to be expected. For the Elitists, imbued with ideological enthusiasm, have an agenda of their own; they want to punish America for its sins, capture the culture, and seize the reins of power from the hands of the business elite. Brooking no opposition, they are engaged in a gigantic struggle with the business class for control of the country. Whether they will defeat the businessman as they have the blue-collar worker cannot now be foretold. But the vigor, tenacity, and ferocity with which the New Elite fights bodes ill for the continued hegemony of the business class, which is divided and does not understand its enemy.

But the odds are not entirely on the side of the New Elite. It too has become divided; it too is having trouble justifying its actions; it too is becoming confused. The problem for the New Elite, in part, is the Chameleon Complex—the emotional and ideological vehicle that the New Elite uses on its road to power. That the Chameleon Complex is a powerful tool in the Elite's war with the business class cannot be denied. Unfortunately, it is a vehicle beset by basic contradictions, inherent flaws that are causing conflict between groups, alienating the Elite from the general public, and creating divisions within the Elite itself. We turn now to the nature of these contradictions and their effects.

PART V

THE CONTRADICTIONS OF ELITE IDEOLOGY

12

Affirmative Inequality

Cynics say that the more things change the more they remain the same. This is a point of view that puzzles many Americans, who see change everywhere, inevitable, rapid, constant and intrusive, touching their lives at almost every point, sometimes creating new and vexatious problems and headaches, at other times bringing with it new opportunities, new sights and new sounds to excite the imagination. But perhaps they are confusing change with mere motion—the flux of fads and fashions.

It is true that every year Detroit turns out cars with changed grills, fenders, colors, and interior decor. Every year, New York dictates new fashions in wearing apparel—skirts with lower or higher hemlines, dresses with padded or natural shoulders, suits with smaller or larger lapels, trousers with cuffs or without. And every year, Hollywood churns out new songs and dances, performed by an ever-changing galaxy of stars whose meteoric rise to popular fame is matched only by their equally rapid fall into obscurity. Of course, none of this necessarily represents serious change; they may only be evanescent sparkles on an essentially still sea. But in fact there have been many changes of true importance—a point this book has gone to some pains to make.

Why then have some observers remarked on the tenacious resistance of American society to change, notwithstanding the repeated

assertions of Americans that things now are totally different from
what they used to be? It is, in part, because they can point to aspects
of American culture that have survived for well over a century with
little apparent change. Take, for example, the contradictions between
merit and equality, and between individualism and conformity. Long
ago Alexis de Tocqueville ruminated on the contradiction between
the emphasis Americans put on merit as the only valid basis for par-
celing out rewards, and their yearning for equality. He also expressed
surprise that Americans had not seen the inherent inconsistency between their insistence on individual freedom and their efforts to impose conformity on dissidents. Tocqueville was not the last to note
these contradictions; similar observations have been made by the
Englishman Denis Brogan and the Americans David Riesman and
Robert Bork.[1]

To these observers it was obvious that merit and equality must be
at loggerheads—the greater the emphasis upon merit, the greater the
inequality. For it is certain that in the race for success the bright and
ambitious sprinter will soon outdistance the dull and lackadaisical laggard. Also, it is hard to deny that however much Americans applaud
individualism, they expect conformity to the popular will, even to the
extent of legislating it. Few countries have sought to restrict what and
how much people drink, eat, and smoke, and with whom they for-
nicate, to the degree that America has. This being the case, why not
admit that contradictions exist in American culture, that efforts to
change them have gone nowhere, and that change is not as great as
most people think?

Partly because the contradictions between merit and equality, and
between individualism and conformity, are in fact truly different today than in the past. For one thing, they originated in different kinds
of societies. Originally they flourished in a country that was still in-
completely industrialized. Competition for work and money was controlled and muted. Large segments of the population—women and
blacks—were excluded from the paid labor force or restricted in what
they could do. Deviants were expected to find outlets for their energies by escaping to the frontier.

Several political parties and religious organizations sharpened and
publicized the contradictions they saw in the culture. Progressives and
Socialists denounced inequality, vigorously hammered away at the
need to reduce differences in wealth, and alerted Americans to the
inconsistency between their advocacy of equality and the inequality

growing throughout the country. As to the conflict between individualism and conformity, it was often a religious group that sought to impose its standards of morality on the general public, notwithstanding the desires of some individuals to go their own way.

The situation today is in some respects significantly different. Political parties and religious groups still influence the culture and try to shape behavior—witness the struggle to abolish or preserve abortion—but there is now a new player on the scene, the New Elite. Today, the cultural contradictions besetting the country—between merit and equality, and between individualism and conformity—are in the main the work of Elitists who, following the dictates of the Chameleon Complex, are seeking to impose their ideology upon the rest of the country.

It is the Elite's commitment to the job of creating an egalitarian society that fuels its determination to wipe out differences in status, wealth, and power. At the same time it insists that merit alone should determine success, the promoter of inequality. And it is the Elite's conviction of their superiority that permits them, unperturbed by counter-argument and scruple, to move against their opponents, ruthlessly stamping out opposition. At the same time, paradoxically, they continue to assert the inalienable right of everyone to think and act as he or she sees fit.

Elitists usually see no contradiction in any of this. Perhaps, if pressed, they will admit to minor inconsistencies, but these are excused as temporary rough spots that will eventually be ironed out. Nonetheless, despite their protestations of innocence, the contradictions are there. Perhaps they can be ignored, dismissed, or denied; but recognized or not they have important consequences. Elitists caught in embarrassing and painful contradictions must devote considerable energy keeping them under control, usually by burying them under denial. But there is a price for this; denial breeds ambivalence and enervating resentment, which require more and more repression to hide.

In addition to their emotional impact on individual Elitists, these cultural contradictions have also created divisions within the New Elite as a whole. Factions within the New Elite argue over the merit of sacrificing merit in order to achieve equality; and they are fighting among themselves over the morality of coercing the individual in the interest of the group. The Elitists are not the only ones distressed by this squabble. Sadly, innocent people are being hurt. When they fight back, the Elitists, surprised that their well-meaning actions are being resisted, move to control dissent, even among groups to whom Elitist squabbles are of little interest.

This chapter examines the clash between merit and equality, and the strife it has produced, both inside and outside the Elitist group. The next chapter will focus on the contradiction between the Elite's stress on individualism and the importance it places on securing absolute conformity to its will. These ideological contradictions embedded in the Chameleon Complex are not only distressing Elitists; they are contributing to the discontent and cynicism now reverberating throughout the country.

INEQUALITY IN AMERICA

Alexis-Henri-Charles-Maurice Clerel was wrong. America was not as equalitarian as he apparently believed. The "general equality of condition among the people" he believed existed during his visit in 1831 was in reality marred by deep-rooted inequalities.[2] In the south blacks were enslaved, treated as chattel that could be bought and sold like cattle, and owned for the most part by a plantocracy whose power and wealth would have brought grimaces of envy from the aristocrats of France's *ancien regime*. Women were not enfranchised, and in some states they lost control of their property upon marriage. The prosperous class, large land owners, merchants and professionals, were wary of the lower orders and carefully built into the electoral system ingenious checks to the common people's full participation in politics.

The bulk of America's free population was composed of farmers, nostalgically remembered as sturdy prosperous yeomen, though in fact their lives were often hard and poverty-ridden. Most shopkeepers and craftsmen in the towns and cities were likewise comparatively poor and had little property besides the stock in their stores and the tools of their trade. Though they vehemently asserted their equality to their neighbors and to the powerful landed proprietors and rich merchants in the cities, poverty sharply limited the independence of many Americans. Clerel knew this, of course. He was neither blind nor a fool. No doubt the United States appeared equalitarian when compared with monarchical France, in which he held the title of Comte de Tocqueville. Nevertheless, all in all, the America of Tocqueville's day was certainly no egalitarian society.

But then most Americans have never wanted complete equality.

Extreme political inequality was unacceptable, and in time they re-moved most of the restrictions against popular participation in the political system. Women and blacks got the vote; senators became elected by popular vote; property requirements for voter eligibility were abandoned. But marked inequality in wealth and income per-sisted—and still persists. Despite the best efforts of reformers, income inequality stubbornly refuses to go away. Indeed, far from disappear-ing, the gap between the rich and the poor has grown in the last two decades. Inequality, which had narrowed during the period from 1929 to 1969, started to widen in the early 1970s. By the mid-1990s, the top 20 percent of American households received eleven times as much income as the bottom 20 percent, up from a multiple of 7.5 in 1969.[3]

At present, the richest quintile of households commands 45 percent of the country's net income, whereas the poorest quintile has only a 4 percent share. The plight of the bottom 20 percent of the popu-lation has been attributed to the growing number of single-parent families, many on welfare, and to a surge in the number of unskilled immigrants whose wages are low.[4] No significant change in their cir-cumstances is in sight. How accurately these statistics describe the true state of inequality in America as a whole is the subject of angry debate. Not everyone believes the poor have become poorer. For instance, sociologist Christopher Jencks thinks the material condition of the poor has actually improved during the past two decades. "Rich families with children do seem to have grown richer," says Jencks, "but poor families did not necessarily grow poorer."[5]

On one fact almost everyone agrees: the rich are getting richer. Take the chief executive officers of large American firms: they are earning ever larger multiples of the wages paid to workers on the factory floor. (Plato thought a fair multiple would be five times as much as the lowliest worker. On this score, as in many others, Amer-icans pay no heed to the Greek philosopher.) A recent study of 292 *Fortune* 500 companies found the ratio of executive salaries to work-ers' wages was 143 to 1 in 1992, approached 185 to 1 in 1995, and it is still growing.[6] Extreme inequality never sat well with liberal re-formers and intellectuals. The populists in the nineteenth century thundered against it; and early in the twentieth century the Socialist Party made money equality a part of its political program. Today, though they differ on how to bring it about, egalitarians believe it is the duty of government to reduce, if not entirely eliminate, inequality in wealth and income.

But most Americans reject absolute equality of wealth. When they speak of equality, they mean the right to equal treatment under the law in an open society where advancement is available to everyone. They emphatically do not mean everyone must live on the same level. Quite the reverse; they readily accept extreme differences in wealth and power. True, some people complain about a rentier class or an international conspiracy of bankers and financiers living off the work of others. But most Americans have never been, and are certainly not now, bent on leveling the entire society.

This has long mystified intellectuals who consider class exploitation a sovereign explanation for popular discontent. Karl Marx, for example, confessed to being nonplussed by the failure of the working class in America to recognize the class roots of their downtrodden condition. The United States, he believed, was ripe for revolution. It had reached the stage that, in his theory, made America an ideal target for revolutionary takeover. It was highly industrialized; it had an urban proletariat living in squalor; and it possessed an educated elite equipped to seize the reins of government. What it lacked was an objectively accurate view of reality. Marx blamed the torpid state of American politics on "false consciousness," the inability or unwillingness of the workers to consider themselves an exploited class whose only chance for improvement was revolution.

Other explanations have been offered. Some critics attribute the workers' stubborn refusal to become revolutionaries to the unexpected ability of the capitalist system to change and grow, producing over time the cascades of wealth that prevented the class polarization Marx had predicted would be the inevitable undoing of capitalist societies. The labor unions also ameliorated life for some workers by winning for them a larger share of the wealth their industry had helped produce. There are other explanations—most notably the high rate of social mobility in the United States that gives workers the hope of becoming rich themselves someday. One study found that in the mid-1980s in a single year 18 percent of families in the bottom income quintile moved up, and that a third of families in the bottom quintile moved into the top half within a single generation.[7] The poor man rising from rags to riches is a familiar figure in American folklore.

You might think most workers would be angry about the enormous disparity between their income and that of the bosses. Perhaps they are, but there is little evidence of it. At the Campbell Soup Company workers did not brandish clubs at chairman David Johnson when the press reported his pay package was $6.6 million in 1995; nor were there demonstrations against chairman Donald Beall of Rockwell International, who pocketed a neat $5.5 million.[8] But this is small beer compared to the total pay of John F. Welch, chairman of General Electric. In 1997 the company announced that it would raise Welch's pay from $22.5 to $30 million. If this announcement raised private hackles, it brought no public protests. Americans seem not to begrudge the rich their wealth as long as the money was fairly earned. Indeed, successful entrepreneurs and managers, even when extravagantly rewarded, are generally admired.

As already noted, there has been from time to time pressure on government to do something about narrowing the money gap between the social classes. In the late nineteenth and early twentieth centuries, union leaders, agrarian populists, and socialist levelers proposed steeply progressive income taxes and heavy inheritance levies to reduce the immense differences in wealth between the rich and the poor, between the workers and the bosses—and for a time this seemed to be working. In 1929 the richest 1 percent of the population held 42.6 percent of the nation's wealth; by 1970 the figure had dropped to 17.6 percent. But then inequality began to rise in the 1970s, and by 1989 the richest 1 percent controlled 36.3 percent of the country's wealth.[9]

Even so there has been no general outcry against inequality. The rich may be envied but they are not the targets of organized animus, since they tend not to be blamed for inequality. Rather, the misfortunes of the poor are generally thought to be of their own making, a result of moral failure, something that government can do nothing about. One poll in 1990 reported that only 29 percent of the people interviewed favored the government taking action to reduce income differentials.[10]

Needless to say, the New Elite considers this attitude callous, morally obtuse, and repugnant. Elitists believe underprivileged groups should not be held responsible for their sad condition. They argue that the responsibility is the government's and that it must act affirmatively to help the poor and disadvantaged and to reduce inequality. Elitists long for equality with a passion akin to that of medieval monks aching for salvation. To Elitists inequality is not simply an economic condition; it is a moral blemish on society, damning evidence of intolerable imperfection. This, of course, they cannot abide. They consider it a flaw to be erased, and consider that task to be their special mission.

But there is more to it than that. By espousing greater equality,

Elitists believe they are demonstrating their own moral superiority over boorish people who lack compassion for the poor and unfortunate. It is this need to prove their superiority, certainly as much as any pain they may feel over the plight of the oppressed, that motivates them. For the feeling of moral superiority is a narcotic to Elitists; they yearn to feel its narcissistic rush. Pushed by this motive and intoxicated by the ideology of equality, they have championed affirmative action to reduce or eliminate inequality in America. They have sought to disarm opponents by defending the practice of preferences and quotas as overdue justice. But only an ideologically intoxicated group driven by a need for perfection could have failed to foresee the controversy their programs would generate. What they call fairness has been called by their opponents reverse discrimination. The normal anxiety created by competition for jobs and advancement has been greatly embittered, and civil discourse has taken on a distinctly uncivil tone.

The controversy over affirmative action is by now a familiar story, the subject of endless discussion in the media and debate in the halls of legislatures. Jobs and money and power are at stake, and few people are neutral on the workings of affirmative action. Some cry foul and call for its abolishment; others say it has not yet had time to fulfill its promise and call for its strengthening. Governments and the courts, responding to public opinion, have taken steps to deal with the matter, generally moving in the direction of curtailing racial and gender preferences, quotas, and set-asides or even eliminating them altogether. This is usually interpreted as a response to economic and political realities; people with political clout feel injured by government-induced equality and want it killed.

But it is a misleading simplification to regard the response to affirmative action as primarily economic or political. As already noted, the economic pie is huge and growing, and Americans have been extraordinarily flexible about how it should be cut up. It is a matter for negotiation. And after some wrangling, the absolute amount allotted to most people has usually been increased, even if their portion relative to that of others has changed little.

What makes affirmative action exceptionally divisive is the growing awareness that more than jobs and money are at stake. A war of values is taking place, a war over the relative value of merit and equality. Increasingly, ordinary people are coming to understand the inherent contradiction between merit and equality. And they now recognize that the Elite seeks the impossible, that its simultaneous championing of merit and equality reeks with hypocrisy, and that it is willing to sacrifice the interests of some groups to further the goals of others. With this perspective in mind, it can be useful to review several examples of the fight over affirmative action. They show that the battle over affirmative action is about something more than money and power—that it is also resisted because it is seen as offensive to the values many people hold dear.

MORE EQUAL THAN OTHERS

Impatient with the slow workings of economic change that seems to have made money inequality worse, dismayed by gross inequities in wealth and income, and passionately convinced of the righteousness of their cause, the New Elite engineered the enactment of legislation designed to improve the social and economic condition of their favorite groups—blacks and women. Building on the welfare legislation of the 1930s and the civil rights acts of the 1960s, they put in place affirmative action programs that have significantly improved the condition of minorities. Quotas were devised to guarantee places in school for minorities. Set-asides were instituted to insure government contracts for minority businesses. And employment practices were modified so that the number of minorities in jobs, in political offices, in cultural affairs, in positions of influence and power in the mass media, and in all institutions of learning will accurately reflect the demographic composition of the population. To paraphrase President Bill Clinton's famous comment about the makeup of his cabinet: the distribution of people holding positions in work, culture, education, and power must look the way America looks— diverse by race and ethnicity and gender.

But there was an unexpected price for the policy; the already tense relationship between blacks and whites, and between men and women, worsened. Men complained when women competed for jobs once considered male prerogatives; they howled angrily when their bosses, wary of tangling with affirmative action regulations, pass them over for promotion in favor of women. On the other hand, women threatened lawsuits when they thought gender discrimination barred their way to employment and promotion, and based their argument upon rules embodied in civil rights legislation. Whites complained that governmental policies gave minorities an unfair advantage in the competition for jobs and contracts. Blacks retorted that the cards have long been stacked against them and now they want a better deal.

Elitists believe that blacks, particularly young, poorly educated black males, need and deserve help. Victims of prejudice, discrimination, and massive economic dislocation, young inner-city black men, many of them school dropouts, unskilled and unaccustomed to the regimentation of daily work, have been devastated by the decline of manufacturing. The rise of the service economy hasn't helped them much. Unfortunately, they often lack the skills needed to find and fill the better paying jobs in the information economy. Many young blacks disdainfully dismiss the idea of working at jobs for "chump change" in garages, cafeterias, fast-food emporia, hotels, laundries, supermarkets, and similar service establishments. Entry level jobs where habits of work and skills at dealing with people can be learned have little appeal.[11]

They have been told by solicitous whites that low-level work is exploitative and demeaning, mere dry bones that whites throw to blacks, not the kind of jobs to which they are entitled. They want real work, good jobs that pay well, jobs that don't require years of training and special skills, jobs that offer benefits and security—in short, the factory jobs they believe were available to everyone a generation ago. But for inner-city blacks these jobs are vanishing, done in by machines or moved to the suburbs and small towns where blacks can't get at them, leaving them isolated and jobless in decaying urban centers. Sociologist William Julius Wilson examined the impact the removal of factories to the suburbs has had on the employment of blacks. He noted that between 1960 and 1984 the percentage of black males in the labor force dropped sharply. In 1984 only 58 percent of all young black males, 34 percent of those aged eighteen to nineteen, and 16 percent aged sixteen to seventeen were employed.[12] The effect of unemployment on the black family has been devastating. Where joblessness is high the number of single parent households rises, school achievement declines, and an explosion of juvenile delinquency, crime, and imprisonment takes place. Of course, older blacks have also been affected by the decline of manufacturing and resulting unemployment, but this change most severely hurt young males, many of whom have never entered the labor force at all.

It was to correct this situation, and other inequities in employment, that Congress amended Title VII of the 1964 Civil Rights Act so that the courts could require employers to "affirmatively" hire blacks (and other minorities, including women) in numbers roughly approximating their representation in the local or regional population. Lyndon Baines Johnson considered affirmative action the crucial weapon in his war on poverty, a war he said he was determined to win.

Did Johnson really believe he could erase poverty? Perhaps not. A son of Texas, raised in a hardscrabble area populated with devout Christians, he must have heard repeatedly that the poor would always be with us. Failure was to be expected. And indeed past wars on poverty had always shown a distressing tendency to peter out in futile gestures of frustration and weary resignation. But he thought it was certainly worth a try. It was also politically canny. The war on poverty would curry favor with the liberal wing of the Democratic party, which had always been cool toward southern politicians in general and Johnson in particular.

In any event, for Johnson, and for the presidents who followed him, the war on poverty in America fared little better than the war in Vietnam. Johnson set the ball rolling by issuing an order in 1965 requiring federal contractors to set "goals and timetables" (in effect, quotas) on the hiring of minorities and women. The courts soon followed the president's lead. Orders from the bench began to lay down guidelines for implementing affirmative action legislation. For example, in 1972 a federal judge told Alabama officials that half of all new state troopers would have to be black until blacks comprised one quarter of the force.[13] Other governmental edicts and judicial orders followed in rapid succession until the effects of affirmative action became abundantly visible.

Under pressure from the government, jobs were given to blacks in corporate offices and manufacturing plants that had never before beheld a single black face. Suits were brought against trade unions forcing them to accept black apprentices in more than token numbers. Doors were open to blacks in colleges and universities that had been reluctant to admit them; places were found for blacks in medical and law schools, even if that meant turning away qualified white applicants and lowering admission standards so that black applicants would qualify. In time and in some places a new black face became visible, a middle-class face, the faces of doctors, lawyers, higher civil servants, and white-collar workers of all types.

The impact of affirmative action was markedly significant in the business world. As a result of affirmative action, government work was awarded to black businessmen, who earlier had never had a chance to even bid on a government contract, let alone win one; and as a consequence the number of black businesses began to grow rapidly. During the five-year period 1982–87 the average annual growth of black businesses nationally approached 8 percent. In Atlanta, Georgia, the rate of growth was somewhat more than 10 percent, the highest in the country.[14]

Atlanta presents an interesting case. When Maynard Jackson entered office in 1974 as the city's first black mayor, he found that less than 1 percent of city contracts were being awarded to black contractors—this in a city whose population was 50 percent black, a proportion that has since grown to 68 percent. He quickly went about remedying this situation. He wrote affirmative action language into city contracts, including fines for noncompliance and enforcement by inspectors and compliance officers, and things began to change. When he left office after three terms, the rate of black participation in city contracts had risen to 35 percent. Almost all the workers employed by black entrepreneurs were black, the mirror image of the situation when whites had hired only people of their own race.

The effect of affirmative action and economic prosperity on black professionals and businessmen can be seen in the black suburbs of southwest Atlanta, where some properties sell for $500,000 to $800,000, approaching the prices of Buckhead, the wealthy white suburb to the north of the city. Atlanta has its black millionaires and multimillionaires, among them the founder of the H. J. Russell construction firm that is America's fourth largest minority-owned company. Another beneficiary, Carl Trimble, head of an architectural firm, demanded that 50 percent of the construction for the Olympic Games in Atlanta be reserved for minorities, in effect for blacks. Although his demand was officially rejected, blacks did end up with about a third of the contracts, including those for constructing the tennis, shooting, and hockey arenas.

White contractors, who once viewed their black competitors with disdain, became upset. One of them, Earl Ehrhart, a power in the Georgia legislature, pushed a bill that would forbid the state to use race, sex, ethnicity, or national origin as criteria for awarding public contacts. When he discussed the effect of affirmative action on the construction business, the word "unfair" appeared a lot. "I'll hire blacks if I can," he said, "but what I remember is that while I worked 60 hours a week, I saw my black friends walk into the grants office and get all they needed, just like that." Mr. Ehrhart denied that he is one of those "angry white males" the press writes about, but he and many of his friends have made clear they feel racial preferences must end.[15]

Rich white contractors have political clout and when riled can make their anger felt in high places. But poor white men, equally upset and if anything far more at risk, feel helpless to do anything when the law pits them against minorities for the same job, while giving their competitor an advantage. A 1995 Washington Post/Harvard University poll found that 86 percent of whites opposed affirmative action and agreed with the statement that "Hiring, promotion and college admission should be based strictly on merit and qualifications rather than on race or ethnicity." Whites who believe that good jobs are scarce and the competition brutal find themselves in a lose-lose situation. If they complain the media call them bigots and racists, pathetic whiners who want only to protect their jobs at the expense of poor minorities. If they remain silent they feel put upon, stupid, and cowardly. Feeling like losers, they are boiling with resentment.

These whites feel trapped. They believe the gate to the middle class is being closed to them and their children, that affirmative action is padlocking them in a stable with people they profoundly dislike—the blacks. They are appalled at the idea of being lumped in the same class with blacks. In the minds of many whites, as Stanley B. Greenberg learned in his study of Macomb County, Michigan, a county made up mainly of white ethnics who climbed into the middle class in one generation thanks to the United Auto Workers and the post-World War II economic boom, "not being black is what constitutes being middle class; not living with blacks is what makes a neighborhood a decent place to live."[16] These whites say they are not racists. They believe the playing field is already level, that equality has been achieved, and that blacks are now seeking special treatment at the expense of whites. They think their jobs are in jeopardy and that whites can't get jobs because the blacks are getting them all. They have come to believe that government bureaucrats (their term for the New Elite) and the blacks are responsible for almost everything that has gone wrong in their lives.

Blacks return white anger with anger of their own. In their view they have actually profited little from affirmative action. They point out that, affirmative action notwithstanding, statistics amply document the disadvantaged position of their race. Average black income is below the national average; blacks are more likely to drop out of school than whites; blacks suffer higher levels of unemployment than whites. But at least affirmative action offers them the possibility of climbing out of the pit of poverty. Why, they ask, is the white man kicking the ladder away just as they are beginning to get started? Don't be misled by the sight of middle-class blacks in the professions or their children in elite universities, say poor blacks. It is true the number of blacks in the middle class is growing. But there are still lots of us at the bottom and we need all the help we can get.

THE MALE BACKLASH

Although working class white males believe affirmative action has mostly benefited blacks, the fact is that women have been its major beneficiaries. And slowly, as yet imperfectly, some men have come to recognize this. As a result, male resentment has grown as men come to feel that women use unfair means to get jobs once held by men and win promotions that only merit should deliver. More and more men now believe political muscle, not merit, has given women the splendid positions they hold in business, in government, in social services, and in education. Angrily, they claim that civil affirmative action gives women an unfair advantage over men. How can men compete with people whose success is guaranteed by government-mandated preferences, set-asides, and quotas? What have women done to deserve their successes except to whine about discrimination, intimidate politicians, and threaten to create a scene if they don't get their way? What has happened, they ask, to the sacred American principle that individual worth, not birth, should determine the prizes awarded to contestants in the game of life.

Some men, singling out a culprit, say they have been injured by the Women's Movement. The movement, they say, has made them the victims of reverse discrimination, and they cite examples of gross unfairness. There is, for instance, the case of Clint Williams, a reporter who was turned down for a job at a newspaper. The problem was not his qualifications, the interviewer explained apologetically, but management's decision that the position must be offered to a minority person, a woman or a black. "In effect," says Williams, "I was told it's too bad you are a white male." Williams eventually found a job with a Southwestern newspaper. He claims not to be angry or bitter, just realistic. "We're paying for the sins of our fathers," he explained resignedly.[17]

Not all men share William's passive point of view. Rather, some men say they are going to fight. If women can take their grievances to court, they reason, so can men. After all, the 1964 Civil Rights Act sought to ensure that people would be judged solely upon their qualifications for the job; race and gender were not to enter the matter at all. That being the case, reasoned eight former employees of Jenny Craig International, a weight loss firm with 600 centers across the country, why should we accept sex discrimination and sexual harassment without a fight? They filed suit in 1995 in Massachusetts Superior Court, complaining that they were denied promotion, sexually harassed, and fired merely because they were men in a corporation whose chief executive officer was a woman, as were most of its employees. The men complained of being treated like outsiders in a female-dominated society. They were asked to perform demeaning tasks not related to their jobs, like shoveling snow, emptying trash, or fixing the boss's car. They were forced to endure comments about "tight buns," excluded from the group when the conversation veered to talk about pregnancy and menstrual periods, and required to wear smocks and neck scarves, the company uniform in which they felt demeaned.[18]

The suit brought by the Jenny Craig Eight, as they have been called, provoked a flurry of inquiries from men with similar experiences. "It's the same stuff," said Jane C. Brayton, an official at the Massachusetts Commission Against Discrimination. "Nothing's changed. The majority keeps putting down the minority."[19] Complaints about being excluded from female chit-chat and made to wear costumes evocative of cross-dressing may appear trivial to an outsider. But insecurity about one's job is another matter—it goes to the heart of the problem. Insecurity balloons into fury when men believe that affirmative action overrides merit and gives women unfair advantage over men.

There is, of course, another side to this—the feminist position. It is all well and good to talk about individual merit, respond the defenders of gender preferences, but in fact change has come much too slowly and against too much opposition from entrenched males for women to be defensive about affirmative action and complacent about the future. Men still see to it that true sexual equality is a distant dream. They still oppress women and still consider themselves superior to women. But far from being a boon to society, men are a burden. As June Stephenson, an American psychologist, sees it, men are not cost-effective. Indeed, men impose heavy costs upon society. For example, they are responsible for 90 percent of all murders and 74 percent of white-collar crimes; they make up 94 percent of all prison inmates. She suggests a special tax be imposed on men to help compensate society for the damage they do.[20]

And so, rather than being satisfied with what has been achieved, feminists advocate even more aggressive programs. Worried about the future, they say this is no time to relax. The gains women have so painfully won may yet be lost to vengeful males furious at being pushed aside and bent on regaining lost ground. After all, say ardent supporters of gender preferences, it was only because affirmative action pressured them to change that men reluctantly agreed to open their ranks to women. The law, not the workings of socio-economic change (a thesis of this book), has given women the leg-up they need to climb the ladder of occupational success.

Even though injury may never have been intended, many men feel injured at the hands of women. For while it is painful to be passed over for promotion, and frightening to lose out in the competition for a job, it is even more infuriating when the decision seems unjust. As a result, affirmative equality is fueling a backlash among men, who have begun to turn their anger against women. Charging that women are unfair competitors, everlasting complainers, and shrill faultfinders, men say they are tired of losing out to women who—adding insult to injury—call them tyrants and oppressors. Enough is enough, they say. Merit, not race or ethnicity or gender, should determine hiring and firing and promotion.

It turns out that the road to a sweetly egalitarian society, free of injustice and conflict, is strewn with disappointments and surprises, as Elitists to their dismay are finding out. They did not expect their good intentions and dreams of a good society would be so badly misread and their well-meaning proposals so harshly rebuffed. They knew their enemies would oppose any move to create a better world, a fair and compassionate society that is fully accepting of pleasure and the pursuit of self-actualization. With their enemies the Elitists were prepared to deal harshly—swiftly, efficiently, and without mercy. But what to do when the objects of their compassion fall out among themselves—when, for example, poor blacks and poor whites, who should be allies, quarrel, when proposals to right ancient wrongs are rejected by the very people they are meant to help?

Elitists thought affirmative action would prevent these conflicts, either by creating a level playing field on which everyone could compete as equals, or by giving the socially handicapped a hand until they could get on their feet and go it alone. They believed that in time people would see the benefits of this policy and accept it; but it hasn't worked out that way. According to the polls many Americans, including some blacks and women, believe affirmative action is unfair and hurtful to the country. Perhaps, as Elitists believe, this attitude is irrational, a visceral response to people of different colors and customs. But the fear may also be rational, a reasoned assessment that affirmative action is an affront to precious values.

For whatever reason affirmative action appears to be on its way out as public policy. Several states, most conspicuously California and Texas, have taken steps to forbid race, ethnicity, and sex from being used as criteria in school admissions and public hiring; and they are curbing the power of the civil rights bureaucracy to promote affirmative action by fiat. Also, the courts have begun to question the constitutionality of preferential treatment for minorities, though, at this writing, it is unclear how far they will go. Possibly the courts are simply following public opinion, as Mr. Dooley asserted, and will go all the way. If so, affirmative action's days are numbered. But it is much too early to sound its death knell. Its supporters actively oppose the demolishment of affirmative action and are taking their protests to the streets and to the courts. Quite possibly, the resolution of this issue will be a long-drawn-out affair.

Even if this is true, it is quite beside the point. Decades of affirmative action have left bitter residues of resentment. And in their resentment many Americans, angry and bewildered, hurt by forces beyond their control, are striking out at targets near at hand, at blacks, immigrants, and women. But apart from the satisfaction derived from giving vent to anger, it is hard to see what the various racial and ethnic and gender components of society gain from attacking one another. For this aggression is ultimately useless, because it does not get at the true cause of the problem: the conflict between egalitarianism and merit rooted in the character and ideology of the New Elite.

Some people have urged the Elite to be less rigid and more willing to compromise. More flexibility, it is said, might prevent the savaging of affirmative action, leading to it being mended, not ended. This argument has little effect on Elitists, for it completely misjudges their motives. Elitists are in the embrace of the Chameleon Complex and its ideology. They must prove the altruism of their motives; they cannot imagine accepting less than what they demand; to do so would smack of betrayal, an acceptance of an imperfect world. Never eager to admit mistakes and passionately certain of their correctness, Elitists respond to any resistance to their plans with disbelief, pique, and impatience. After some reflection, including a spell of denial (e.g., the resistance is temporary, the negative effects will go away), the New Elite has concluded that its critics simply misunderstand the benevolence of its intentions, the correctness of affirmative action, and its long-term benefits. As the Elite sees it, people have been persuaded to oppose programs in their own interest.

What the Elite cannot see or will not admit, for to do so would shake them to the core of their character, is the contradiction embedded in their demands for both merit and equality. They do not yet realize that their desire to create a completely just and thoroughly egalitarian society has generated widespread cynicism and conflict. Whatever the cost, however, they are determined to plow ahead. But the price of this determination is not only conflict with outsiders, which they are willing to accept as the price of change, but also within the Elite itself. This conflict has come to them as a complete surprise. We will analyze this development when we examine the conflict between individualism and conformity, the subject of the next chapter.

13

The New Conformity

Revolutions invariably surprise their makers. Idealistic rebels eager to build a new and peaceful society soon discover that the fighting does not end with the overthrow of the old order. The killing goes on long after the supporters of the hated old regime have fled or been shot. Inevitably, new ideologies arise to challenge revolutionary dogma, and new enemies replace old ones. Friction develops between rival factions, and the battle for power becomes deadly. Naive idealists fall victim to ambitious and unscrupulous rivals. Relentlessly the revolution devours its children.

Even when they manage to survive the early blood-letting, many slogan-intoxicated revolutionaries live long enough to see their ideas become pretexts for class privilege and personal tyranny. Tragically, the world they had fought so hard to build eludes them; the world they actually made is far different from the one they expected. Reality mocks their illusions, change spins out of control, and dreams become nightmares.

Fearing this fate, the New Elitists, themselves rebels against the old order, are taking steps to stamp out dissent. They know their rebellion can only succeed if their ideology, a web of ideas and aspirations embedded in the Chameleon Complex and congruent with Elitist needs, becomes the new dogma of society. But this brings them smack up against a painful contradiction inherent in their ideology—

the clash between individualism and conformity. In a world not yet in their control and hence dangerous, many Elitists feel they must opt for conformity, even though they profess to despise it. Individualism is their credo and heart's desire. As narcissists, they emphatically celebrate the right to do their own thing, a right they would like to extend to everyone. But as chameleons, they know that only conformity ensures safety.

As youths they delighted in shocking authority—parents, teachers, police, and other agents of the repressive old order. They were free spirits, defiantly unwilling to truckle under to the demands of authority. Flouting convention was their right, achieving a fully actualized self their goal, conforming to society's expectations their aversion. But as grownups, enjoying power and eager to win more, they must give greater play to the conformist side of their character. For without conformity the enemies of the revolution would be free to propagate hateful ideas, free to resist the attainment of a just and egalitarian society.

Convinced of the nobility of their goals, some Elitists are claiming the right to enforce conformity to their credo. They try to smooth over the contradiction between individualism and conformity by arguing that the need to enforce conformity is only temporary. After the revolution is secure, a thousand flowers may bloom unmolested, and individualism will once again be welcomed. But until that time comes they are prepared to employ severe measures to exact unquestioned obedience to Elitist expectations. Whatever the cost and no matter how much it conflicts with treasured individualism, Elitists assert that conformity to their credo is obligatory.

The Elite's insistence on others conforming to its wishes, even as it professes allegiance to individual freedom, alienates lots of people. For one thing, the Elitists' airy proclamation of everyone's right to do their own thing puts off most lower- and middle-class conservatives. It appears to them thoroughly crazy and altogether unacceptable. These classes have long been champions of conventional morality, and to their minds unfettered individualism evokes images of moral chaos and social breakdown. Believing themselves faced with this prospect, conservatives grow resentful and punitive. They want laws passed; they want the police called out; they want right upheld and wrong punished. For its espousal of untramelled individualism alone, the Elite is suspect. When, on top of this, the Elite ignores its championship of individuality and demands conformity, it leaves itself open to the charge of hypocrisy.

Perhaps this was foreseen and discounted. What truly surprised the New Elite is the effect that the contradiction between individualism and conformity has had on its own ranks. The New Elite has become divided over the need to enforce conformity to its credo; it is not at all sure what to do about the inherent conflict between individualism and conformity. This is a most uncomfortable situation for the New Elite to be in because it once thought it knew exactly what needed to be done and how to do it—but no longer. Elitists are now arguing angrily over goals, the measures to achieve them, and the pressures that must be put on others to exact obedience to Elitist wishes.

The problem is that although most Elitists agree on the sanctity of the individual, they have to face the unpleasant fact that what is an inalienable right to some Elitists strikes other Elitists as a violation of their own rights. For example, abortion to a pro-life Elitist is a denial of the right of the fetus to life, not the mother's right to privacy as pro-choice Elitists maintain. Pornography to certain feminists is nothing less than violence against women, not the exercise of free speech as civil libertarians would have it. And while the right to protect and celebrate minority cultures seems eminently reasonable to multicultural Elitists with separatist inclinations, it seems to other Elitists to be an invitation to anarchy and national dissolution.

This chapter focuses on the conflict that the contradiction between individualism and conformity produces within the Elite, a noisy brawl grandiloquently called a war, though in some ways it more closely resembles a nasty family spat. This war is said to have engulfed the entire country, a typical piece of Elitist exaggeration—the Elite cannot imagine that anything concerning it is of little moment to others. But as yet, most of the country is unaware of the war between Elitists, just as much of the country is insufficiently aware of the contradictions inherent in Elitist ideology. Still, what affects Elitists will eventually affect the rest of the country, and for that reason it deserves analysis.

Although only two elitist groups—feminists and Afrocentric blacks—have been selected for analysis, I believe the character of the conflict is essentially the same for other groups within the Elite. First I will look at several examples of the Elite's attempt to enforce conformity to its code on the general public. They illustrate the seri-

ousness with which the Elite takes its mission to impose conformity
on others. But this will not delay us long.[1]

WATCH YOUR TONGUE, MIND YOUR MANNERS

Many members of the New Elite hold jobs which require them to
collect data about all forms of bias and discrimination. Some Elitists
work in public or private bureaucracies, where they zealously enforce
laws meant to reduce discrimination and promote cultural diversity.
Ever vigilant to further the interests of egalitarianism, more than
ready to denounce the moral obtuseness of anyone insufficiently
sensitive to other cultures, they endeavor to sniff out any sign of
prejudice or discrimination anywhere, even in the most innocent-
appearing settings. In effect, they constitute a diversity police, or a
self-righteous vigilante force that wants to impose a politically correct
code on everyone. They will not hesitate to quickly bring the full
weight of the law down on anyone who stands in their way.

Some Elitists sell programs to schools and universities, designed to
promote multicultural sensitivity; frequently, they service private corporations whose fear of running afoul of anti-discrimination laws and
minority group opinion keeps management in a constant tizzy. As
diversity experts, these Elitists offer seminars to small groups, give
lectures to large audiences, or set up role playing dramas in which
employees take part as actors—all meant to increase the sensitivity of
the majority to the feelings of minorities. For their services they earn
fat salaries. At a lower level of entrepreneurial skill are the multilin-
gual teachers in the public schools and cultural diversity advisers in
colleges who lobby to keep the multiculturalism flourishing in the
classroom and on the campus because their livelihoods depend on the
public's willingness to fund their programs.

Diversity-mongers among the New Elite wish to appear tolerant,
inclusive and benign. Their goals, they say, are entirely compatible
with America's history, which has long been marked by pluralism.
They want only to promote openness to different points of view, to
make people more appreciative of the enormous diversity of cultures
that exists in American life, and to bring into the country's mainstream all the minorities, especially women and people of color, that
have been excluded in the past. In this respect, their goals would seem
to be simply an extension of the civil rights movement of the 1960s.

And indeed this association with the civil rights movement has given the New Elite legitimacy, particularly among the baby-boomers for whom the civil rights movement remains the redeeming experience of their generation.

In fact, the Elite's benign face is a fake, a chameleon-like assumption of the popular garb of tolerance. Behind the facade of openness and tolerance lie boundless ambition, a yearning for power, venomous hostility for any viewpoint outside its purview, and a fervent, self-righteous wish to make the world over in its own image, which is to say, to make the world egalitarian, fair, and perfect. For those who have not observed Elite diversity-mongers close up, the following descriptions of some of their capers may shed light on the war being waged between the Elite and the general public and between factions of the Elite itself. Two are particularly significant. The first is the attempt to purge the language of unwelcome words; the second is the ongoing effort to rewrite history to make it conform to Elitist ideology.

The New Elite seems almost playful when it seeks to free the language of terms hurtful to disadvantaged groups or of connotations brimming with racist or sexist bias. If that is the goal, it can be argued that cleaning up the language does no harm. For instance, what harm can it do (and think what good it might do) to call crippled people vertically challenged or differently abled? Presumably cripples dislike being reminded of their condition. A gentler, less invidious word, a clever euphemism helps soothe tender feelings, or so it is thought. Sensitively correct language protects fat people, who are now to be called "big boned" or "differently sized" from invidious comparisons; the dumb, now labeled "exceptional" or "cognitively challenged," need not feel badly; and the ugly, the aged, the infirm, and all minorities can also find shelter under some linguistically correct tent.

Where's the harm in all this? It seems more comical than tragical, and indeed journalists and comics have had a field day making fun of political correctness. Surely, nothing horrific can come of it. Unless, of course, you are J. Donald Silva. He was not amused when the University of New Hampshire suspended him without pay from his position as a professor of technical writing and directed him to undergo counseling at his own expense. Professor Silva's crime was to compare focus in writing to focus in sex. In another lecture, he used a description of belly dancing as an example of simile, saying it was like Jell-O on a plate with a vibrator under the plate. Some female students complained that the vibrator in the simile was a reference to a sexual gadget and said the professor's language was a form of sexual harassment. Professor Silva refused to undergo counseling and sued for back pay and damages. On September 19, 1994, Federal Judge Shane Devine ordered Silva's reinstatement and strongly indicated that his lawsuit would be successful if it went to court. The trustees of the University of New Hampshire agreed to pay professor Silva $60,000 in back pay and damages, plus $170,000 in legal fees. Even so, Silva could not have found the entire affair funny.

Then there is the matter of the Western Civilization program at Yale University, a particularly interesting case because it shows that when the Elite wants something badly enough money is no object—not even 20 million dollars. This is the amount Texas oil billionaire Lee M. Bass gave to his alma mater, Yale University, for the explicit purpose of shoring up its program in Western Civilization. Once an unchallenged staple of the university's curriculum, the course on Western Civilization was under attack from politically correct elements in the faculty. News of this reached Lee Bass' ears and he decided to do something about it. Despite misgivings, the university accepted the gift. (How could it not? Even rich Yale has money problems.) But this decision immediately ran into flack from some Elitists on the faculty, who grumbled that the university was already offering more than enough courses on the Western Tradition.

Facing determined faculty opposition, the university dawdled and procrastinated for four years. Bass' requests for action went unheeded. Finally, hearing about faculty discontent and perhaps fearing that the purpose of his grant would be subverted, he announced that he wanted a voice in deciding who would teach the course. Yale recoiled in horror at this request. It said its integrity was at stake; it said there were things money could not buy; it said its virtue was not for sale. No one could tell this august university who might teach a course. And so on. Whereupon Bass said he wanted his money back, and in March of 1995 Yale complied, though not without pointing self-righteously to its obligation to defend academic freedom from outside interference. The media approved; the *New York Times* ecstatically endorsed Yale's decision—Texas plutocrats have never been popular among members of the Eastern elite press.

This little morality play should amuse anyone with firsthand knowledge about the workings of a modern American university. The notion that a university is, or should be, beyond the reach of money is unrealistic and hilarious. Money lubricates the machinery of higher learning in the United States—and always has. In the past great wealth built great universities. Standard Oil money founded the University of Chicago; tobacco money turned a small obscure college into Duke University; and Western Union money helped establish Cornell University. Big money keeps them running today. Moreover, most universities, even the most prestigious, routinely accept donations with strings attached. Donors like to know how their money is being used, and universities try to work within the parameters laid down by the giver, while holding on to as much independence of action as possible. And yet Yale would not come to terms with the Texas billionaire. Why was that?

Was it that Bass had been too aggressive, too up-front in his demands, in the traditional Texas way? No one has claimed this. (Some donors, notably the Japanese, show great subtlety and delicacy in the way they award money. But there is seldom any doubt about how they want their money used, and they are quite successful in achieving their ends. Is it just coincidence that many professors holding chairs in Japanese studies established with Japanese money turn out to be ardent supporters of all things Japanese, including Japanese trade policies?) Perhaps there was something in Bass' approach that offended Yale administrators, but more likely it was what he sought to do, not his manner, that caused Yale to balk. He tried to counter the anti-Western bias in some sections of the Yale faculty—this in a university notable for deconstructionism and political correctness—and he lost. He took his marbles back, but he could not change the game.

Consider also the way the Elite seeks to rewrite history. There is, for example, Martin Harwitt, the director of the Air and Space Museum, a division of the Smithsonian Institution, who tried to give a politically correct coloration to one of history's momentous events— the dropping of an atomic bomb on Hiroshima. Harwitt and his staff wanted to mount an exhibition commemorating the fiftieth anniversary of this event, which seemed to be a timely and appropriate thing to do. What was not acceptable to many people was what the museum wanted to say about the bomb and the entire war with Japan.

The museum planned to display the "Enola Gay," the B-29 that dropped the bomb, accompanying it with an analysis of the bombing of Japan and its legacy. As originally planned, the analysis would have questioned the need to drop the atomic bomb, saying that far fewer Americans would have died in the invasion than had been originally estimated, perhaps no more than 75,000, not the 500,000 to 1,000,000 the military had predicted. And besides, an invasion was not really necessary because Japan was on the verge of surrender anyway, or so the museum and some other history revisionists believe. Not only was dropping the bomb unnecessary, the script would have said, it was yet another example of America's bloodthirsty hunger for revenge. Seen from this perspective, it was clear that the Americans had completely distorted the history of the war and its antecedents. The exhibition would have argued that the Japanese were actually victims of American aggression, and that the Japanese were merely defending themselves against western imperialism.

Many veterans were outraged. They believed the proposed script was blatantly anti-American. They considered the museum's director and his staff defamers of American motives and honor, and the entire exhibition a plot to vilify their country. They wondered at the museum's failure to mention that the war had begun with the Japanese bombing of Pearl Harbor; they marveled at the museum's apparent indifference to the atrocities committed by the Japanese in China and Indonesia; and they were furious at the museum's insensitivity to the death of tens of thousands of Americans in the Pacific war.

As to how many Americans would have been killed in an invasion of the Japanese mainland, obviously no one at the time could really have known. But the experience of taking Iwo Jima was not reassuring. This tiny island, hundreds of miles from the Japanese main islands, not heavily populated, of little significance other than its location, was the scene of one of the bloodiest battles in the Pacific War. American marines landed on the island on February 19, 1945, and immediately encountered fierce resistance. Most of the Japanese fought to the death. They had to be rooted out of their bunkers and caves and killed one by one with flame-throwers, machine guns, or in hand-to-hand combat. The bloodletting was horrendous. After 36 days of continuous fighting, the island was finally taken, at the cost of 6,821 American lives and more than 16,000 wounded. Of the original Japanese force of 22,000, only 1,083 survived. Whatever made Mr. Harwitt and his staff believe that the Japanese would have fought any less ferociously and courageously for the main islands, for Tokyo and Kyoto, for their homes and families, for the burial places of their ancestors?

Perhaps the veterans did not know it, but they had run smack into a passel of Elitists busy rewriting history to conform to their ideology.

The intent of this revision was to praise a foreign culture and malign America by depicting the Pacific war as an example of American aggression and imperialism. The veterans would have none of it. They took their case to Congress, won the support of key politicians, and forced the museum to back down. The exhibit was reduced and objectionable material eliminated, and a few months later Director Harwitt resigned. In a rare display of organized resistance, ordinary people had forced the Elite to back down.

Most Elitists want to remake America, not separate themselves from it. But some Elitists cannot bring themselves to conform to any system still in the hands of white males, even though these be fellow Elitists. As they see it, individual freedom must suffer in a system dominated by white men, and conformity to its rules cannot help but be abhorrent. These rebels, mostly members of racial or ethnic minorities or disaffected white women, are separatists. They want to create a subsociety of their own, subservient to their needs and wishes, and free of interference from outside groups. They want to separate themselves culturally, psychologically and, if possible, physically from the dominant system. Echoing the language of Orwell's dystopia, individual freedom to these Elitists is submission to the rules of their new order. Only in such a society can individualism flourish; only in such a society can conformity be applauded; only in such a society can the contradiction between individualism and conformity be resolved.

LOOKING FOR A WAY OUT

Separatists call America a failed society. Chanting a litany of hate, they charge America with a long list of sins and an even longer list of victims. The American Dream, they say, is a hoax. America's promise of a just society is fraudulent, and its history is a bloody tale of exploitation, aggression, and war. At home, racial and sexual minorities—people of color, homosexuals, women—are oppressed, denied jobs, paid less than the dominant majority (white heterosexual males) for comparable work, kept out of the corporate boardroom, treated with intolerable contempt, and rejected as equals in social encounters.

Murder and genocide, separatists go on to say, make laughable America's claim to being a nation of peace-lovers. The very boundaries of the nation are testimony to American aggression and imperialism. The land called the United States was stolen from its original owners, the Native Americans, who were brutally crushed, harried, rounded up and put in reservations. America's southern neighbor, Mexico, was forced at gunpoint to cede huge portions of its territory to land-hungry, imperialist Yankees. And the only reason Americans are not now ensconced in Montreal and Toronto, the separatist adds, not without glee, is that the Canadians twice threw back invasions from the south, and because the British controlled the seas and threatened to intervene, effectively discouraging further military adventures.

Abroad, America casts a dark shadow. Weaker nations are at its mercy. Its actions are never disinterested or benign. America, it is charged, supports tyranny and treats dictators as friends whenever profit or political advantage can be gained by doing so. If it sends aid to Third World nations, such as Haiti or Somalia or Bosnia, it is solely for economic and geopolitical reasons, though these reasons are seldom spelled out in detail. It is simply assumed that America being what it is—a money-hungry, imperialist nation—some ulterior motive must be at work.

In some ways the separatists resemble other Elitists. They, too, tend to have university degrees, often work at trades that require skill in speaking and writing, and sometimes hold jobs in schools and colleges. But here the resemblance ends. Separatists tend to be younger and not yet atop the greasy pole of success. They are more likely than the mainstream Elitist to be female, black, or Hispanic, openly gay or lesbian and intent on promoting a homosexual agenda; they also tend to be drawn to administrative positions which permit them to implement their agenda. Jobs managing diversity training in schools and corporate offices appeal to them. Positions in governmental bureaucracies that oversee the protection of minorities also fit neatly into their plans.

These plans are radical—nothing less than the dismantling of the entire white male establishment will satisfy them. Politically they tend toward left-liberalism, sometimes toward a sub-species of Marxism that has proven resistant to experience and history. They are usually dedicated utopians. Nothing will erase their yearning for a world in which virtue triumphs over evil and the wicked get their comeuppance. They make no bones about their hostility to cultural conservatism; they want to put quits to traditional values and replace them with ideals more in keeping with their own needs—millenarian and egalitarian.

Power is the name of the separatist's game. True, separatists say they wish only to create a just society, and they skillfully use the rhetoric of equality to further their aims, all the while pointing to victimhood as justification for their actions; but it is not simply equality, not even revenge and restitution, they seek—it is power. With power will come position and the heady joys of being in charge of one's own fate and that of one's group. This power will come at a price, however. Even now, it is bringing bitter arguments with old friends and allies: a constantly escalating war over curriculum and placement in schools and colleges, over jobs, set-asides, and other entitlements tied to race, gender, and ethnicity; and most seriously, angry disagreements over the wisdom and right of minorities to separate themselves from the rest of society.

Separatists believe the white male business establishment has lost its right to govern and to control dissent; misjudgment, moral obtuseness, and a failure of will has undermined its ability to rule. As the separatist sees it, the white establishment is little more than a band of self-important men, who lack all passion or desire except to be left in peace to enjoy their wealth. They no longer have the ability to inspire others: the people have been left in the lurch at a time when guidance is most needed. As a result, the establishment can no longer channel the energies of rebellious youths away from pursuing their own dream of self-fulfillment, can no longer motivate them to follow the old ethic of work and achievement, which had once given cultural focus to the country. So goes the separatists' complaint against the establishment.

But this is mostly rhetoric. What separatists really want is to be able to celebrate themselves and to require others to do so. What they demand is more respect, more jobs, more money for themselves and their group.[2] These objectives, entirely normal in the United States, are not in themselves thought objectionable. What causes trouble is whom separatists threaten and the methods they use to attain their aims: rumor and gossip, physical harassment, legal actions that can be frivolous and vicious, and a pervasive attack upon the dominant culture.

To gain their ends separatists attack, often with consummate skill, the idea of objective truth. They deny that valid standards exist—

indeed, can ever exist—with which to evaluate individuals and groups. This challenge to the idea of objective standards is buttressed by the work of scholars and literary critics influenced by French intellectual fashion, most notably the deconstructionist theories of Michel Foucault and Jacques Derrida. Using the techniques of literary deconstruction, combined with radical feminist critiques, Afrocentrism, and mystical environmentalism, separatists have challenged the idea of objectively measuring value in human expression and endeavor. As separatists with deconstructionist inclinations see it, no aspect of culture, whether it be Herman Melville's *Moby-Dick* or an advertisement for Calvin Klein's jeans, is intrinsically superior to any other. Truth, beauty, and morality are entirely relative.

Even modern science has come under attack. Mystics, phenomenologists, and romantic humanists insist on the priority of intuition over reason. Science, particularly big science enshrined in multi-million-dollar laboratories and prestigious institutes, is on the wrong track, they say. Despite the best efforts of science, nothing can be shown to be more true than anything else; only thinking makes it so. As a result, science, the last refuge of the rationalist, no longer enjoys immunity to attack from the forces of unreason; it is no longer a privileged temple for the priests of high science pursuing truth. Today it is under attack not only from superstitious know-nothings but also from politicized academics in the university.

Shorn of the protective cover of objectivity, art and literature are revealed for what they truly are: mere social constructions, the tools of a white patriarchal elite that imposes its values on others. When the myth of standards is discarded, all cultures, native or foreign, male or female, black or white, are of equal value. To believe otherwise is to play into the hands of the oppressor, the white male ruling class, which uses its standards to put down the achievements of women and minorities in order to keep them firmly under control. Such is the gospel according to the separatist.

If morality, beauty, and truth are relative and their measurement utterly subjective, if the standards of Western civilization are mere social fictions without objective foundation, then no culture can prove its superiority over any other. Without objective standards, statements about a group's performance, morality, and culture, upon which claims to superiority or charges of inferiority rest, evaporate into mere clouds of bigotry. This being the case, white male Eurocentric culture need not be the measure of all things. Blacks, Indians,

Hispanics, women, and other minorities need not feel inferior to white males. Precious self-esteem, a crucial concern of minorities and the golden fleece of Elitists in search of self-realization, need not be held hostage to the opinions of dominant white males. Every group is thus free to proclaim its equality to other groups, including those that once denigrated it.

This has enabled separatists to argue that blacks, Native Americans, lesbians, gays, Hispanics, Asians, women, and other minority groups have a right to separate identities and unique cultures. But most separatists recognize the folly of alienating public opinion and wisely seek to win over public opinion to their point of view. This they do by appealing to the American sense of fair play, emphasizing that blacks, women, and other minorities are not receiving a fair deal, that the cards are stacked against them, that they are victims of a game rigged to make them into losers. Women trying to rise in the corporate hierarchy report bumping up against a glass ceiling put there by males; blacks and Hispanics say that prejudice and discrimination relegate them to menial jobs; gays and lesbians complain of being locked out of mainstream society—all say they are treated as second-class citizens. The game, they argue, unfairly favors white males.

There is a measure of truth in these allegations, of course. That discrimination worked against women, nonwhites, and homosexuals in the past cannot be denied; and it is true that bias has not disappeared from the American scene. But it is also true that women, especially educated black women, have made phenomenal gains in the past few decades, and to a lesser extent so have college-educated black males. And the country is moving, albeit slowly, to an acceptance of unconventional sexuality. It can, therefore, be argued that the social condition of minorities has markedly improved over the last several decades.

But separatists say these gains are pitifully small when judged against past and present injustices. Prejudice and discrimination still deeply stain the fabric of American society. And injustice, the separatist insists, is the key to understanding American history, which is little more than a long record of cruelty and rapacious exploitation that has densely populated the country with victims. The list of victims is long and growing longer, as the separatist, ever inventive in finding new sufferers of white male savagery, enlarges the definition of victimhood and scurries about to uncover new evidence of villainy. The mission of the separatist is to alert the victim to his rights and remind the oppressors (white people in general, white males in particular) of their responsibility for the victim's plight, impressing upon them the need to mend their ways and pay for their mistakes and heinous crimes.

Getting people to admit their mistakes is never easy; getting them to pay up voluntarily is harder still. But there is a way—make the oppressor feel guilty. This has proven easier than expected, because large numbers of Americans, especially in the educated white upper-middle class, are afflicted with what the historian C. Vann Woodward calls "The New Guilt," a gnawing sense of remorse that is "congenital, inherent, intrinsic, collective, something possibly inexpiable, and probably ineradicable."[3] One need only mention the terrible things Americans have done to minorities since the founding of the Massachusetts Bay Colony—the slaughter of Indian braves, the enslavement of blacks, the denigration of women, the harassment and exploitation of lesser breeds from Latin America, Asia, and Eastern Europe—to reduce some middle-class whites to pitiable lumps of guilt.

The genius of the separatists was their ability to sell a guilt-ridden public a bill of goods, a way whereby the sinner could reduce guilt, though never entirely eliminate it, by making atonement for the sins of the past. How exactly can the sinner atone for his sins? First by admitting his guilt and then quickly performing acts of expiation and contrition. Restitution must be made to the victims of oppression, compensation must be paid for their injuries, and programs must be devised to prevent any further harm.

When opponents attack their programs, separatists take cover under the mantle of victimhood. They point to the harm prejudice and discrimination have inflicted upon their clients, and ask for understanding, sympathy, and submission to their demands. When this isn't forthcoming, they call their opponents racists, homophobes, and sexists. This usually works like a charm, especially with white Elitists, since most of them are liberals or former liberals, and being called a racist is a label no liberal can accept lightly. A scarlet "A" sewn on his or her jacket would be easier to bear.

Paradoxically, though they call themselves a beleaguered minority, separatists have become a sub-rosa establishment. In the last decade, without calling attention to themselves, they have infiltrated schools, universities, foundations, and governmental organizations. And because they often work as directors of diversity programs, they are well situated to promote their agenda through an artful manipulation of ideas and policies. Proclaiming their powerlessness, they have become powerful; surreptitiously undermining the established order, they boast of their openness; describing themselves as victims of discrimination, they discriminate against their opponents. They have quietly achieved powerful positions from which to wage war against their enemies in the hated white male establishment.

It would be a mistake to believe that separatists are easily beaten or that they will not put up a knock-down, drag-out fight before going down to defeat. In reality, they more often win than lose, and even when losing they usually leave their opponents shaken and frightened and embittered, with little appetite for the next fray. Their success stems from more than an uncanny skill at working surreptitiously and quietly, evading confrontation when possible in the hope of gaining their ends before anyone notices. More important is the separatist's ability to use against their opponents the best in the American character—an openness to change, a tolerance of cultural differences, a belief in the importance of a level playing field on which anyone can compete.

However, when appeals to the better angels of the American nature do not bring desired results, separatists will freely employ threats and invective to cow their opponents. They are perfectly willing to call their opponents bigots and racists—epithets and labels most Americans will do almost anything to avoid—if that will help their cause. Even then, of course, the fight may still be lost. Win or lose, they severely bruise and demoralize people who oppose them and may permanently divide a community into irreconcilable factions.

In the battle to gain power and to establish the autonomy of their own culture, the separatists so far hold a tactical edge. In the opening rounds of the war they astutely captured the moral high ground. Cloaking their program in the mantle of the civil rights movement, they portray themselves as the defenders of virtue, champions of a just society in which advancement is open to all. They proclaim their intention to level all barriers against women, gays and lesbians, Hispanics and blacks and other people of color; to see that old injustices are faced and restitution made; to give free rein to the creative forces of racial and ethnic cultures. Fairness and equality demand no less.

BOOSTING MINORITY SELF-ESTEEM

These measures, the separatist points out, though necessary and long overdue, will not fully compensate the victims for their most grievous injury—the rape of their self-respect at the hands of a cruel majority. Whatever the cost, the victim must be made whole again. This can happen only if the victim as well as the victimizer changes. The victims must be re-educated and re-invigorated, made strong and confident, secure in their own self-worth and proud of their group identity. To correct the harm done to the victim and prevent further damage, the separatist proposes major surgery; the malignancy of self-hatred must be cut out. The victim's group culture must be rehabilitated and its history, long ignored and hidden by the oppressor, rediscovered. Only then will the victim recover from the damage done to his or her self-esteem.

No one should doubt the importance of self-esteem. Wound self-esteem, create doubts about self-worth, and the entire structure of personality will shake and perhaps topple. Separatists maintain that women and victimized minorities suffer from the crippling effects of shaky self-esteem. Handicapped by feelings of inferiority, consumed with anxiety, and expecting to fail, they tend to approach competition with members of the dominant group with self-defeating timidity. But give them a sense of pride in their origins, a sense of belonging to a group with a rich culture and noble history—in short, give them an identity in which they can take justifiable pleasure—and self-esteem will flourish. With strong self-esteem they will become strong competitors, a credit to their group, a contributor to its glory. Enhanced self-esteem and group separation go together. Improve the group's status and its members will feel better about themselves. So argues the separatist.

This argument is not as naive as it may sound. Though hard to pin down, group membership bears a strong relationship to self-esteem. Admittedly, the process through which self-esteem develops is complex and the role of group membership in the process is not well understood, but there are good reasons for believing that group membership is an important part of self-esteem. To begin with, it is generally recognized that self-esteem grows out of interaction with significant persons, and that we tend to see ourselves as they see us— or as we think they do. And how people see us reflects to some extent their assessment of the groups to which we belong. A group held in high regard may cause its members to receive favorable treatment and hence feel good about themselves. In contrast, belonging to a despised group may mean that its members often meet with rebuff, causing self-doubt or in some cases self-hatred.

Since belonging to a despised group can damage self-esteem, separatists have decided to change the public's image of their group. (As noted, the focus in this chapter is on feminists and black separatists, but the analysis would apply to other disadvantaged minority groups as well.) They have set up programs to educate the public into an understanding of the true virtues of the minority, to create a favorable picture of their group, and in this way to elevate the minority's opinion of itself. But to do this they must first take control of the schools where culture is taught. Only then can they put into the curriculum the good news about the accomplishments of their group: its long and glorious history, its many achievements in the arts and sciences, its contributions to the nation and to the well-being of humanity in general.

It was expected that the white male majority would resist separatist aims; but what the separatists did not anticipate was that they would create a power struggle within the Elite structure itself. On one side are mainstream Elitists—mainstream in the sense that they support the traditional literary-artistic culture, not that they are members of the business class—who defend some aspects of the white male establishment culture; on the other are the separatists who attack it completely and without reservation. In a way this battle is paradoxical, for the two sides had once joined hands to fight a common enemy; bigotry and discrimination. Together they sought to encourage the state to care for sick and needy, the old and indigent; and to push for greater governmental support of the arts and humanities. Now they are at each other's throats.

They are fighting, in part, over what should constitute the canon of the culture, the body of art and literature they believe every educated person should know and appreciate. Also important, they are fighting over the insistence of separatist Elitists that mainstream Elitists conform to separatist rules, values, and expectations. This strikes mainstream Elitists as unreasonable, even though as Elitists they have been exposed to the latent emphasis on conformity in Elitist ideology. But most important, they are fighting over the right of separatist Elitists to opt out of the nation and go into business for themselves, to establish a separate society. Mainstream Elitists, though in principal opposed to establishment society, are appalled at the thought of national division, and now find themselves, paradoxically, defending certain values of the white male majority. Once compatriots in Elitehood, mainstream and separatist Elitists are now engaged in serious combat with each other.

Mainstream Elitists tend to be white, successful and upper-middle class. They write for national newspapers and magazines, or hold fellowships in think tanks, or teach in prestigious colleges and universities. Some are politically conservative, some are liberal—a diversity of opinion that confuses outsiders who have come to think of all Elitists as like-minded liberals. But whatever their political or economic views, mainstream Elitists tend to be traditionalists in matters of culture, and the vehemence of the attack against the literary idols and standards of their youth has shocked them into action.

Belatedly, they are defending the traditional culture, the glue that once bonded the nation together, against the depredations of the separatists, whose attacks have raised the specter of national disintegration. The result is a nasty war. But it is not the war commonly supposed—the war between Elitists and the general public—it is a war between members of the Elitehood itself. Because this war is being led by intellectuals trained to defend their ideas, the fighting has become an unrelenting polemical exchange filled with innuendo and cutting sarcasm that is sometimes masked as light-hearted wit. But do not be taken in by artful poses and smooth talk; the stakes are high and the combatants are deadly serious.

THE WAR BETWEEN ELITE WOMEN

Division within the Elitehood is one of the prices Elitists are paying for the contradictions in their ideology. Consider the fractiously torn and anguished Women's Movement. The insistence on conformity at the expense of individualism is dividing feminists into angry, disputatious factions. Elite feminists feel pulled in opposite directions. On the one hand, feminists treasure individualism's promise of untrammeled self-exploration and free expression. On the other hand, they belong to a movement that demands conformity to its expectations and standards. Fair enough, many feminists think; a movement needs the cohesion that conformity to group goals will generate.

But conformity to what? As individualists, feminists have created different goals and diverse routes to their attainment. It is not always apparent which goals are correct. Moreover, when the goals are mutually contradictory, vicious fighting can break out as one faction seeks to impose its will upon the other. Sadly, this has been the fate of the Women's Movement. To the dismay of people friendly to the aspirations of women, the Women's Movement is now split into two fiercely antagonistic groups—equity feminists and gender feminists— each determined to get its own way.

According to Christina Sommers, a self-avowed feminist, equity feminists cleave to the tradition of Elizabeth Cady Stanton and Susan B. Anthony, founders of the Women's Movement.[4] Under their direction the little group of women who met on July 14, 1848, in Seneca Falls, a small industrial city in upstate New York, to found the Women's Movement never asked for favors or special consideration. What they wanted was equality with men in law and in work, exactly as described in the Declaration of Independence, the inspiration for their own declaration of independence. Preferential treatment was no part of their thinking. The early leaders of the Women's Movement understood quite well the opposition their movement would face from traditional men (and women) and carefully avoided any suggestion of preferment for women over men. Nor were they seeking revenge. Their goal was not to inflict injury upon men but to free women from the unfair restrictions of a prejudiced society. Least of all were they exponents of separatism.

Equity feminists, who think of themselves as the true descendants of the Women's Movement's founders, seek no war with men, hold no grudges, desire no reparations for past discrimination. They only want fair treatment on a level playing field where they can compete with men, whom they consider fellow workers, not enemies. Gender feminists view the world very differently. Sommers maintains that gender feminists hate men or at the very least view them with a degree of suspicion that borders on paranoia. To feminists such as Catherine MacKinnon, Paula Rothenberg, Elizabeth Minnich, Eleanor Smeal, Diana Scully, doyenne of gender feminism, men are oppressors and natural brutes. Gender feminists believe men don't just have sex with women, they rape them. Even voluntary sex is nothing less than rape, for what is sexual penetration but a violation of a woman's bodily integrity? That some women obstinately insist on having sexual relations with men baffles gender feminists, who see it as just another form of male oppression.

Women who voluntarily choose the homemaker role trouble gender feminists even more, perhaps because in choosing the home over outside employment the stay-at-home woman is refuting the feminist argument that only male coercion keeps women at home. To the gender feminist, angry and exasperated almost to tears, the traditional homemaker seems a spiritless ninny, a simple-minded baker of cookies and dispenser of milk (to paraphrase Hillary Rodham Clinton's famous remark) who hasn't the wit, courage, or ambition to test herself against the challenge of the marketplace. To these feminists, genderistic beliefs about men and traditional women are obvious truths, and they insist that other feminists conform to their point of view.

As long as they were a small embattled group, the feminists could not afford the luxury of fighting among themselves. But success has brought the contradictions and the conflict inherent in Elitist ideology into the open. Some feminists now direct at each other the fury they once hurled solely at men. Equity feminists charge their opponents with ignoring the dictates of biology, with denigrating the family, with misusing school curricula for ideological purposes, and with building empires solely to accumulate money and power. They charge the gender feminists with betraying the Women's Movement.

Gender feminists have not taken the attacks against them lying down. Piggybacking their dogma on the civil rights movement, they justify their program to remake society as a simple extension of the fight against prejudice and discrimination. They describe themselves as agents of benign change, supporters of cultural diversity, and champions of tolerance and inclusiveness. Highly organized and well-funded by foundations, universities, and departments of education, they have insinuated themselves into positions of power and are pushing their agenda with vigor and success.

Gender feminists are especially strong in elite colleges and universities where critical theory, literary deconstructionism, and multiculturalism have taken hold. They dominate women's studies programs, and have strong influence in English and history departments, and in law and divinity schools. They are disproportionately represented in Dean of Students offices, in dormitory administration, in offices devoted to discovering and punishing sexual harassment, in offices of multiculturalism, and in various counseling centers. Skillful at administration and committed to gaining control of the curriculum, they use their influence to denounce phallocentric oppression. They demand more money for women's studies, and set up seminars to examine the ways in which male-dominated institutions work to exclude women from jobs and positions of power.

For quite a time gender feminists met little opposition. Males in the faculty and administration usually kept quiet, frightened of being called sexists and harassed if they objected to genderistic excesses. Some of those who spoke up were shouted down in the classroom and sometimes abused by enraged students who made threats. This usually scared the men into silence. Academics are not trained to be warriors. On leaving home, they preferred graduate school to boot camp. In most cases when violence threatens, they opt for withdrawal; silence seems to them the better part of valor. As for most women academics, they played along, not wanting to appear disloyal to the Women's Movement. Many of their students, attracted to the ideology of sexual equality, enrolled in women's studies courses and became disciples of gender feminism.

But a reaction has set in. Some women, mostly outside the academy, all prominent writers and critics such as Camille Paglia, Katie Roiphe, Midge Decter, and Jean Kirkpatrick, to name only a few, have begun to decry the excesses of gender feminism. They accuse gender feminists of subordinating scholarship to ideology, of recruiting students to the extreme wing of the women's movement, and of stirring up hatred between the sexes. In articles, books, and lectures before large audiences, they attack the genderist viewpoint as manipulative sophistry intended to advance personal campaigns for attention and influence. They are making it clear that gender feminists do not speak for all women and certainly not for them. They will not conform to gender feminism's ideology.

Had the feminists been content to keep their differences within their own community, a clash might have been avoided. In a permissive society everyone is entitled to her own viewpoint and choices. But feminists have not been reticent about expressing their opinions. Each side insists that the other conform to its ideological perspective. They have taken their quarrel to the public and are engaged in a donnybrook that is having consequences not only for the Women's Movement but for society as well. A large dollop of discord has been injected into the life-stream of a nation that already suffers from a surfeit of disharmony. Like a low-grade fever, the fight between feminists debilitates the spirit and weakens the body politic.

THE AFROCENTRIC CONTRETEMPS

Nothing so clearly illustrates the contradiction between individualism and conformity in Elitist ideology as the current angry debate between the mostly black Afrocentric Elite and their erstwhile allies, the predominantly white mainstream Elite. Cherishing the uniqueness of their culture, Afrocentrists are promoting their own individuality and threaten to establish a separate society unless they get their way. But despite their devotion to individualism, they demand conformity from whites and blacks alike to Afrocentric visions, rules, and values, and attack anyone who will not conform.

Afrocentrists explain that they are acting to counteract the psychological damage the white majority has visited on blacks. They cite studies which show that belonging to a disparaged group can damage self-esteem. For example, an early study of inner-city blacks found that black men suffer from the "mark of oppression," the result of living in a country dominated by whites who hate the black race and show their contempt in prejudice-laden language, cultural stereotypes, and discrimination in housing and work. The psychic damage of this mauling had been devastating. The blacks in this study who had internalized the white man's hateful image of their race felt defeated, weak, frightened, and were filled with a consuming rage they could not safely express.[5]

Afrocentrists say they are only seeking to neutralize the effects of prejudice by projecting an image of black culture and history that will strengthen black self-esteem and refute the hateful stereotypes of the black man cherished and promoted by some whites. To this end they emphasize the part blacks played in the nation's development, giving to blacks a heroic stature not found in previous accounts of the American experience; more to the point, they try to infuse school curricula with favorable information about African Americans. Surprisingly, their efforts have met little resistance. In some parts of the country, particularly where blacks are numerous and in elite schools where a we-are-all-guilty spirit prevails, Afrocentrists have been able to fashion curricula much more to their liking.

Afrocentrists are a bold and feisty lot, not given to understatement and debilitating modesty. They will, for example, blithely ditch scholarly exactitude in the interest of creating black counterparts to the national heroes in the white pantheon. Afrocentric blacks are writing their own histories, trying to put their own mark on the American memory. "We've got to stop waiting for white folks to put us in their history books," said one Afrocentrist, Professor Jacob Gordon of the University of Kansas.[6] And so, for example, in the spirit of giving the black man his due, the Afrocentric account of the American Revolution has been given to Crispus Attucks a significance rivaling that of Paul Revere.

Not content merely to rewrite American history, they have undertaken to reexamine the origins of Western Civilization itself. Their explorations have uncovered, so they say, vital truths about the past that white scholars have deliberately ignored or concealed. The cradle of Western Civilization, it turns out, was not Greece, as white Eurocentric classicists maintain, but Egypt, an African nation peopled by blacks. According to some Afrocentrists, for example Molefe Kete Asante, head of the African-American Studies department at Temple University, the great contributions to philosophy, mathematics, and science long attributed to the ancient Greeks were in fact stolen from blacks by Greeks during their visits to Egypt. Thales, Homer, Pythagoras, Isocrates, Plato, and Aristotle had studied in Egypt, Afrocentrists assert, and it was in a black African land that they learned philosophy, astronomy, geometry, medicine, architecture, and law. This knowledge the Greeks pilfered and passed off as their own—to their everlasting shame and to the profound diminishment of black history.

Egyptologists and classicists react to this story with shocked disbelief, mingled with impatience at sloppy scholarship. They point out that the Afrocentric argument rests on two highly dubious assumptions: first, that the people of ancient Egypt were black; and second, that the Greek philosophers accused of theft had in fact visited Egypt. But there is no evidence to support either assumption. As to the first assumption—the black racial composition of ancient Egypt—Frank J. Yurco, an Egyptologist at Chicago's Field Museum of Natural History, believes the evidence derived from mummies, statues, and paintings indicates the ancient Egyptians were much like their present-day descendants, whose skin color ranges from light on the Mediterranean coast to a darker shade in upper Egypt to a dark brown near Aswan. Professor Alaf Marsot of the Near-East Center of the University of California at Los Angeles concurs. He calls the idea that ancient Egyptians were black a "myth, based on the flimsiest kind of evidence. The Egyptians were a mixed population, as all Mediterranean people are mixed."[7] As to the charge that the ancient Greeks purloined Egyptian knowledge during their visits to Egypt, not an iota of evidence exists that these worthy gentlemen ever set foot on Egyptian soil. Aristotle, for instance, could hardly have stolen Egyptian knowledge during a visit to the famed library at Alexandria, as Afrocentrists claim, since, as classics scholar Mary Lefkowitz points out, the library had not yet been built during his lifetime.[8]

But this does not discomfit Afrocentrists in the slightest. They understand, even if their opponents may not, that they are not engaged in scholarship. Myth making is their business, and business is good. Factually correct or not, their ideas about the black contribution to world culture are being incorporated into the curricula of public schools in several major cities—Baltimore, Chicago, Detroit, Camden, Milwaukee—with the specific purpose of enhancing the self-esteem of black children. But mainstream Elitists are finding it hard to accept the Afrocentrists' argument. For what began as an effort to put the place of African-Americans in American history in better perspective, to reveal their true contribution to American history and culture, has become an attack upon whites.

Emerging from these attacks is a picture of white people that is offensive to white sensibilities. (Disparaging someone's race, as all the world must know by now, is a game two can play; blacks have learned a lot from whites.) It is not a pretty picture. In the Afrocentric view whites are one-dimensional figures, all action and no affect; cold and cruelly domineering, indifferent to beauty, and incapable of human warmth. White people live emotionally flat, dreary lives. Only materialism and aggression excites them; their greatest pleasure is to control and exploit the weak, especially people of color, who live under the yoke of white rule.

As Afrocentrists see it, white people cannot help being what they are, given their origins. According to Leonard Jefferies, a professor of African-American studies at the City College of New York, whites are "ice people," whose ancestors lived in dark, cold caves, a cold-hearted people who have brought the world only exploitation and destruction. In contrast, say Afrocentrists, blacks descend from a warm, superior people who grew up in the African sunlight. Protected by skin-darkening melanin, blacks became "sun people," warmly compassionate toward all people who suffer under white oppression.

The power of melanin and sunshine in Afrocentric ideology is impressive. According to Afrocentrists, it is to melanin and sunshine that blacks are indebted for their gift for rhythm and dance, their good-natured disposition, their capacity for creative thought. It is due to sunshine and melanin that blacks are able to escape the white man's icy linear way of thinking; blacks can intuitively understand things hidden from whites dependent upon cold reason. It is because of sunshine and melanin that blacks can infuse experience with a humane warmth found only outside the rigid boundaries of cold reason. Cold logic, a specialty of whites, has brought humanity nothing but sorrow, for the white people's ice-bound nature distorts their view of the world—a sad limitation for whites and a tragedy for anyone who falls into their hands.

If this harangue had been mere rhetoric, perhaps no serious damage would have been done. In America groups have been slandering each other for generations, and the republic still stands. Is not the current contretemps between the races simply one more example of Americans slinging mud and making threats rather than engaging in rational debate? And are not the separatists mere hucksters and hustlers, con artists using racial injuries to justify extravagant claims to lush rewards? It is tempting to think so. After all, money and fame await the separatist who has demonstrated exceptional skill at stirring up racial hatred and focusing anger on the white majority—the putative cause of the minority group's troubles. A good living can be made succoring the oppressed. Organizations can be built, offices staffed, foundation grants garnered, conferences held at luxurious hotels in elegant surroundings on tropical isles, speeches given for high fees to enthusiastic audiences, and interviews granted to attentive reporters with assured access to the public. Outside of political office, what other job offers such generous rewards for so little work?

And it is true that the threats of separation have come from only a few black spokesmen, not the rank and file. Who are these spokesmen? Who gave them the right to make charges, to formulate programs, to take actions in the name of all blacks? No one, actually. Apart from a few elected officials (who presumably represent a mixed bag of constituents), most minority spokesmen are either entirely self-appointed or selected by small organizations which represent only themselves or at most very narrow interests. Gunnar Myrdal dismissed the "leaders" of the new ethnicity movement as a "few well-established intellectuals, professors, writers" obsessed with "upper-class intellectual romanticism."[9] Were he alive today he would have to modify this statement.

It is true that most separatists are obsessed with the Elitist ideology integral to the Chameleon Complex, which is romantic in its narcissistic, perfectionist view of human nature. But then so are most of their opponents in the mainstream Elite. And it may well be that some separatists are hustlers, motivated only by a hunger for power and money. It would be naive to believe that the mainstream is without such people. In fact it is more likely that most separatists, and their opponents among the white New Elite, are sincere and fierce, determined advocates of ideas and programs intrinsic to their character and ideology.

That contradictions in this ideology require them to be both individualists and conformists only makes them more unbending. The common response to internal conflict, the consequence of living with contradiction, is ambivalence and emotional rigidity, a paralyzing fear that compromise will cause things to fall apart. It is this ambivalence that makes it so painful for Elitists to acknowledge the contradictions in their beliefs and behavior. And it is this rigidity that makes it so difficult for Elitists, Afrocentric and mainstream alike, to find negotiated solutions to conflict and the threat of separation.

Some Afrocentrists have gone beyond mere rhetoric; they are founding organizations based on the premise that between ice people and sun people there can be no accommodation, no integration, no assimilation. Afrocentrists argue that blacks must separate themselves from the white man's world—physically, wherever possible; culturally, whenever possible; psychologically, as much as possible. There is no living with white people. To mix with whites is to suffer humiliation and exploitation. Blacks must be black, must protect their blackness, must treasure their uniqueness. Anything less means inevitable extinction, not only for the group but also for the individual, a slow withering of emotional vitality and the drawn-out decline and eventual death of black culture and identity. The only solution is to put as much distance as possible between themselves and whites, to create a black world, and to keep the white man out.

Friendly whites react to Afrocentric separatism with pained surprise and alarm. Why, they ask, are we being attacked? What have we done wrong? Why are blacks doing this? That these whites feel puzzled and hurt is understandable. They thought they had been doing the fair thing; they thought that fairness means opening the gates to everyone, keeping no one out because of race, religion, or creed. But now some blacks say they don't want in; they want out. Echoing sentiments dating from the time of Marcus Garvey and before, Afrocentrists speak of founding a black nation in North America, independent of white society and dedicated to the advancement of black people. It's not the white man's acceptance they want; it's separation, independence, and national sovereignty.

THE ELITISTS' DILEMMA

The call for separation perplexes mainstream Elitists. They believe it has always been the American ideal to be inclusive, to welcome everyone into the common fold, to build a new American identity out of the diverse materials taken from many cultures. The process, as aptly expressed in Israel Zangwill's 1908 play *The Melting-Pot*, was to dump everyone into a crucible, expose them to the fiery blast of American culture, burn off all foreign impurities, and pour out a new product—a new American who, culturally speaking, closely resembled the old American, the dominant White Anglo-Saxon Protestant.

The melting pot ideal was never wildly popular among all ethnics, many of whom held on to their customs, stubbornly resisting the quick march into assimilation.[10] Nonetheless, with relatively few exceptions, most groups moved into the cultural mainstream, usually within a generation or two. The exceptions isolated themselves in small enclaves where they continue to follow their own ways almost unnoticed by the larger society. Small in number, often immersed in their religion, determinedly anti-modern and sometimes quaintly attired, they pique the interest of tourists, who see in their desire to be left alone no threat to the nation.

Mainstream Elitists are generally sympathetic to the idea that a group has the right to develop its own culture and identity. It is part of their code of individualism. But the notion that a large group can go its own separate way is intolerable. They charge Afrocentrists, gender feminists, and any ethnic group possessing separatist elements with fomenting disunion, with emphasizing group differences, with seeking to split the country into antagonistic groups, each with its own political agenda and territorial ambition. They say that this is more than the country can take. They urge people to agree upon a common culture and a national identity—and conform to it. Without common values and ideals, without the common mystic chords of memory that bind people together, a racially and culturally hetero-geneous nation could well fall apart.

However, the people seem blissfully unaware of the nation's im-minent dissolution. They know they are beset with problems thrown up by traumatic economic change. The Second Great Transforma-tion has given them more than enough to worry about. The idea of cultural separation would only compound their anxiety—if they knew about it, but relatively few of them do. The controversy over con-formity to a single cultural standard is not as widely publicized as Elitists believe; it is largely an intramural argument within the New Elite about which most people know little and care even less. That the Elitists, despite their commitment to individual choice, are urging each other to conform to their own particular culture is not generally viewed as a matter of national concern.

Thus when mainstream Elitists insist that the separatists drop their demands for cultural autonomy the people concur. But they cannot see what the fuss is about. It seems mostly talk to them—that is, when they hear of it. Perhaps they would be more concerned if they knew that separatists are making plans to break away, and that appealing to them to desist their attacks upon the establishment is futile. Sep-aratists have their own notions of individualism and conformity. They are not interested in unity; it is disunion they are seeking. They ex-pect to pick up the pieces, use what they need to bolster their group's power, and throw the rest away.

It can be argued, of course, that the threat of separation is nothing new to America. Why is it creating so much alarm among Elitists now? Is the country more vulnerable to divisive demagoguery today than in the past? More so than in the tumultuous 1890s? Probably not. But some danger there is and it needs to be understood. For what makes the present turmoil unique is the confluence of two his-torically important forces: the triumph of the techno-service econ-omy, which created unnerving economic change, and the emergence of a new character type—the New Elitist—whose ideas and actions are stirring up conflict.

The techno-service economy wounded many people, making them feel like losers at a time when they thought they had a chance to become winners. And some Elitists rubbed salt in the wound by ques-tioning the blue-collar workers' and the blacks' ability to cope with the challenges of the information society. When still other Elitists, the separatists, came along and counseled separation, the scene was set for a new drama, the epic of a fragmented America. How this play will turn out is a question that should concern every American. For, quite deliberately, the separatists are seeking to create a contentious tribalism that would divide the nation into conflicting groups, each set apart by a separate identity, each jealously guarding its own culture, each determined to enforce its claim on the nation's patrimony and wealth.

These are potentially dangerous tactics. The separatists are assaulting a strongly held value: that all groups—class, sectional, religious, sexual, ethnic, racial—must subordinate their parochial concerns to the national interest; and that the first goal of the nation is to weld together from widely different materials a common national identity. Caught up in their own contradictions, torn between individualism and conformity, the Elitists are fighting over the right of groups to go their own way. Nothing enduring may come of all this. But even if this fracas should turn out to be temporary, it will leave scars. It is altogether likely that the contradictions inherent in the Elitist ideology and the fractious nature of the New Elite itself will throw up new problems and new battles.

PART VI

CONCLUSION

14

Letting the Light In

When people are uneasy, plagued by doubt and cynicism, they usually want to know why and what to do about it. But not always. Sometimes they deny that a problem exists or refuse to deal with it, tucking it away in some dark recess of the mind. Even when convinced that they need help, they quickly grow weary of complex explanations and clamor for a quick fix to drive the ache away. But this is self-defeating—denial or demands for magic solutions will not do the trick.

The truth of the matter is that much of the unease prevalent in some circles today is caused by the conflicts produced by the Second Great Transformation: the clash between different cultures and character types, the competition for power between new and old elites, the struggle within the minds of individuals pulled in opposite directions, the fight between the winners and the losers who have been made to feel out of place and unwanted, no longer comfortable in their own country.

In this book I have sought to shed light on the fallout produced by the explosive social changes embodied in the Second Great Transformation. These changes affect how people feel about themselves, how happy they are with the groups to which they belong, and how well their own needs fit the needs of the new society. Sad to say, not everyone has benefited from the Second Great Transformation; some people are winners, some are not.

The winners run the new techno-service society; they have the traits, talents, and skills needed to function well in an information-based economy. They are skilled at information collection and processing, adept at manipulating abstractions and symbols, exceptionally proficient in the use of words and images. Society rewards them with generous amounts of money, power, and status. But equally important, they are given something most people believe essential to their peace of mind—respect—a prize awarded to them because of their contributions to the successful functioning of the information economy.

I call these winners Elitists, in part because they believe superior merit alone accounts for their success; in part because they evaluate themselves and others in terms of merit badges accumulated—promotions, awards, diplomas and advanced degrees, money, homes in prestigious neighborhoods, and other similar marks of success; in part because they decide who shall be admitted into their ranks; but mostly because they believe they know what is best for society—and do not hesitate to say so. Slowly these people are coalescing into a group increasingly identifiable as the New Elite.

The losers are drawn from diverse groups. Many are blue-collar workers who have been hurt by the relative decline of manufacturing; they feel their old world, linked to manufacturing, has been emasculated. Many are poorly educated young men who have been unable to find a foothold in the new information system and are unneeded in the manufacturing economy. These dispossessed people have either lost their jobs in the old system or have never been able to make a place for themselves in the new. They had been promised that the good times would go on forever, getting better with each new generation, only to see the old economy shoved aside by the new one created by the Second Great Transformation.

Americans have never had much time for losers. Being in second place or entirely out of the running may win sympathy, but only winners get the big prizes. It is the gold medal that most contestants strive for; anything less feels like a consolation prize. Blue-collar workers doing routine work, white-collar clerks performing perfunctory tasks, traditional people desperately clinging to old-fashioned ideas, under-educated youths unable to learn the skills required to succeed in a high-tech world—all these and other losers win no medals in the new information economy.

Losers don't feel comfortable in the information society; their values and character traits fit poorly with the needs of the new system. And yet, like everybody else, they need to feel that society values their work and has a place for them. But this is exactly what they are being denied. The respect they once enjoyed has been taken away—and a loss of status respect inevitably engenders anger and bitterness, doubt and cynicism.

As though all of this were not bad enough, the losers have been enfiladed in a war between mainstream Elitists trying to hold on to their position and the new separatist Elites who want to usurp it. As in all wars, the cultural war has its casualties. But these seldom include the combatants, who shed little besides ink, lose little besides reputation, suffer little besides wounds to their pride. The true victims of the fighting are the working and lower-middle classes whose values are being rubbished and whose interests are being ignored. They may sense that something strange is going on around them—echoes of the war reach their ears when television and the print media make a point of reporting the fighting—but they are generally at a loss to understand what the fuss is all about.

Who precisely the fighters are and what exactly they are fighting about is not clear to most outsiders. Convoluted arguments over which books belong in the literary canon usually pass the public by. Restrictions on language to make it conform to the strictures of political correctness, to the extent that the public has heard of them, seem petty and silly. Changes in the curriculum to include more multicultural materials would interest them if they knew of it; but unless they attend school board meetings or closely follow discussions of school issues in the press, the chances are that they know little of the furor multiculturalism is causing within the academy and between various factions of the New Elite.

What they know for sure is that governmental agencies have promulgated rules that affect how they may treat one another—on the factory floor and in the office. These rules have made them vulnerable to lawsuits, and this frightens them. Comments that only yesterday seemed trivial, or at worst in bad taste, have become criminal offenses. They are learning that charges of racism or sexual harassment, sometimes on the flimsiest evidence, may cost them heavily. But they feel they have little say in the matter.

Most damaging of all, they feel manipulated and deceived, permitted to see and read only what the media Elite think suitable, and much of that false and harmful. The media warn them that the country has been put in peril by their past and present failures and sins. Many working-class and middle-class whites feel indicted, tried, and convicted of crimes against blacks, Indians, Hispanics, homosexuals, and women, committed in their name and without their knowledge or consent. Although they feel like victims, they are condemned as victimizers.

The losers are finding Elitist dominance particularly hard to bear. They quite naturally resent the manners, airs, and values of the affluent New Elite, which, still new to its eminence and visibly pleased with itself, makes no effort to hide its contempt for people who lack the human capital to buy their way into the Elite. Moreover, the losers have learned to be wary of Elitists, who, armored by the conviction of the purity of their motives, have shown no compunction in crushing their opponents.

Since most Elitists have been amply rewarded with wealth and influence and respect—winners take most of society's prizes; after all, it was created by and for them, its work fits their skills, its culture suits their needs, its money flows abundantly into their pockets—why then are so many of them uneasy and anxious? Because, operating in an intensely competitive environment and tending to see treachery everywhere, they have taken refuge in the Chameleon Complex; they are caught in its toils, and are plagued by its demands and contradictions. Chameleonism generates anxiety, the result of a nagging fear of being unmasked, and a mind clouded by confusion about one's true identity. They have sought solace in a search for perfection, but they cannot reconcile their need for a perfect world with the imperfect one they have created. They feel disappointed with themselves, and guilty.

The ideological contradictions embedded in the Chameleon Complex pull them in opposite directions, now toward meritocratically based success, now toward equality irrespective of merit; now toward individualism and freedom of choice, now toward conformity and obedience to the will of the group. Guilt, ambivalence and a tendency to self-flagellation for every imperfection in themselves and the world form the basic stuff of anxiety among Elitist winners.

Winners and losers alike have taken to fighting among themselves. Working class losers—whites and blacks, Latinos and Native Americans, men and women—compete for the same jobs, and have taken to hurling charges and insults at each other. As for the winners, they have split into warring factions and are vindictively attacking each other: gender feminists against equity feminists, separatist Elitists against mainstream Elitists, men against women. These attacks evoke counterattacks and cause bitter feelings, bruised egos, and occasionally shattered bodies. The clash of ideas, the clangor of charges and counter-charges, the unyielding insistence on having one's own way, threaten to undermine the belief among some Americans that they have built a common identity from many disparate parts.

That all this has produced anxiety, doubt, and cynicism is hardly questionable. The pressing question is what to do about it? Unfortunately, diagnosing a problem is far easier than prescribing a workable cure. And even more distressing, there is no magic bullet. Even if surefire solutions were available (which they are not), it would take far more space to describe them than that allotted to me in this book. Still, it is my hope that focusing light on the problem will help. Once people understand the true causes of their distress—not the spurious ones spread by irresponsible provocateurs seeking to stir up trouble, and by groups eager to promote their own interests—then the torment caused by rapid social change will subside somewhat. To some degree the terror of anxiety lies in its mystery. Some people feel worried, angry, and betrayed; they know that things are not going as well as they expected, but they cannot put their finger on what has gone wrong.

But once people understand the true nature of the predicament they are in—that they are caught up in a massive restructuring of the economy that began before many of them were born and will in all likelihood continue long after their death—they may see the futility of beating their breasts, of making impossible demands and accusations, and of lashing out at innocent bystanders, many of them fellow victims. Then they can take steps to alleviate the misery of rapid social change. But first they must understand that they cannot prevent change. The techno-service revolution will continue whether it suits everyone's interests or not. There is no place to stop and get off. But we can soften the revolution's effects and make whatever good use of change we can. Here are some things we can do.

First of all, don't panic—we have been there before and survived. The First Great Transformation was also a jarring experience. When manufacturing triumphed over farming, many people felt the ground cut out from under them: craftsmen lost their trades; farmers had to leave their beloved countryside and move to the inhospitable city; migrants felt alone in the new industrial world, unwanted, unappreciated, uncomfortable. They had been trained to function in a rural-small town economy. But now they were in an urban, industrial world, and they felt out of place. They could not understand what was wanted, what to believe, what to feel. The suffering was great, but the overwhelming majority made the transition to the new society, and their children or grandchildren flourished in it. A similar process is underway today. Slowly, a new symmetry is developing between the needs of the new techno-service society and the needs of the individual. The process of adjustment is painful and far from over, but with luck the turmoil stirred up by the Second Great Transformation will be overcome.

Second, help the losers. Help may not turn every loser into a winner, yet it *is* possible to palliate the effects of unbridled social change. Money will help, but money alone will not do the job. Most of today's losers are not economically deprived. In many cases their problems are less financial than psychological and cultural. Most of them have jobs; and more jobs, many of them good ones, are being created everyday. Unemployment is at its lowest level in years. Some people described as losers are not doing all that badly, economically speaking; some are doing quite well, despite the endlessly reiterated assertion that they are not, that they are falling behind, that they are becoming poorer. It is true that income inequality has increased, but this is because the rich have become richer; the poor, on average, have not become poorer.

Losers have been disoriented by exceedingly rapid social change, and their problems are not going to be easily solved by government grants and handouts. Still, in some cases more money, more schooling, and wider, stronger safety nets will soften the pain felt by workers alienated and marginalized by technological change. Some of these people are truly in a bad way through no fault of their own—for example, workers whose unemployment insurance has run out, who have lost their medical insurance and cannot replace it. For these people the safety net can and should be strengthened. Legislatures are taking steps in that direction and no doubt will take more.

The under-educated or redundant blue-collar workers whose skills are outdated and who may have difficulty learning new ones present a much more complicated problem. They are victims of technological change and need help. But what to do for them is far from obvious. Apprenticeships for the young, an idea former Secretary of Labor Robert Reich borrowed from Germany, may help, but it is unclear whether it is feasible here. The Germans are talking of reducing their apprenticeship program or abandoning it altogether. And whether laid-off machinists can be taught the data processing skills that are marketable in the information economy is problematical. But perhaps it is worth a try.

The saddest losers in society—the flotsam and jetsam of the underclass, the drug addicts who haunt needle parks, the juvenile delinquents, the teenage unmarried mothers, the murderous thugs who prey upon the helpless in the inner city—present a far more difficult problem. To some extent their troubles have been exacerbated by the Second Great Transformation; many of them are certainly in a bad way. But how to help them is a conundrum that still baffles the most skilled of society's social analysts.

Still, something can in fact be done that is certain to raise the spirits of almost all losers: restore to them the status respect they once enjoyed. Manual workers once esteemed for their strength and mechanical skills, and white-collar workers—people holding down jobs in lower level clerical, sales, personal service work and proud of their clean hands and tidy surroundings—no longer receive the kind of respect formerly accorded them. With the triumph of the techno-service economy their skills seem inconsequential compared to the grandeur of information collection and processing, and as a result their contributions to society have been devalued.

The principal agent of this devaluation has been the New Elite, which looks down, with a condescension bordering on contempt, on people who have not mastered the art and uses of information processing. Such ineptitude is seen as symptomatic of the intellectual deficiency that marks non-adepts as losers, a flaw that prevents them from gaining membership in the Elite's meritocracy, and hence a sign of shameful inferiority—a terrible indictment, of course, but this can be changed. Since the New Elite establishes the criteria for garnering status respect, it can change those criteria so as to enhance the status of people it now considers losers. It can, for example, express admiration for someone who makes machinery and keeps it in repair; it can show its appreciation to the people who do the thousand and one things that bring food to our tables, safeguard our person and property, perform routine service work in large and small organizations, and care for our bodies when sickness strikes. These are things the Elite now takes for granted, to the exasperation and fury of blue-collar workers and lesser service personnel.

If changing the criteria for winning respect is to work—and it will be a slow process, expect no miracles—it must not be a parade of pious fatuities and airy platitudes. Change must take visible and concrete form. For instance, the New Elite can establish ties with organized labor, which it avoided when unions were seen as barriers to the advancement of blacks and women. This alone would do much to heal the breach between the unionized blue-collar worker and the New Elite. It can take seriously the complaints of white males that affirmative action programs violate the Elite's claim to value merit above ascription, that what matters is not the workers' color or gender but how well they do their jobs; it can halt and perhaps reverse the process of isolating itself in guarded communities, select schools, clubs and service organizations. And perhaps most importantly, it can show that it respects the values of traditional people—their patriotism and devotion to family and religion.

The beauty part of all this is that restoring respect to the losers costs nothing, a not inconsiderable factor at a time when social programs are being curtailed or eliminated to save money. But in a way it is the most costly of all because it requires major changes in social attitudes, not something easy to do. And yet, it may happen when New Elitists recognize that the price they are now paying for the luxury of lording it over less smart people is prodigious—that is, having to live in society with many embittered people who feel badly treated and who may someday turn their anger against the Elite.

Third, it would help enormously if the people who base their security on the Chameleon Complex could be persuaded that they have condemned themselves to a lifetime of disappointment. Though mostly members of the New Elite and winners by conventional criteria, the practioners of the Chameleon Complex have chosen a losing strategy for achieving peace with themselves and with others. Chameleonism may ward off danger in the short run, but its long-term effects are crippling. Chameleons are burdened with narcissistic perfectionism—the pursuit of an ideal self and a flawless society. Sadly, perfection will forever be beyond their reach. They blame themselves and berate others for standing in the way of their impossible dream. Paradoxically, though winners in the new social system, they think of themselves as losers in the race that matters most to them: the dash for the gold medal of a fully realized self in a flawless society. And since they believe the medal is theirs by right, they are filling the air with cries of betrayal.

Since the Chameleon Complex is deeply rooted in personality, it will be difficult to relinquish. Chameleons adore their ideal selves and cherish the ideal of a flawless world. They will fight to keep them. But if they can be convinced that the Chameleon Complex is self-defeating, they may perhaps substitute the real world, which affords them many satisfactions, for a fantasy that brings them pain. Sometimes the shocking discovery that one has an unreal view of oneself and the world will vanquish defensive distortion, and perhaps Elitists will suffer enough shocks to bring this about. After all, Elitists are highly intelligent; with the right approach they may be persuaded to come to their senses.

Finally, all parties can lower the decibel level. The din of battle between groups competing for jobs, money, and power is drowning out pleas for compromise and conciliation. The plaintive voice of reason cannot be heard above the noise of angry voices shouting for redress of their grievances. If voices were lowered, sanity might emerge. Then it would be recognized that status-seeking middle-class women, ambitious blacks, working-class Latinos, and immigrants are only trying to get a foothold in the new system. They can hardly be blamed for doing what America has always urged its citizens to do—strive to get ahead, make something of yourself, be successful.

But when groups stake out positions that have no reasonable chance of being accepted they only encourage the disappointment of futile dreams. Whites cannot retreat to a pristine area in the Northwest, there to set up their own Aryan nation. Blacks cannot retreat into an all-black society in the South. Women and men cannot do without each another, even though organized groups have made it difficult for them to iron out conflicting claims for jobs and power. The New Elite cannot dispense with blue-collar whites or even with the business class; they are needed to build cars, maintain the roads, keep the economy running. The country cannot do without the New Elite, no matter how much this would please the blue-collar class and traditional folk, for the Elitists are needed to run the new information society.

Of course, it is unrealistic to expect the fighting to stop merely because some dreams are impossible and conflict is dangerous. People are fighting for the power to control the culture, to define the American character, and to set the direction of the country. These are matters of paramount importance. The future of the country is at stake, and hence the fight will go on. The issues are too vital to be dismissed with polite shudders and weary sighs about how people are being unreasonable and making dangerous demands. The demands are in fact often unreasonable and dangerous, but saying so will not make them go away. Nevertheless, doing nothing is also dangerous, and so is the unwillingness to understand the nature of the changes roiling society today. Denial and ignorance can only make matters worse.

Americans will have to learn to live with rapid social change. But acceptance of change does not mean passive resignation to its unfortunate consequences. Something can be done about them. But it is wise to recognize that the effects of change are deeply entrenched and will not quickly disappear. Still, the pain of change will in all probability decline when the needs of the individual and those of the social system come into better complementarity, as they most likely will in time. The fighting will also slacken when a victorious group finally takes over. Then the question of who should control the culture will have been answered, at least for a time. In the meantime we can try to fathom the workings of change, so as to better understand what is happening to us as a people. This will not be easy, but it can be done. It would also help if we face up to the fact that for the indefinite future Americans will continue living in interesting times.

Notes

CHAPTER 1. THE LOSER'S LAMENT

1. As far back as 1981, a Gallup Poll found that 81 percent of the respondents were "dissatisfied with the way things were going in the United States." Cited in Peter Clecak, *America's Quest for the Ideal Self* (New York: Oxford University Press, 1983), p. 7. For other comments on the nation's disgruntlement, see a Gallup Poll reported in the *New York Times*, March 4, 1990, and the Wirthlin Group Poll reported in the *New Republic*, October 17, 1994, p. 18.

2. Lamar Alexander, *The Economist*, August 20, 1994, p. 27.

3. Bill Clinton, reported in the *New York Times*, September 22, 1995, p. 1.

4. *U.S. News and World Report*, October 24, 1995, p. 72.

5. John Chancellor, in *Social Problems: Annual Edition, 93/94* (Guilford, Conn.: Dushkin Publishing Group, 1993).

6. James W. Michaels, "Oh My Aching Angst," *Forbes*, September 14, 1992, p. 48. The statistics on the American economy in this book are mainly based on work by government departments, principally the Commerce Department and the Department of Labor. Economic data appear in a variety of official public reports, some of which may be found in the annual *Statistical Abstract of the United States*. These data are not always fully disaggregated and analyzed. I also use data presented in magazines like *The Economist*, *Forbes*, *Business Week*, and the weekly news magazines. See also Robert J. Samuelson, *Newsweek*, March, 2, 1992, p. 35; James Lincoln Collier, *The Rise*

of Selfishness in America (New York: Oxford University Press, 1991); Stanley Lebergott, *Pursuing Happiness* (Princeton, N.J.: Princeton University Press, 1993); "The Global Economy," *The Economist*, October 1, 1994, p. 15.

7. Rollo May, *The Meaning of Anxiety* (New York: Ronald Press, 1950), p. 349. A discussion of theories of anxiety can be found in Calvin S. Hall and Gardner Lindzey, *Theories of Personality* (New York: John Wiley, 1957); Christopher F. Monte, *Beneath the Mask* (New York: Praeger, 1977); and Salvatore R. Maddi, *Personality Theories* (Homewood, Ill.: Dorsey Press, 1980).

8. G. D. H. Cole, "Industrialism," in the *Encyclopedia of the Social Sciences*, one-volume edition New York: Macmillan, 1973), p. 18. For a fuller presentation of the Parsonian position, see Talcott Parsons, *The Social System* (Glencoe, Ill.: Free Press, 1951); also C. Wright Mills, *The Sociological Imagination* (New York: Oxford University Press, 1959), p. 31; Dennis Wrong, *The Problem of Order* (New York: Free Press, 1994), pp. 132–133. A more psychoanalytic exposition of this basic argument can be found in Erich Fromm and Michael Maccoby, *Social Character in a Mexican Village* (Englewood Cliffs, N.J.: Prentice-Hall, 1959).

9. *The Economist*, in the "Food Survey," December 4, 1993, p. 15.

10. Quoted in Mickey Kaus, *The End of Equality* (New York: Basic Books, 1992), p. 19.

11. Quoted by Kaus, *The End of Equality*, p. 27.

CHAPTER 2. ROUND UP THE USUAL SUSPECTS

1. This description of conditions in American schools appears in *The Economist*, July 24, 1993, p. 31.

2. Gannett News Service, October 21, 1994. The Department of Education reported that for the school year 1995–1996 in 29 states and the District of Columbia 6,276 students were expelled for bringing guns and other weapons to school. *Ithaca Journal*, June 17, 1997, p. 1B.

3. A brief summary of conditions in the contemporary family can be found in "The Disappearing Family," *The Economist*, September 9–15, 1995, pp. 25–29.

4. A good, if somewhat lurid, sketch of the history of crime in America can be found in Ovid Demaris, *America the Violent* (New York: Cowles, 1969).

5. Charles Silberman, *Criminal Violence, Criminal Justice* (New York: Random House, 1978), p. 22.

6. Donald J. Mulvehill and Melvin M. Tumin, co-directors, *Crimes of Violence. Staff Report to the National Commission on the Causes and Prevention of Violence* (Washington, D.C.: U.S. Department of Justice, 1969), p. 51.

7. David Herbert Donald, *Lincoln* (New York: Simon and Schuster, 1995), p. 80.

8. Herbert J. Croly, *Promise of American Life* (Hamden, Conn.: Archon Books, 1963, originally published in 1903); pp. 95–96.

9. James Lincoln Collier, *The Rise of Selfishness in America* (New York: Oxford University Press, 1991), p. 5.

10. Ralph Blumenthal, *New York Times*, August 26, 1990, p. E6.

11. Ibid.

12. Demaris, *America the Violent*.

13. Bill Bryson, *Made in America* (London: Secker and Warburg, 1994), p. 166.

14. Blumenthal, *Times*.

15. Silberman, *Criminal Violence, Criminal Justice*, p. 6.

16. Sean Wilentz, "Bombs Bursting In Air, Still," *New York Times Magazine*, June 25, 1995, p. 40.

17. Silberman, *Criminal Violence, Criminal Justice*. See also National Center for Health Statistics, *New York Times*, August 13, 1995, p. 18.

18. Time/CNN Poll, *Time Magazine*, January 30, 1995, p. 63.

19. United States Department of Justice, *The Economist*, October 15, 1994, p. 21.

20. *Time Magazine*, January 30, 1995, p. 63.

21. *New York Times*, October 24, 1993, Section 4, p. 1.

22. L. P. Hartley, *The Go-Between* (London: Hamish Hamilton, 1953), quoted in John Steele Gordon, "The Problem of Money and Time," *American Heritage*, May-June 1988, p. 57.

23. "The Global Survey," *The Economist*, October 1, 1994, p. 4.

24. Data on the improvement of women' earnings are taken from Bureau of Labor Statistics, as reported in the *New York Times*, February 25, 1996.

25. *New York Times*, August 13, 1995, p. 26.

26. Robert J. Samuelson, *The Good Life And Its Discontents* (New York: Times Books, 1995), p. 70.

27. *Time*, January 30, 1995, p. 60.

28. Floyd Norris, "Week in Review," *New York Times*, December 1, 1996, p. 4; see also Robert J. Samuelson, *Newsweek*, September 25, 1995, p. 63.

29. Susan Dentzer, *US News and World Report*, March 11, 1996, pp. 58–60.

30. John Cassidy, "All Worked Up," *The New Yorker*, April 22, 1996, pp. 51–55. Robert J. Samuelson agrees with this conclusion. See his article in the May 6, 1996, issue of *Newsweek*, p. 51.

31. *The Economist*, February 24, 1996, p. 30.

32. Census Bureau data reported by Marc Levinson, "Hey, You're Doing Great," *Newsweek*, January 30, 1995, p. 42.

33. *The Economist*, January 28, 1995, p. 25.

34. *The Economist*, February 24, 1996, p. 15.

35. *The Economist*, February 18, 1995, p. 63.

36. John Cassidy, "The Growth Fallacy," *The New Yorker*, August 12, 1996, p. 35.

37. Richard L. Berke, *New York Times*, October 10, 1994, p. 1.

38. *The Economist*, June 5, 1993, p. 22.

39. "The Global Survey," *The Economist*, October 1, 1944, pp. 3–38.

40. Estimates of past American economic growth vary. Jeffrey Madrick puts it higher than the 2 to 2.5 percent figure usually given. The true figure, he says, is 3.4 percent. See his *The End of Affluence* (New York: Random House, 1995), pp. 4–5. For a review of estimates of economic growth, see Cassidy, "The Growth Fallacy."

41. Robert J. Samuelson, *Newsweek*, September 25, 1995, p. 63.

42. *Newsweek*, June 8, 1992, p. 42; *New York Times*, May 20, 1993, p. A8.

43. "Back On Top?" *The Economist*, September 16, 1995, pp. 3–10.

44. *New York Times*, December 31, 1995, Section 3, p. 5.

45. *The Economist*, February 24, 1995, p. 30.

46. *New York Times*, December 31, 1995, Section 3, p. 1

CHAPTER 3. WE'VE BEEN THERE BEFORE

1. John Kenneth Galbraith, *The Affluent Society* (New York: Houghton Mifflin 1958), p. 38.

2. Quote in Samuel Eliot Morison and Henry Steele Commager, *The Growth of the American Republic* (New York: Oxford University Press, 1937), p. 123.

3. Bruce Catton, *The Civil War* (New York: American Heritage Books, 1960), p. 15.

4. David Herbert Donald, *Lincoln* (New York: Simon and Schuster, 1995), p. 67.

5. Ernest L. Bogart and Donald L. Kemmerer, *Economic History of the American People* (New York: Longmans, Green, 1947), p. 368.

6. The population figures in this section were drawn from the following sources: Wolf Schneider, *Babylon Is Everywhere, The City as Man's Fate* (New York: McGraw-Hill, 1963); Adna Weber, *The Growth of Cities in the Nineteenth Century* (Ithaca, N.Y.: Cornell University Press, 1965); *The Determinants and Consequences of Population Trends*, United Nations, Department of Economic and Social Affairs, Population Studies Publication No. 50, 1973; Charles Abrams, *The City Is the Frontier* (New York: Harper Colophon Books, 1965). Overviews of urban growth in the United States can be found in Philip M. Hauser and Leo F. Schnore (eds.), *The Study of Urbanization* (New York: John Wiley, 1996); Raymond W. Mack and Calvin P. Bradford,

Transforming America (New York: Random House, 1979). Paul Johnson, *A History of the American People* (New York: HarperCollins, 1997). For an examination of the process and effects of urbanization and industrialization, see separate articles by J. R. T. Hughes and Wilbert Moore in the *Encyclopedia of the Social Sciences* (New York: Crowell Collier and Macmillan, 1968).

7. Eric Homberger, *Scenes from the Life of a City* (New Haven: Yale University Press, 1995), quoted by William Marshall, *New York Times*, Book Review Section, January 1, 1995, p. 14.

8. James Lincoln Collier, *The Rise of Selfishness in America* (New York: Oxford University, Press, 1991) p. 10.

9. Samuel P. Hays, *The Response to Industrialism, 1885–1914* (Chicago: University of Chicago Press, 1957), p. 113.

10. Quoted in Bernard C. Rosen, *The Industrial Connection* (New York: Aldine, 1982), p. 24.

11. Catton, *Civil War*, p. 9.

12. Quote in Henry Bamford Parks, *The American Experience* (New York: Random House, 1947), p. 243.

13. Collier, *Rise of Selfishness*, p. 21.

14. For a more detailed description of the putting-out system see Max Weber, *The Protestant Ethic and the Spirit of Capitalism* (New York: Scribner's 1948), pp. 66–67.

15. Quoted in Morison and Commager, *American Republic*, p. 124.

16. Arthur Cecil Bining and Thomas C. Cochran, *The Rise of American Economic Life* (New York: Scribner's, 1964), p. 239.

17. Morton Peto, *Resources and Prospects of America* (London, 1866), cited in Bining and Cochran, *American Economic Life*, p. 242.

18. James McPherson, *The Battle Cry of Freedom* (New York: Oxford University Press, 1988), p. 11.

19. Morison and Commager, *American Republic*, pp. 106–107.

20. Ibid., p. 128.

21. Data on agricultural change are taken from John A. Garraty, *The New Commonwealth, 1877–1890* (New York: Harper and Row, 1968), pp. 33–37.

22. George Soule and Vincent P. Caroso, *American Economic History* (New York: Dryden Press, 1957), p. 211.

23. Morison and Commager, *American Republic*, pp. 278, 288–301.

24. Soule and Caroso, *American Economic History*, p. 210.

25. Ibid., pp. 210–211; also Robert F. Spencer, "Agriculture," in *Dictionary of American History*, vol. 1 (New York: Scribner's, 1976), p. 38.

26. Quoted in Morison and Commager, *American Republic*, p. 238.

27. A contemporary description of the Haymarket Riot can be found in George M. McLean, *The Rise of Anarchy in America* (Chicago: R. G. Badoux, 1890; for a more recent view see H. W. Brands, *The Reckless Decade* (New York: St. Martin's Press, 1995).

28. Bogart and Kemmerer, *Economic History of the American People*, p. 475.

29. Alfred Mazels, *Industrial Growth and World Trade* (Cambridge: Cambridge University Press, 1963).

30. Cited in Mack and Bradford, *Transforming America*, p. 5.

CHAPTER 4. PROGRESS AND DARWINIAN MAN

1. For classic descriptions of the role of achievement and success in American life as seen by outsiders, see Alexis de Tocqueville, *Democracy in America* (New York: Vintage Books, 1954); Dennis W. Brogan, *The American Character* (New York: Knopf, 1948); Geoffrey Gorer, *The American People* (New York: W. W. Norton, 1948).

2. Irwin G. Wyllie, *The Self-Made Man in America* (New Brunswick, N.J.: Rutgers University Press, 1954.

3. Robert K. Merton, "The Self-Fulfilling Prophecy," *The Antioch Review* (Summer 1948), p. 199.

4. Alan M. Kraut, *The Huddled Masses* (Arlington Heights, Ill.: Harlan Davidson, 1982), quoted in James Lincoln Collier, *The Rise of Selfishness in America*, (New York: Oxford University Press, 1991), p. 29.

5. Neil Sheehan, "Annals of War," *The New Yorker*, January 20, 1988, p. 35.

6. Richard H. Tawney, *Religion and the Rise of Capitalism* (New York: Harcourt, Brace, 1926), p. 23.

7. Theories of the idea of progress are described in Robert Nisbet, *History of the Idea of Progress* (New York: Basic Books, 1980). Quotation is from p. 11.

8. John Bagnell Bury, *The Idea of Progress* (New York: Macmillan, 1932).

9. This account of Condorcet is taken from *The Encyclopedia Britannica*, 13th edition, vol. 6, p. 853. It is not certain what caused his death. Perhaps it was exposure and exhaustion or possibly it was poisoning.

10. For an account of the reaction to Social Darwinism, see Richard Hofstadtler, *Social Darwinism in American Thought, 1860–1915* (Philadelphia: University of Pennsylvania Press, 1944).

11. John Kenneth Galbraith, *The Affluent Society* (New York: Houghton Mifflin, 1958), p. 55.

12. Robert Green McCloskey, *American Conservatism in the Age of Conservatism* (Cambridge, Mass.: Harvard University Press, 1951).

13. Will Durant, *The Story of Philosophy* (New York: Simon and Schuster, 1926), pp. 431–432.

14. John W. Osborne, *The Silent Revolution* (New York: Scribner's, 1970), p. 17.

15. See Max Weber, *The Protestant Ethic and the Spirit of Capitalism* (New

York: Scribner's, 1948), p. 55. See also Robert A. Le Vine, *Culture, Behavior and Personality* (Chicago: Aldine, 1974), p. 105. These theorists were echoing Aristotle. See his *Politics* (Oxford: Oxford University Press, 1948), p. 390.

16. Galbraith, *Affluent Society*, p. 59.

17. McCloskey, *American Conservatism*, p. 36.

18. Henry Ward Beecher, quoted in Richard Brookhiser, *The Way of the Wasp* (New York: Free Press, 1991), p. 77.

19. Joseph Epstein, *Ambition* (New York: E. P. Dutton, 1980), p. 1.

20. Tom Lutz, *American Nervousness, 1903* (Ithaca, N.Y.: Cornell University Press, 1991).

21. Seymour Martin Lipset, *The First New Nation* (New York: Basic Books, 1963), pp. 114–115.

22. George M. Beard, *American Nervousness: Its Causes and Consequences* (New York: Putnam's, 1881), p. 104.

23. Ibid., p. 105.

CHAPTER 5. THE NEW ELITE

1. Descriptions of the rise of the service economy can be found in the following sources: Victor Fuchs, *The Service Economy* (New York: Columbia University Press, 1968); Thomas Weiss, "Service Sector," in Glen Porter (ed.), *Encyclopedia of American Economic History* (New York: Scribner's, 1980), pp. 413–426; Stephen S. Cohen and Joseph Zysman, *Manufacturing Matters* (New York: Basic Books, 1987).

2. *The Economist*, February 20, 1994, p. 63; March 19, 1994, pp. 91–92.

3. *New York Times*, April 24, 1994, Business Section, p. 11.

4. *Statistical Abstract of the United States* (Washington, D.C.: U.S. Department of Commerce).

5. Samuel M. Ehrenhalt, "Work-Force Shifts in the 80s," *New York Times*, August 15, 1986; *Newsweek*, November 27, 1995, p. 98.

6. George Gilder, *Wealth And Poverty* (New York: Basic Books, 1981), p. 213.

7. Alan Gartner and Frank Riessman, *The Service Economy and the Consumer Vanguard* (New York: Harper and Row, 1974).

8. David Cay Johnston, "The Servant Class Is at the Counter," *New York Times*, August 27, 1995.

9. Quoted by Louis Uchitelle, "Economic Scene," *New York Times*, Business Section, December 1, 1986.

10. Bery Sprinkel, "Let's Not Torpedo the Growth of Jobs," *New York Times*, June 5, 1987.

11. *The Economist*, March 19, 1994, pp. 91–92.

12. Daniel Bell, "The Social Framework of the Information Society," in

Michael Dertouzos and Joel Moses, *The Computer Age* (Cambridge, Mass.: M.I.T. Press, 1979), p. 178. See also M. Porat and M. Rubin, *The Information Economy* (Washington, D.C.: U.S. Department of Commerce, 1977); Stephen Saxby, *The Age of Information* (New York: New York University Press, 1990); Michael Dertouzos, *What Will Be* (San Francisco: Harper Edge, 1997).

13. Arno Anzias, *Ideas and Information* (New York: Simon and Schuster, 1989), p. 10.

14. Daniel Bell, in Dertouzos and Moses, *The Computer Age*, p. 178.

15. Herbert Dordick and Georgette Wang, *The Information Society* (Newbury Park, Calif.: Sage Publications 1993) pp. 2, 10; also *The Statistical Abstract of the United States, 1991*; p. 432.

16. Robert B. Reich, *The Work of Nations* (New York: Knopf, 1991), p. 179.

17. Jerry Adler, "The Overclass," *Newsweek*, July 31, 1995, p. 34.

18. Steve Lohr, "Suiting Up for America's High-Tech Future," *New York Times*, December 1, 1995, Business Section, p. 14.

19. Adam Smith, *New York Times*, October 8, 1995, Book Review Section, p. 35.

20. Connie Bruch, "The World According to Soros," *The New Yorker*, January 23, 1994, p. 53.

21. Joseph Glassman, *The New Republic*, July 1, 1994, p. 14.

22. Michael Lind, *The Next American Nation* (New York: Free Press, 1995), pp. 141–150; see also Jerry Adler, "The Overclass," *Newsweek*, July 31, 1995, pp. 33–46.

23. Adler, "The Overclass," p. 44.

24. This indictment of the New Elite appears in Christopher Lasch, *The Revolt of the Elite and the Betrayal of Democracy* (New York: W. W. Norton, 1995).

CHAPTER 6. THE CHAMELEON PERSONALITY OF OUR TIME

1. David Riesman et al., *The Lonely Crowd* (New York: Doubleday) 1950.

2. See L. A. Festinger, *A Theory of Cognitive Dissonance* (Stanford Calif.: Stanford University Press, 1957).

3. There are several versions of the Narcissus story, but they all agree it ends unhappily. See Edith Hamilton, *Mythology* (New York: Mentor Books, 1953), pp. 87–88.

4. Sigmund Freud thought a certain amount of self-love was healthy. See his "On Narcissism," in *Works of Sigmund Freud: Standard Edition*, vol. 9 (London: Hogarth Press, 1957).

5. The theme that rampant consumerism is ruining America occurs often

in criticisms of American culture. See, for example, Christopher Lasch, *The Culture of Narcissism* (New York: W. W. Norton, 1978), p. 65.

6. The major theorists of self-fulfillment psychology are examined in Salvatore R. Maddi, *Personality Theories* (Homewood, Ill.:Dorsey Press, 1980).

7. This is a major theme of Sigmund Freud's *Civilization and Its Discontents* (New York: W. W. Norton, 1930).

8. See Erich Fromm, *The Sane Society* (New York: Rinehart, 1950).

9. For an analysis of the pain that perfectionism inflicts when permitted to dominate the individual, see Karen Horney, *Our Inner Conflicts* (New York: W. W. Norton, 1945).

10. Karen Horney, *The Neurotic Personality of Our Time* (New York: W. W. Norton, 1937).

CHAPTER 7. THE ROOTS OF THE CHAMELEON COMPLEX

1. For a sympathetic portrayal of the family's plight, see Christopher Lasch, *Haven in a Heartless World* (New York: Basic Books, 1977).

2. For a summary of statistics on the American family, see "The Family: Home Sweet Home," *The Economist*, September 9, 1995, pp. 25–29.

3. An analysis of the impact of industrialization on the family appears in Bernard C. Rosen, *The Industrial Connection* (New York: Aldine, 1982). See also William Goode, *World Revolution and Family Change* (New York: Free Press, 1963).

4. AARP survey reported in *New York Times*, December 31, 1995.

5. This analysis is influenced by Warren Bennis and Phillip E. Slater, *The Temporary Society* (New York: Harper and Row, 1968); see also Alan C. Kerkhoff, *Socialization and Social Class* (Englewood Cliffs, N.J.: Prentice-Hall, 1972).

6. Bennis and Slater, *Temporary Society*, p. 37.

7. Ibid., p. 43. The discussion in this chapter on the experiential chasm is especially indebted to the work of Philip E. Slater.

8. For an analysis of the familial origins of achievement, see Bernard C. Rosen and Roy D'Andrade, "The Psycho-Social Origins of Achievement Motivation," *Sociometry* 23:3 (September 1959), pp. 185–218.

9. Basil Bernstein, "Elaborated and Restricted Codes: Their Social Origins and Consequences," in J. J. Gumpery and D. Hymes (eds.) *The Ethnography of Communication, American Anthropologist* 66: (November 6, 1964).

10. The liberal viewpoint is examined in Ruth Wisse, *If I Am Not for Myself* (New York: Free Press, 1992).

11. For a review of research on moral development see Lawrence Kolhberg, "The Development of Moral Character and Moral Ideology," in

Martin L. Hoffman and Lois Wladis Hoffman (eds.), *Review of Child Development Research* (New York: Russell Sage Foundation, 1964), pp. 383–431.

12. For an extensive treatment of the ages at which societies begin to impose restrictions of children, see Rosen, *The Industrial Connection*, pp. 176–181.

13. Margery Wolf, *Women and Family in Rural Taiwan* (Stanford, Calif.: Stanford University Press, 1972).

14. T. W. Maretski and H. Maretski, "Taira: An Okinawan Village," in Beatrice Whiting, *Six Cultures* (New York: Wiley, 1963), pp. 367–531.

15. David Landy, *Tropical Childhood* (Chapel Hill: University of North Carolina Press, 1959), p. 99.

CHAPTER 8. THE IDEOLOGY OF THE NEW ELITE

1. Janny Scott, "At Appomatox in the Cultural Wars," *New York Times*, May 25, 1997, Section 4, p. 1; see also Rhys M. Williams, *Cultural Wars in American Politics* (Hawthorne, N.Y. Aldine de Gruyter, 1997).

2. John Leo, *U.S. News and World Report*, July 15, 1994, p. 8.

3. For a discussion of Kerouac's and Mailer's politics see Norman Podhoretz, *Breaking Ranks* (New York: Harper Colophon Books, 1979); see also William G. McLoughlin, *Revivals, Awakenings and Reform* (Chicago: University of Chicago Press, 1978), pp. 196–199.

4. The discussion of Parisian Bohemia draws upon the work of Cesar Graña. See his *Bohemians Versus Bourgeoisie* (New York: Basic Books, 1973).

5. Ibid., p. 74.

6. Ibid., pp. 68–69.

7. An excellent analysis of modernism, on which this section draws heavily, can be found in Daniel Bell, *The Cultural Contradictions of Capitalism* (New York: Basic Books, 1976), Part One.

8. Graña, *Bohemians*, p. 95.

9. D. H. Lawrence, *Lady Chatterley's Lover* (New York: Penguin Books, 1946), p. 108.

10. Graña, *Bohemians*, p. 189.

11. Ibid., p. 172.

12. This section draws upon Bell, *Cultural Contradictions*.

13. Bell, *Cultural Contradictions*, p. 46.

14. Robert Hughes, *The Shock of the New* (New York: Knopf, 1981).

15. Graña, *Bohemians*, p. 41.

16. Hughes, *Shock of the New*, p. 61.

17. Richard Grenier, *Capturing the Culture* (Washington, D.C.: Ethics and Public Policy Center, 1991), p. xxxix.

18. Quoted in Bell, *Cultural Contradictions*, p. 76.

19. *Ithaca Journal*, April 7, 1997, p. 2A.

20. J. D. Plumb, *England in the Eighteenth Century* (London: Penguin Books, 1950), p. 161; see also Kenneth Clark, *Civilization* (New York: Harper and Row, 1969), Chapter 12.

21. Moses I. Finely, *Economy and Society in Ancient Greece* (New York: Viking Press, 1982), p. 105. See also his *Politics in the Ancient World* (New York: Cambridge University Press, 1983), p. 125. On the other hand, many poets, playwrights, and philosophers supported the ruling aristocratic class. See Arnold Hauser, *The Social History of Art* (New York: Vintage Books, 1957), pp. 83–84.

22. Luigi Barzini, *The Italians* (New York: Atheneum, 1967), p. 310.

23. Antonio Gramchi, *Letters from Prison* (New York: W. W. Norton, 1973).

CHAPTER 9. WOMEN AS WINNERS

1. Bernard C. Rosen, *Women, Work and Achievement* (New York: St. Martin's Press; and London: Macmillan, 1989), Chapter 5.

2. Bettina Berch, *The Endless Day* (New York: Harcourt, Brace, Jovanovich, 1982); Elyce J. Rotella, *From Home to Office* (Ann Arbor, Mich.: UMI Research Press, 1981); Bureau of Labor Statistics, *Employment and Earnings*, vol. 34, no. 1 (January 1987); *The Economist*, March 15, 1994, p. 80.

3. Quoted by William Serrin, *New York Times*, November 25, 1984.

4. Michele Ingrassia and Pat Wingert, "The New Providers," *Newsweek*, May 22, 1995, p. 37.

5. Janet Norwood, *Monthly Labor Review*, December 1985, pp. 3–4, cited in Andrew Hacker, "Women at Work," *New York Review of Books* 14 (August 1986), p. 29.

6. For a description of women executives in major American corporations and the prospect of more to come, see articles in the *New York Times*, May 11 and May 14, 1995; also *The Economist*, June 8, 1996, pp. 7–8.

7. Sources of information about female participation in the paid workforce are Alice Kessler-Harris, *Out To Work* (New York: Oxford University Press, 1982) and Julie A. Matthaei, *An Economic History of Women in America* (New York: Schocken, 1982).

8. Barbara Welter, "The Cult of True Womanhood," in Michael Gordon (ed.), *The American Family in Social-Historical Perspective* (New York: St. Martin's Press, 1978).

9. Charles R. Morris, *A Time of Passion* (New York: Harper and Row, 1984), p. 230.

10. For a detailed analysis of trends in fertility and divorce, see J. Ross

Eshlemann, *The Family* (Boston: Allyn and Bacon, 1985); also Ben J. Wattenberg, *The Birth Dearth* (New York: Pharos Books, 1987).

11. Quoted by Robert A. Bennet, *New York Times*, June 20, 1986.

12. Bureau of Labor Statistics, July 1984, cited by William Serrin, *New York Times*, July 31, 1984; see also article on women's future in the workforce in *U.S. News and World Report*, February 8, 1993.

13. This research is reported in Rosen, *Women, Work and Achievement*, p. 127.

14. See Jean Lipman-Blumen, *Gender Roles and Power* (Englewood Cliffs, N.J.: Prentice-Hall, 1984), p. 76.

15. Walter Karp, *New York Times*, August 17, 1986, Book Review Section, p. 24.

16. This study by Julie Brines, a sociologist at the University of Washington, is cited in Ingrassia and Wingert, "The New Providers."

CHAPTER 10. BLUE-COLLAR BLUES

1. Cover of *U.S. News and World Report*, January 22, 1996.

2. The growth rate in income was part of a long-term process. From 1839 to 1886 real income doubled, and between 1913 and 1950 the Gross Domestic Product grew an average of 1.6 percent annually, which is striking considering that this period included the Great Depression. See Paul Krugman, *Peddling Prosperity* (New York: W. W. Norton, 1994), p. 3; see also *The Economist*, June 5, 1993, p. 22.

3. Steven Ratner, *New York Times Magazine*, September 19, 1993, p. 96. See also Robert J. Samuelson, *The Good Life and Its Discontents* (New York: Times Books, 1995), p. 114.

4. Data on the effects of foreign competition on American workers were taken from "Global Survey," *The Economist*, October 1, 1994, p. 32.

5. Steven Ratner, *New York Times Magazine*, September 19, 1993, p. 96.

6. For data on downsizing, see *The Economist*, July 31, 1993, p. 59; and Jon D. Hull, "The State of the Union," *Time*, January 30, 1995, pp. 53–75. For a description of its often cruel and demoralizing effects, see William Hoffman et al., "Impact of Plant Closings on Automobile Workers and Their Families," *Journal of Contemporary Human Services*, February 1991, pp. 103–107; Barry Bluestone and Bennett Harrison, *The Deindustrialization of America* (New York: Basic Books, 1982), p. 32; and Kevin Kelly, *Business Week* (Industrial Technology Edition), March 9, 1992, p. 33.

7. The quotations on downsizing are taken from George J. Church, "We're No. 1," *Time*, October 24, 1994, pp. 51–56.

8. Quoted in ibid.

9. Ibid.

10. *The Economist*, March 19, 1994, p. 91.

11. Isabel Wilkerson, "How Milwaukee Boomed But Left Its Blacks Behind," *New York Times*, March 19, 1991, pp. A1 and D22.

12. *New York Times*, November 27, 1990, pp. A1 and B10.

13. Ibid.

14. *The Economist*, December 3, 1994, p. 29.

15. Judith H. Dobrynski, "The New Jobs: A Growing Number Are Good Jobs," *New York Times*, July 21, 1996, Section 3, p. 1.

16. Dirk Johnson, "Chicago on Trade Accord: A Split Along Class Lines," *New York Times*, November 14, 1993. Quotations on the trade accord are taken from this article.

17. *The Economist*, June 17, 1995, p. 29.

18. *New York Times*, December 25, 1994, p. 17.

19. Richard J. Herrstein and Charles Murray, *The Bell Curve* (New York: Free Press, 1994).

CHAPTER 11. THE BUSINESS CLASS
UNDER ATTACK

1. The charge that businessmen conspire against the public interest is as old as capitalism itself. For examples of this kind of thinking, see C. Wright Mills, *The Power Elite* (New York: Oxford University Press, 1956), Chapters 6 and 7; and Lewis Lapham, *Money and Class* (New York: Heidenfeld and Nicolson, 1988).

2. A detailed analysis of the Greek ethos can be found in C. M. Bowra, *The Greek Experience* (New York: World, 1957), and in Edith Hamilton, *The Greek Way* (New York: W. W. Norton, 1942). See also Robert Garland, *The Greek Way Of Life* (Ithaca, N.Y.: Cornell University Press, 1990).

3. Moses I. Finley, *The Ancient Economy* (Berkeley: University of California Press, 1973).

4. Francis Geis and Joseph Geis, *Cathedral, Forge and Watermill* (New York: HarperCollins, 1994), p. 10. Upper-class Greeks were particularly inclined to think that physical labor degraded the mind. Arnold Hauser attributed the low status of sculptors in ancient Athens to the fact that they worked with their hands. The genius Phidias was treated as a mere workman by Athenian aristocrats. See Hauser's *The Social History of Art*, vol. 1 (New York: Vintage Books, 1957), pp. 113–120.

5. The condition of the merchant class in medieval Europe is described at length in Fernand Braudel, *Civilization and Capitalism* (New York: Harper and Row, Perennial Library Edition, 1985); see also Friedrich Heer, *The Medieval World* (New York: Mentor Books, 1963); P. Boisonnade, *Life and Work in Medieval Europe* (New York: Harper Torchbooks, 1964).

6. Marc Bloch, *The Medieval Society* (Chicago: University of Chicago Press, Phoenix Edition, 1964), pp. 298–299.

7. Henri Pirenne, *Economic and Social History of Medieval Europe* (New York: Harcourt, Brace, 1937), pp. 28–29.

8. Paul Veyne, *A History of Private Life*, vol. 1 (Cambridge, Mass.: Belknap Press, 1987), p. 123.

9. Wat Tyler and the fury he unleashed in the Peasant Revolt are described by Arthur Bryant in *The Age of Chivalry* (New York: New American Library, 1963), pp. 532–539.

10. Quoted by Daniel Bell, *The Coming of the Post-Industrial Society* (New York: Basic Books, 1973), p. 188.

11. See Irving Kristol, *Two Cheers for Capitalism* (New York: Basic Books, 1978), Part Three.

12. This description of the Ball family and of Muncie is taken from Robert S. Lynd and Helen M. Lynd, *Middletown* (New York: Harcourt, Brace, 1929), and the companion volume, *Middletown in Transition* (New York: Harcourt, Brace, 1937).

CHAPTER 12. AFFIRMATIVE INEQUALITY

1. Denis W. Brogan, *The American Character* (New York: Knopf, 1944); David Riesman, Nathan Glazer, and R. Denny, *The Lonely Crowd* (New York: Doubleday, 1950); Robert Bork, *Slouching Toward Gomorrah* (New York: Regan Books, 1996).

2. Quote from Robert J. Samuelson, *The Good Life and Its Discontents* (New York: Times Books, 1995), p. 178.

3. Statistics on income inequality are taken from *Statistical Abstract of the United States*, 1995, p. 478; Mickey Kaus, *The End of Equality* (New York: Basic Books, 1992), pp. 29–30; "Inequality," *The Economist*, May 5, 1994, pp. 19–21; Sheldon Danziger and Peter G. Gottschalk, *America Unequal* (Cambridge, Mass.: Harvard University Press, 1995).

4. These explanations for the growth of income inequality were offered by Robert J. Samuelson, "Great Expectations," *Newsweek*, January 8, 1996, p. 31.

5. Christopher Jencks, *The Homeless* (Cambridge, Mass.: Harvard University Press, 1994), quoted in *U.S. News and World Report*, July 25, 1994, p. 33.

6. *Time*, February 5, 1996, p. 45.

7. *The Economist*, November 5, 1994, p. 21.

8. *Time*, February 5, 1996, p. 40.

9. This estimate, based on 1990 census data, was made by Claudia

Golden, Bradford DeLong, and Edward Wolff and reported in the *New York Times*, August 6, 1992, Week in Review Section, p. 3.

10. *The Economist*, November 5, 1995, p. 20.

11. A conclusion reached by Myron Magnet, *The Dream and the Nightmare* (New York: W. Morrow, 1993).

12. William Julius Wilson, *The Truly Disadvantaged* (Chicago: University of Chicago Press, 1987), p. 43.

13. Andrew Hacker, *Two Nations* (New York: Scribner's, 1992), p. 20.

14. Data on the effects of affirmative action in Atlanta are taken from *The Economist*, April 15, 1995, p. 22.

15. Ibid.

16. Stanley Greenberg, *Middle Class Dreams* (New York: Time Books, 1995), cited in Nicolas Lemann, "Taking Affirmative Action Apart," *New York Times*, June 11, 1995, p. 36.

17. Quote from Marmer Solomon, "Are White Males Being Left Out?" *Personnel Journal*, November 1991, p. 88.

18. Jane Gross, "Now Look Who's Taunting, Now Look Who's Suing," *New York Times*, February 26, 1995.

19. Ibid.

20. Jane Stephenson, *Men Are Not Cost Effective* (New York: Harper-Collins, 1995).

CHAPTER 13. THE NEW CONFORMITY

1. Numerous books on the cultural war have appeared in recent years. They are much alike, differing mostly in political orientation. See, for example, Dinesh D'Souza, *Illiberal Education* (New York: Free Press, 1991), which looks at the war from the political right; while Todd Gitlin, *The Twilight of Common Dreams* (New York: Metropolitan Books, 1995) covers the same ground from the political left.

2. Richard Bernstein, *Dictatorship of Virtue* (New York: Knopf, 1994).

3. C. Vann Woodward, quoted in William A. Henry, *In Defense of Elitism* (New York: Doubleday, 1994), pp. 46–47.

4. The fighting between different factions of the Women's Movement is described by Christina Hoff Sommers, *Who Stole Feminism?* (New York: Simon and Schuster, 1994).

5. Abram Kardiner and Lionel Ovesey, *The Mark of Oppression* (New York: W. W. Norton, 1951).

6. From Arthur Schlesinger, *The Disuniting of America* (New York: W. W. Norton, 1992), pp. 61–62.

7. Ibid., pp. 77–78.

8. Mary Lefkowitz, *Not Out of Africa* (New York: Basic Books, 1996).

9. Quoted in Schlesinger, *Disuniting of America*, p. 42.

10. For an analysis of the resistance to assimilation and its effects, see Nathan Glazer and Daniel Patrick Moynihan, *Beyond the Melting Pot* (Cambridge, Mass.: M.I.T. Press, 1963); Michael Novak, *The Rise of the Unmeltable Ethnics* (New York: Macmillan, 1992); Seymour Martin Lipset, *American Exceptionalism* (New York: W. W. Norton, 1996).

Selected Bibliography

Abrams, Charles. *The City Is the Frontier*. New York: Harper Colophon Books, 1965.

Anzias, Arno. *Ideas and Information*. New York: Simon and Schuster, 1989.

Aristotle. *Politics*. Oxford: Oxford University Press, 1948.

Barzini, Luigi. *The Italians*. New York: Atheneum, 1967.

Beard, George M. *American Nervousness: Its Causes and Consequences*. New York: Putnam's, 1881.

Bell, Daniel. *The Coming of the Post-Industrial Society*. New York: Basic Books, 1973.

———. *The Cultural Contradictions of Capitalism*. New York: Basic Books, 1976.

Bennis, Warren, and Phillip E. Slater. *The Temporary Society*. New York: Harper and Row, 1968.

Berch, Bettina. *The Endless Day*. New York: Harcourt, Brace, Jovanovich, 1982.

Bernstein, Richard. *Dictatorship of Virtue*. New York: Knopf, 1994.

Bining, Arthur Cecil, and Thomas C. Cochran. *The Rise of American Economic Life*. New York: Scribner's, 1964.

Bloch, Marc. *The Medieval Society*. Chicago: University of Chicago Press, Pheonix Edition, 1964.

Bluestone, Barry, and Bennett Harrison. *The Deindustrialization of America*. New York: Basic Books, 1982.

Bogart, Ernest L., and Donald L. Kemmerer. *Economic History of the American People*. New York: Longmans, Green, 1947.

Boisonnade, P. *Life and Work in Medieval Europe*. New York: Harper Torch-books, 1964.

Bork, Robert *Slouching Toward Gomorrah*. New York: Regan Books, 1996.

Bowra, C. M. *The Greek Experience*. New York: World, 1957.

Brands, H. W. *The Reckless Decade*. New York: St. Martin's Press. 1995.

Braudel, Fernand. *Civilization and Capitalism*. New York: Harper and Row, Perennial Library Edition, 1985.

Brogan, Dennis W. *The American Character*. New York: Knopf, 1944.

Brookhiser, Richard. *The Way of the Wasp*. New York: Free Press, 1991.

Bryant, Arthur. *The Age of Chivalry*. New York: New American Library, 1963.

Bryson, Bill. *Made in America*. London: Secker and Warburg, 1994.

Bury, John Bagnell. *The Idea of Progress*. New York: Macmillan, 1932.

Catton, Bruce. *The Civil War*. New York: American Heritage Books, 1960.

Clark, Kenneth. *Civilization*. New York: Harper and Row, 1969.

Clecak, Peter. *America's Quest for the Ideal Self*. New York: Oxford University Press, 1983.

Cohen, Stephen S., and Joseph Zysman. *Manufacturing Matters*. New York: Basic Books, 1987.

Collier, James Lincoln. *The Rise Of Selfishness in America*. New York: Oxford University Press, 1991.

Croly, Herbert J. *Promise of American Life*. Hamden, Conn.: Archon Books, 1963, originally published in 1903.

Danziger, Sheldon, and Peter G. Gottschalk. *America Unequal*. Cambridge, Mass.: Harvard University Press, 1995.

Demaris, Ovid. *America the Violent*. New York: Cowles Book Company, 1969.

Dertouzos, Michael. *What Will Be*. San Francisco: Harper Edge, 1997.

Dertouzos, Michael, and Joel Moses. *The Computer Age*. Cambridge, Mass.: M.I.T. Press, 1979.

Donald, David Herbert. *Lincoln*. New York: Simon and Schuster, 1995.

Dordick, Herbert, and Georgette Wang. *The Information Society*. Newbury Park, Calif.: Sage, 1993.

D'Souza, Dinesh. *Illiberal Education*. New York: Free Press, 1991.

Durant, Will. *The Story of Philosophy*. New York: Simon and Schuster, 1926.

Epstein, Joseph. *Ambition*. New York: E. P. Dutton, 1980.

Eshlemann, J. Ross. *The Family*. Boston: Allyn and Bacon, 1985.

Festinger, L. A. *A Theory of Cognitive Dissonance*. Stanford: Stanford University Press, 1957.

Finley, Moses I. *The Ancient Economy*. Berkeley: University of California Press, 1973.

———. *Politics in the Ancient World*. New York: Cambridge University Press, 1983.

Freud, Sigmund. *Civilization and Its Discontents*. New York: W. W. Norton, 1930.

———. *Works of Sigmund Freud: Standard Edition*, vol. IX. London: Hogarth Press, 1957.

Fromm, Erich. *The Sane Society*. New York: Rinehart, 1950.

Fromm, Erich, and Michael Maccoby. *Social Character in a Mexican Village*. Englewood Cliffs, N.J.: Prentice-Hall, 1959.

Fuchs, Victor. *The Service Economy*. New York: Columbia University Press, 1968.

Galbraith, John Kenneth. *The Affluent Society*. New York: Houghton Mifflin, 1958.

Garland, Robert. *The Greek Way of Life*. Ithaca, N.Y.: Cornell University Press, 1990.

Garraty, John A. *The New Commonwealth, 1877–1890*. New York: Harper and Row, 1968.

Gartner, Alan, and Frank Riessman. *The Service Economy and the Consumer Vanguard*. New York: Harper and Row, 1974.

Geis, Francis, and Joseph Geis. *Cathedral, Forge and Watermill*. New York: HarperCollins, 1994.

Gilder, George. *Wealth and Poverty*. New York: Basic Books, 1981.

Gitlin, Todd. *The Twilight of Common Dreams*. New York: Metropolitan Books, 1995.

Glazer, Nathan, and Daniel Patrick Moynihan. *Beyond the Melting Pot*. Cambridge, Mass.: M.I.T. Press, 1963.

Goode, William. *World Revolution and Family Change*. New York: Free Press, 1963.

Gordon, Michael (ed.). *The American Family in Social-Historical Perspective*. New York: St. Martin's Press, 1978.

Gorer, Geoffrey. *The American People*. New York: W. W. Norton, 1948.

Gramchi, Antonio. *Letters from Prison*. New York: W. W. Norton, 1973.

Graña, Cesar. *Bohemians Versus Bourgeoisie*. New York: Basic Books, 1973.

Greenberg, Stanley. *Middle Class Dreams*. New York: Time Books, 1995.

Grenier, Richard. *Capturing the Culture*. Washington, D.C.: Ethics and Public Policy Center, 1991.

Hacker, Andrew. *Two Nations*. New York: Scribner's, 1992.

Hall, Calvin S., and Gardner Lindzey. *Theories of Personality*. New York: John Wiley, 1957.

Hamilton, Edith. *The Greek Way*. New York: W. W. Norton, 1942.

———. *Mythology*. New York: Mentor Books, 1953.

Hartley, L. P. *The Go-Between*. London: Hamish Hamilton, 1953.

Hauser, Arnold. *The Social History of Art*, vol 1. New York: Vintage Books, 1957.

Hauser, Philip M., and Leo F. Schnore (eds.). *The Study Of Urbanization*. New York: John Wiley, 1966.

Hays, Samuel P. *The Response to Industrialism, 1885–1914*. Chicago: University of Chicago Press, 1957.

Heer, Friedrich. *The Medieval World*. New York: Mentor Books, 1963.

Henry, William A. *In Defense of Elitism*. New York: Doubleday, 1994.

Herrstein, Richard J., and Charles Murray. *The Bell Curve*. New York: Free Press, 1994.

Hoffman, Martin L., and Lois Wladis Hoffman (eds.). *Review of Child Development Research*. New York: Russell Sage Foundation, 1964.

Hofstadtler, Richard. *Social Darwinism in American Thought, 1860–1915*. Philadelphia: University of Pennsylvania Press, 1944.

Homberger, Eric. *Scenes from the Life of a City*. New Haven: Yale University Press, 1995.

Horney, Karen. *The Neurotic Personality of Our Time*. New York: W. W. Norton, 1937.

———. *Our Inner Conflicts*. New York: W. W. Norton, 1945.

Hughes, Robert. *The Shock of the New*. New York: Knopf, 1981.

Jencks, Christopher. *The Homeless*. Cambridge, Mass.: Harvard University Press, 1994.

Kardiner, Abram, and Lionel Ovesey. *The Mark of Oppression*. New York: W. W. Norton, 1951.

Kaus, Mickey. *The End of Equality*. New York: Basic Books, 1992.

Kerkhoff, Alan C. *Socialization and Social Class*. Englewood Cliffs, N.J.: Prentice-Hall, 1972.

Kessler-Harris, Alice. *Out to Work*. New York: Oxford University Press, 1982.

Kraut, Alan M. *The Huddled Masses*. Arlington Heights, Ill.: Harlan Davidson, 1982.

Kristol, Irving. *Two Cheers for Capitalism*. New York: Basic Books, 1978.

Krugman, Paul. *Peddling Prosperity*. New York: W. W. Norton, 1994.

Landy, David. *Tropical Childhood*. Chapel Hill: University of North Carolina Press, 1959.

Lapham, Lewis. *Money and Class*. New York: Heidenfeld and Nicolson, 1988.

Lasch, Christopher. *Haven in a Heartless World*. New York: Basic Books, 1977.

———. *The Culture of Narcissism*. New York: W. W. Norton, 1978.

———. *The Revolt of the Elite and the Betrayal of Democracy*. New York: W. W. Norton, 1995.

Lawrence, D. H. *Lady Chatterly's Lover*. New York: Penguin Books, 1946.

Lebergott, Stanley. *Pursuing Happiness*. Princeton, N.J.: Princeton University Press, 1993.

Lefkowitz, Mary. *Not Out of Africa*. New York: Basic Books, 1996.

Le Vine, Robert A. *Culture, Behavior and Personality*. Chicago: Aldine, 1974.

Lind, Michael. *The Next American Nation*. New York: Free Press, 1995.

Lipman-Blumen, Jean. *Gender Roles and Power*. Englewood Cliffs, N.J.: Prentice-Hall, 1984.

Lipset, Seymour Martin. *The First New Nation*. New York: Basic Books, 1963.

———. *American Exceptionalism*. New York: W. W. Norton, 1996.

Lutz, Tom. *American Nervousness, 1903*. Ithaca, N.Y.: Cornell University Press, 1991.

Lynd, Robert S., and Helen M. Lynd. *Middletown*. New York: Harcourt, Brace, 1929.

———. *Middletown in Transition*. New York: Harcourt, Brace, 1937.

Mack, Raymond W., and Calvin P. Bradford. *Transforming America*. New York: Random House, 1979.

Maddi, Salvatore R. *Personality Theories*. Homewood, Ill.: Dorsey Press, 1980.

Madrick, Jeffrey. *The End of Affluence*. New York: Random House, 1995.

Magnet, Myron. *The Dream and the Nightmare*. New York: W. Morrow, 1993.

Matthaei, Julie A. *An Economic History of Women in America*. New York: Schocken, 1982.

May, Rollo. *The Meaning of Anxiety*. New York: Ronald Press, 1950.

Mazels, Alfred. *Industrial Growth and World Trade*. Cambridge: Cambridge University Press, 1963.

McCloskey, Robert Green. *American Conservatism in the Age of Conservatism*. Cambridge, Mass.: Harvard University Press, 1951.

McKenna, Elizabeth P. *When Work Doesn't Work Anymore*. New York: Delacorte Press, 1997.

McLean, George M. *The Rise of Anarchy in America*. Chicago: R. G. Badoux, 1890.

McLoughlin, William G. *Revivals, Awakenings and Reform*. Chicago: University of Chicago Press, 1978.

McPherson, James. *The Battle Cry of Freedom*. New York: Oxford University Press, 1988.

Mills, C. Wright. *The Power Elite*. New York: Oxford University Press, 1956.

Monte, Christopher F. *Beneath the Mask*. New York: Praeger Publishers, 1977.

Morison, Samuel Eliot, and Henry Steele Commager. *The Growth of the American Republic*. New York: Oxford University Press, 1937.

Morris, Charles R. *A Time of Passion*. New York: Harper and Row, 1984.

Nisbet, Robert. *History of the Idea of Progress*. New York: Basic Books, 1980.

Novak, Michael. *The Rise of the Unmeltable Ethnics*. New York: Macmillan, 1992.

Osborne, John W. *The Silent Revolution*. New York: Scribner's, 1970.

Parks, Henry Bamford. *The American Experience*. New York: Random House, 1947.

Parsons, Talcott. *The Social System*. Glencoe, Ill.: Free Press, 1951.

Pirenne, Henri. *Economic and Social History of Medieval Europe*. New York: Harcourt, Brace, 1937.

Plumb, J. D. *England in the Eighteenth Century*. London: Penguin Books, 1950.

Podhoretz, Norman. *Breaking Ranks*. New York: Harper Colophon Books, 1979.

Polyani, Karl. *The Great Transformation*. New York: Rinehart, 1944.

Porat, M., and M. Rubin. *The Information Economy*. Washington, D.C.: Department of Commerce, 1977.

Porter, Glen (ed.). *Encyclopedia of American Economic History*. New York: Scribner's, 1980

Reich, Robert B. *The Work of Nations*. New York: Knopf, 1991.

Riesman, David, Nathan Glazer, and R. Denny. *The Lonely Crowd*. New York: Doubleday, 1950.

Rosen, Bernard C. *The Industrial Connection*. New York: Aldine, 1982.

———. *Women, Work and Achievement*. New York: St. Martin's Press, and London: Macmillan, 1989.

Rotella, Elyce J. *From Home to Office*. Ann Arbor, Mich.: UMI Research Press, 1981.

Samuelson, Robert J. *The Good Life and Its Discontents*. New York: Times Books, 1995.

Saxby, Stephen. *The Age of Information*. New York: New York University Press, 1990.

Schlesinger, Arthur. *The Disuniting of America*. New York: W. W. Norton, 1992.

Schneider, Wolf. *Babylon Is Everywhere, The City as Man's Fate*. New York: McGraw-Hill, 1963.

Silberman, Charles. *Criminal Violence, Criminal Justice*. New York: Random House, 1978.

Sommers, Christina Hoff. *Who Stole Feminism?* New York: Simon and Schuster, 1994.

Soule, George, and Vincent P. Caroso. *American Economic History*. New York: Dryden Press, 1957.

Stephenson, Jane. *Men Are Not Cost Effective*. New York: HarperCollins, 1995.

Tawney, Richard H. *Religion and the Rise of Capitalism*. New York: Harcourt, Brace, 1926.

Tocqueville, Alexis de. *Democracy in America*. New York: Vintage Books, 1954.

Veyne, Paul. *A History of Private Life*, vol. I. Cambridge, Mass.: Belknap Press, 1987.

Wattenberg, Ben J. *The Birth Dearth*. New York: Pharos Books, 1987.

Weber, Adna. *The Growth of Cities in the Nineteenth Century*. Ithaca, N.Y.: Cornell University Press, 1965.

Weber, Max. *The Protestant Ethic and the Spirit of Capitalism*. New York: Scribner's, 1948.

Whiting, Beatrice. *Six Cultures*. New York: Wiley, 1963.

Williams, Rhys M. *Cultural Wars in American Politics*. Hawthorne, N.Y.: Aldine de Gruyter, 1997.

Wilson, William Julius. *The Truly Disadvantaged*. Chicago: University of Chicago Press, 1987.

Wisse, Ruth. *If I Am Not for Myself*. New York: Free Press, 1992.

Wolf, Margery. *Women and Family in Rural Taiwan*. Stanford, Calif.: Stanford University Press, 1972.

Wood, Gordon S. *The Radicalism of the American Revolution*. New York: Vintage, 1993.

Wrong, Dennis. *The Problem of Order*. New York: Free Press, 1994.

Wyllie, Irwin G. *The Self-Made Man in America*. New Brunswick, N.J.: Rutgers University Press, 1954.

Index

About the Author

BERNARD CARL ROSEN is Emeritus Professor of Sociology at Cornell University. He has been the director of research projects on the causes and effects of social change in five countries and three continents. He is the author of four books, including *The Industrial Connection* (1982) and *Women, Work and Achievement* (1989), as well as numerous journal articles.